History of the

Southbridge, Massachusetts

By Felix Gatineau

On the occasion of the 50th anniversary of the Notre Dame Parish,
the Golden Anniversary of the St.-Jean-Baptiste Society, and the
return of our soldiers who served in the World War.
First Published by Lakeview Press
Framingham, Massachusetts
1919

Translated by Dr. Elizabeth Blood, Salem State University,
with an Introduction by Dr. Leslie Choquette,
French Institute, Assumption College
Republished in English, 2018

Introduction

By Dr. Leslie Choquette, French Institute, Assumption College

I am delighted to introduce Dr. Elizabeth Blood's new translation of Felix Gatineau's *History of the Franco-Americans of Southbridge, Massachusetts,* first published in French in 1919. A century later, this chronicle of an immigrant community at its height provides important insights about the process of becoming American. It also highlights the contribution of an ethnic group that has often been a "quiet presence" in the United States.[1]

By the numbers, French Canadians are one of the largest immigrant groups of the 19th and 20th centuries, surpassed only by the Irish, Germans, Italians, and eastern Europeans. Between 1840 and 1930, about one million French Canadians immigrated to the United States, over two-thirds of them to nearby New England. As Gatineau explains, their motivations were both political and economic. The "troubles in Canada in 1837-1838," failed revolts against British colonial rule (Quebec had been a British colony since 1763), gave rise to the first wave of immigrants, who were soon joined by economic migrants, families of "day-laborers and ruined farmers" from the Quebec countryside.

Discontent with authoritarian government culminated in the Patriot Rebellions of 1837 and 1838, which were particularly intense in the Richelieu Valley, the countryside northeast of Montreal. Patriots took up arms in favor of a democratic republic, but the British Army put them down by force. Twelve Patriots were hanged, fifty-eight were deported to penal colonies in Australia, and a thousand

---

[1] Dyke Hendrickson, *Quiet Presence: Histoires de Franco-Américains en New England* (Portland, ME: Gannett, 1980). Hendrickson describes Franco-Americans as "the invisible minority group of New England" (p. viii).

were imprisoned. Many more fled, on foot or by horse and buggy, to the United States, where they found work in the growing industrial economy of places like Southbridge.

French Canadians continued to leave home for economic reasons. By the mid-19th century, the best farmlands in the St. Lawrence Valley were fully occupied, leaving only marginal agricultural areas for the expanding rural population. Meanwhile, commercial farming required capital investments in land and equipment that were beyond the reach of most *habitants,* as Quebec farmers were known. Rural society grew more stratified, with a large pool of landless laborers and small-holders who found it increasingly hard to make ends meet.

The Civil War was a watershed event for French-Canadian immigration to the United States. This bloody conflict put four million men into battle and cost the lives of more than 600,000. The resulting hunger for manpower triggered a mass exodus of French Canadians which would last until the Great Depression of the 1930s. Nearly 20,000 French Canadians served in the Union Army between 1861 and 1865, volunteering either from their new homes in the United States, where tens of thousands already lived, or directly from Quebec, where U.S. Army recruiters plied their trade in defiance of British law.[2] New England mill owners also recruited aggressively in the Quebec countryside to fill labor shortages caused by the draft. Mass immigration was facilitated by the railways, which connected the U.S. to Canada by the 1850s.

Between 1860 and 1900, New England's French-Canadian population jumped from 37,000 to 573,000. In Southbridge, a burgeoning center of the textile and optical industries, the French-Canadian community grew from 500 to 6,000, while climbing from

---

[2] Jean Lamarre, *Les Canadiens français et la guerre civile américaine (1861-1865)* (Montreal: VLB, 2008).

twelve to sixty per cent of the town population. Like Gatineau himself, most of Southbridge's French Canadians came from farms in the Richelieu Valley, heavily touched by the rebellions and economic change. A transnational network of family, friends, and neighbors linked "the Eye of the Commonwealth" to a cluster of parishes around Sorel and St. Ours, fueling the phenomenon known as chain migration.

The French Institute at Assumption College possesses several archival collections related to French Canadians in Southbridge: the Felix Gatineau Collection, which includes correspondence and diaries by the author of this history; the Harpin Sansoucy Family Archive, featuring dozens of letters exchanged between the immigrant family and the family in Canada; and the Hus Lemoine Family Archive, containing deeds and other papers from the Lemoine homestead in Canada. It is no accident that they all document aspects of this chain migration, which involved whole families as well as single young men.

Felix Gatineau was born in St. Victoire de Sorel in 1857 and immigrated to Southbridge at the age of twenty. He worked in a cotton mill, pharmacy, and grocery store before opening his own grocery store, which he eventually sold to work full time for a Franco-American mutual aid society, the Union St. Jean Baptiste d'Amérique (USJB).

Napoleon Sansoucy and his wife Corinne Harpin married in St. Ours, the parish to the south of St. Victoire, in 1886 and immigrated to Southbridge in 1909 with nine of their eleven children, aged three to twenty. Two of their teenage daughters remained for a time in Canada. Napoleon's sister Roseanna and her husband Pierre Harpin had already immigrated to Southbridge in 1897 with eight of their nine children, aged two to eighteen. By 1900, they owned a house in the "flats" of Little Canada, where Pierre was a butcher, and three of the children worked at American

Optical. In Southbridge, Napoleon worked as a laborer in cement, while two of his children found jobs at American Optical. In 1916, the family purchased a farm in Shrewsbury, where son Maxime opened a contracting business and daughter Antoinette a hat shop in the 1920s.[3]

Joseph O. Lemoine was born in St. Robert, the parish to the east of St. Victoire, in 1898. Like Felix Gatineau, he immigrated as a single young man, first to Millbury, then to Southbridge, where he worked at American Optical before opening a furniture store, eventually the largest in town.

As Dr. Blood explains, immigrants like these had a dual identity. They were *loyaux mais français*, loyal but French, as fellow Franco-Americans in Lewiston, Maine expressed it.[4] Bilingual, they participated actively in American politics and institutions. Gatineau emphasizes the prominent role that Southbridge's Franco-Americans, "full of energy and initiative, have always played in civic affairs." Indeed, he writes in his history that "almost all of the most important positions are in the hands of our fellow citizens." Gatineau himself served four terms in the Massachusetts House of Representatives.

Southbridge's Franco-Americans dominated town politics because they made up a majority of the population, a relatively unusual situation in New England. In nearby Worcester, where French Canadians supported four thriving parishes in the early 20th century, they comprised less than fifteen per cent of the total population so wielded less political clout. Nonetheless, the Southbridge

---

[3] Jacqueline Lessard Finn, *From Habitants to Immigrants: The Sansoucys, the Harpins, and the Potvins* (Lulu Publishing, 2017).
[4] Mark Paul Richard, *Loyal but French: The Negotiation of Identity by French-Canadian Descendants in the United States* (East Lansing: Michigan State University Press, 2008).

immigrants' pattern of adaptation, acculturation, and contribution to community was common throughout New England, wherever French Canadians settled. The ethnic world they created and celebrated formed a colorful tile of the American mosaic. Though it would eventually succumb to assimilation, there has been no shortage of equally colorful tiles to take its place.

Translator's Preface

by Dr. Elizabeth Blood, Salem State University

When I first visited Felix Gatineau's statue on Main Street in Southbridge, at the start of this translation project, I was delighted to see that his achievements were documented in both French and English. English on the front of the statue base, and French on the back, with a bronze bust of the man himself towering above. Upon closer inspection, however, I discovered that the English text on the front of the statue was completely different from the French text. It was not a translation, but rather an attempt to convey the complex identity of this local Franco-American icon. Gatineau was both a French-speaking "French-Canadian" and an English-speaking "American," equally devoted to the French-Canadian homeland and to the adopted country of many French-Canadians, the United States. The front-facing side of the statue chronicles Gatineau's contributions to American political life, while the reverse speaks to his involvement in Franco-American clubs and institutions in Southbridge.

For a time, I wondered how it could be possible that someone could so strongly identify with his homeland and care so deeply about French-Canadian identity and contemporary political issues within Canada and also identify so proudly as an American citizen and be so engaged in local, state and national social and political issues, but then, thinking of today's immigrants from the Dominican Republic or Haiti or the Congo or Syria, I realized that this is completely natural. To adopt full citizenship in the United States does not imply abandoning one's maternal language, nor does it imply replacing one's cultural heritage with a new one, nor does it imply that one no longer cares about political or social issues in one's homeland, where many relatives still reside and where issues of political, economic or social justice still matter.

Gatineau's hybrid identity is completely understandable, especially given the political climate in Canada at that time and the proximity of New England Franco-Americans to their homeland. In reading Gatineau's account of life in Southbridge in the late 19th and early 20th centuries, I came to understand that his dual allegiances to French Canada and the U.S., far from competing with each other, in fact overlapped and even coalesced in Gatineau's mind. French Canada was not an autonomous nation. The French had lost their holdings in Canada to the British at the end of the Seven Year's War, a war known to most French-Canadians as the "British Conquest," in 1763. French-Canadians living in the region that is today the Province of Québec suffered oppression, discrimination, and lack of economic opportunities under British Canadian rule. By the early-19th century, French-Canadians had organized and the French-speaking "Patriotes," a political movement to fight Anglophone domination in Canada, launched several failed rebellions against the British in 1837-1838, the time of the first major wave of French-Canadian immigrants to Southbridge. It seems obvious that French-speaking Canadians seeking political rights and economic opportunities in the late 19th century would choose to emigrate to the United States, a country that had already overthrown British rule and had established an open and free society where new citizens shared equal rights, regardless of religion, maternal language, or ethnic heritage. Although, as Gatineau will tell you, many Canadians initially considered their stay in the U.S. temporary, and many did eventually return to Canada, but those who chose to naturalize, become citizens, and raise American children here became full patriotic Americans, even though many never relinquished their allegiance to their homeland.

Initially, many French-Canadian immigrants were factory workers. Eventually, however, they became involved in politics, built churches and schools, opened businesses, created programs to support the arts, founded social clubs and mutual aid societies, and many voluntarily joined the U.S. military to fight during the Civil War and World War I. You will learn all of this, in detail, by reading Gatineau's history, for Gatineau loved lists. Many of the chapters in this book simply list names, dates and facts about French-Canadians and Franco-Americans in Southbridge. While reading such lists can be tiresome (not quite as tiresome as retyping them!), they are a true treasure trove for anyone seeking to learn about the contributions of their ancestors to the town of Southbridge. I wish I knew what social clubs and political committees my grandparents belonged to in their Franco-American community in upstate New York! I wish I knew how they lived, what stores they shopped in, what plays they saw, how they celebrated and mourned; I really wish I knew silly little stories about them, like what happened the time that too many pies were ordered for a 4th of July festival. I wish that all Franco-Americans had a Felix Gatineau to chronicle the history of their ancestors in their little corner of the world.

In addition to those with a personal connection to Southbridge's Franco-American community, this book will also be of interest to anyone who wants to learn more about the history of Southbridge, about Franco-American heritage, or about how immigrant groups organized themselves to support each other and provide their community with social, cultural and economic opportunities in the early 20th century.

I would like to thank Alan Earls, publisher of this work and descendant of Southbridge Franco-Americans, for giving me the opportunity to translate this text and to live for a little while in 1919 Southbridge. And, of course, to Felix Gatineau, who cared so much about Franco-Americans to offer us this chronicle of early Franco-American life, *un grand merci!*

ACKNOWLEDGEMENTS

The publisher wishes to acknowledge the vital assistance and encouragement provided by Margaret Morrissey, Director of the Jacob Edwards Library in Southbridge, and her staff. Additionally, a note of appreciation is due to Louise Tremblay Cole for early advice and input on this project.

TO THE READER
By Felix Gatineau

My goal, in publishing this modest volume, was to transmit to future generations all that relates to the birthplace and the humble beginnings of the colony of people of French-Canadian origin in Southbridge, Mass., and this with the hope that the young generation, following the examples and noble lessons offered by the pioneers of our ethnicity, may be able to perfect the work that began so nobly.

I ask indulgence of the reader if my work is not as perfect as even I myself would have liked; to trace the history of a municipality over the course of one hundred and fifty years is not the easiest of tasks, and please know, dear reader, that this undertaking cost me many hours of painstaking work.

I would have liked to have documented in a more concrete way my most sincere gratitude to a certain number of our compatriots who, for fifty years, have dedicated themselves to and sacrificed themselves for the advancement of our people, but they will understand that I had to focus on the history of the colony, without entering into too many individual details.

I must thank those who helped me complete my memoir; there are among them some who are in eternal sleep in our cemeteries, but who provided me with very precise information before leaving us.

In particular, I thank Mr. Joseph Gélinas, Mr. Louis Métivier and Mr. Joseph Langevin, who arrived here before 1850, and who were for me a "true encyclopedia"; furthermore, my gratitude is to Mr. Norbert Duval, Mr. Joseph Berthiaume, Mr. Daniel Dumas, Mr. Clément Bégin, Mr. Gilbert Thériault and others.

I must thank especially the Rev. R. A. Laporte, who helped me so zealously with the editing of the manuscripts.

I pay homage to Rev. Fr. L.O. Triganne, devoted priest of our parish, who furnished me with precious information from the parish registers.

Finally, to all my collaborators, to all those who helped me to publish and to publicize this "souvenir volume," I say: *Merci beaucoup!*

FELIX GATINEAU

CONTENTS

AUTHOR'S INTRODUCTION

By Felix Gatineau

Fifty years ago, the parish of Notre-Dame of Southbridge, Massachusetts, had just opened its doors. Already a half century has passed since Canadians laid the groundwork for a strong parish here. Fifty years of struggles, of work and of merit! 1919! We salute you, jubilee year!

On the occasion of the jubilee festivities, which our city will experience this year, we thought to engage the French-Canadian citizens of Southbridge by dedicating this work to them, entitled: *"History of the French-Canadians of Southbridge."*

The task that we have imposed upon ourselves is a very pleasant one, since it involves telling of the deeds and accomplishments of those who were our forefathers; it has also been a long and tiresome chore, since it has meant collecting documents and notes for over twenty years. After having assembled all of these facts into one work, we dare to share it with you, begging for your indulgence and asking you to consider our good intentions.

In this volume, after describing the establishment of the first settlers and above all the first Canadians in Southbridge, we will tell you in *the first part* (a) all that they have done in the religious realm, and in *the second* (b) all that they have done in society and politics, for the past fifty years.

What hearts of gold did our brave compatriots have, those who came to settle here in great number from Canada, battling against misfortune and poverty! The youth, who today have only to reap the harvest grown from the seeds scattered in the furrows by our forefathers more than a hundred years ago, will be able to learn some useful and productive lessons in reading these lines and will come to understand above all that this heritage is being given to them not so that it can disappear but rather so that it can be handed down in turn for all posterity!

Our forefathers were sincere Christians and fervent patriots[5]: the contents of this little book will convince even the most skeptical. Rarely do we see a group of Canadians so united, and that is the secret to all of the successes that they have had in the political arena and in the religious realm. In all instances, they let themselves be guided by their priests, and they only served their country so well because they always carried high and strong the flag of their beliefs and always fought for and defended their native language. In this year of festivities, 1919, from the church to the city hall, the Canadians of Southbridge reach out to each other. They hold great authority in municipal affairs and impose their will everywhere. Southbridge is really just a little corner of the Province of Québec, where the sublime starred flag is harmoniously framed by the maple leaf, emblem of the incessantly renewed vitality of our ethnicity!

---

[5] Translator's note: This is the first of Gatineau's many references to the "patriotism" of Franco-Americans in Southbridge. For Gatineau, patriotism meant unfailing support of French-Canadian autonomy in the face of British control and oppression in Canada, but also unbridled loyalty to the United States, adopted home to French-Canadian emigrants and a country founded on rebellion against the British crown. Allegiance to French Canada and allegiance to the United States, far from being competing or contradictory notions, instead overlap and even coalesce in Gatineau's mind and in his recounting of Franco-American life in Southbridge.

PART ONE

CHAPTER I

Southbridge – The First Settlers – The Beginning

There is no village more stylish or more prosperous in all of Worcester county than Southbridge, whose origins we endeavor to recount. This village, today large enough to be considered a city, has a population of about 15,000 inhabitants, of which the vast majority are of French-Canadian origin, and it is situated twenty miles from Worcester. The history of Southbridge began long before it was recognized as a separate village, and this is because the municipality included parts of Dudley, Charlton, and Sturbridge back then.

As early as 1633, John Oldham, known throughout history for his trade relations with the natives, wanted to make a journey with three other men through the lands of the natives, which spanned from Massachusetts Bay to the Connecticut River. These travelers arrived in "Tantusque," the name given to this territory by the Indians, which today encompasses Sturbridge and Southbridge. These were the first white colonists who visited and explored the lands where we live. In 1644, John Winthrop Jr. was granted a plot of land on which the lead mines of Sturbridge were later discovered.

The picturesque site of our village and the many advantages that it promised in terms of industry and commerce quickly drew a flock of colonists to the area such that by 1796 they had become quite numerous and, wanting to have a church where they could worship God in their own way, spoke of separating from the municipalities of Sturbridge, Dudley and Charlton.

They at first erected a temple on high ground, on the property of Captain Marcy. This temple was dedicated on July 4th, 1797, one year after work had begun on it. It would be hard to find a more dignified a way to celebrate our national holiday than to erect a temple to God's glory on that day.

The first inhabitants of Southbridge were not satisfied with this initial success; they were active and courageous people who were deterred by nothing, and thanks to their initiative and to their tenacity, on February 15, 1816, the municipality of Southbridge became a reality.

Next it came time to baptize our village, and do not think that this was any banal or easy affair to settle. At first they called it "Honest Town," then "Vienna," but this Austrian name did not seem to please; the debates were animated, which proves that back then, like today, the citizens of this village never agreed to any project, to any undertaking, without having carefully thought through the details.

On January 20, 1815, they adopted the name Southbridge and to our knowledge there is no other place in the United States that bears this name, so circumspect was this choice.

At the first municipal meeting, which occurred on March 6, 1816, the following officials were elected: Captain Gershom, Major Samuel Fiske, Joshua Mason, Wm. Morris and Fordyce Foster. This basic information about the political history of Southbridge is shared here in order to shed light on the important and nearly exclusive role that Canadians play in politics here today.

James Dennison, after whom the Dennison District is named, was probably the first colonist to settle in this region. He came from Medfield and arrived here in 1730; for two years, he lived in a kind of grotto, that can be seen even today, near the road that extends along the properties of Willard V. Morse and Mrs. Vernon Chamberlain. Before 1744, Mr. Samuel Freeman was the first citizen whose home was located in the actual town center of Southbridge.

They say that John Gray, who sold clothing, was the first to do business in our village, around 1790; Oliver Plympton opened the first store in 1791.

The first cotton mill in the area was built in 1811 in the location called Westville today. This mill, it seems, cost almost $6,000; the first wool manufacturer was established in 1813 near the location where today we find "Central Mills."

The "Globe Manufacturing Co." was incorporated by an act of the Legislature in the year 1814, and it was this company that gave the name "Globe" to the part of the village on which it stood. At that time, Southbridge was on the fast track to progress and was claiming its place in the spotlight; industry was changing our village from one day to the next. The cotton and wool mills had many supporters and by 1818, just two years after the incorporation of the village, the important Dexter, Harrington & Sons cutlery factory was established. A century later, this prosperous company is still run by members of the Harrington family.

But, without a doubt, the industry that made Southbridge famous and gave it a dominant ranking in the manufacturing world was the eyeglasses and optical instruments industry. They called it the Eye of the Commonwealth (*l'Oeil de la République*).

Southbridge is not the "City of Light," we have no such pretention, but we can happily call it the eyeglasses-city, the city where you can find what you need "to see better," *to make things clear!* This industry was not born in Southbridge, as one might easily imagine; they started manufacturing lenses here in the year 1833, thanks to the efforts and initiative of William Beecher. From that time until 1869, the year in which the American Optical Company was formed, the eyeglasses industry passed through several hands, and the last to run it was Robert H. Cole, who became President of the American Optical Company, along with his associates George W. Wells, Assistant, and E. M. Cole, Treasurer.

We could provide you with additional interesting details about the origins of our city, but since we want to focus on the history of the Canadians of Southbridge, we will now enter into the heart of our subject, and we hope that the reader will be grateful to have these preliminary facts.

However, before speaking of the Dugas family, the first family of French origin in the Southbridge area, and the family of Abraham Marois, the first Canadian family, we would like to list the names of the first colonists of our city, no matter their background. They are: Bacon, Chamberlain, Newell, Cheney, Marcy, Cady, Carpenter, Clark, Marsh, McKinstry, Perry, Amidown, Pratt, Vinton, Dresser, Streeter, Putney, Edward, Cummings, Merritt, Dunbar, Elles, Litchfield, Paige, Morse, Plimpton, Fiske, Mason, Morris, Foster, Hooker, Joslin, White, Harding, Lamb, West, Potter, Hartwell, Durfee, Wolcott, Sumner, Baylies, Angel, Park.

From 1816, the year of the incorporation of the municipality of Southbridge, to 1830, we find several French names on the registers, including: Allard, Graton, Fortune, Pagé, Chapin, Léonard, Chamois, Blanchard, Adam, Amidon, Blain, Bacon, Boulton, Carpentier, Clemence, Dugar, Masson, Poirier, Goddard, Trusdel, etc.

Several of these people belonged to Acadian families, but most were Huguenot descendants from the colony of Oxford who moved here due to unforeseen circumstances, and some of them had already anglicized their names.

It is without a doubt that several of these individuals who changed their names subsequently lost their faith and are now buried in the "Oak-Ridge" cemetery, next to their fellow Protestants.[6] A meticulous study of the headstones in that cemetery confirms this sad belief, and it's a

---

[6] Translator's note: A common saying among Franco-Americans at the turn of the 20th century was *"Qui perd sa langue, perd sa foi"* ("If you lose your language, you'll lose your faith"). The French language and the Catholic faith were intertwined in early French-Canadian identity and were central to that identity. Gatineau, dedicated to the preservation of French-Canadian heritage in Franco-American communities, here references this belief.

terrible lesson for our compatriots who think they will differentiate themselves by changing their names. They say that there is over $1,500,000 unclaimed in the country's treasury in Washington belonging to heirs of French ethnicity, and it's there because they anglicized their names. The heirs have never been found. As far as we are concerned, we have only contempt and disdain for those compatriots among us who are embarrassed by their origins, by their names, and by their faith. They are a disgrace to our ethnicity.

CHAPTER II

The first Canadians – Date of their arrival

According to precious documents that we possess, the first family that spoke French and came to live in our vicinity was the family of Claude Dugas, who settled in Sturbridge in the year 1754. Elsewhere, we see that this happened in 1755, which we believe is correct because this family had been recognized as being neutral, having left Acadia at the request of the Governor before the deportation of the Acadians, which occurred in the fall of 1755.[7]

The Dugas Family

Claude Dugas was born in Port-Royal, Nova Scotia on January 14, 1710; he was the son of Abraham Dugas and Madeleine Landry. He married Josephte Melançon in Annapolis Royal on May 29, 1731; he died on September 3, 1792 and his wife died on October 19, 1793 in Saint-Jacques-de-l'Achigan, Montcalm County, Québec Province.

From their union were born several children:

Marie, August 21, 1732 in Annapolis Royal, Nova Scotia.

Osethe, December 18, 1734 who married Chas. Belliveau on January 20, 1755 in Annapolis. The couple and their children were in Sturbridge in May 1757; the mother died in Saint-Jacques, Québec Province, on January 20, 1820.

Marguerite was born July 21, 1737 and married Armand Bourgeois in New England in 1766; she also died in Saint-Jacques-de-l'Achigan.

Madeleine, born November 16, 1739; she was disabled and married Joseph Leblanc, in our vicinity, and died in the same parish as the others.

Charles, born on January 24, 1743.

Cécile, who was mentally retarded, born January 30, 1746 and died

---

[7] Translator's note: Between 1755 and 1764, the vast majority of French settlers living in Acadia (roughly the region that is today New Brunswick, Nova Scotia and Prince Edward's Island) were expelled by British forces. This event, called *"le Grand dérangement"* or the Great Deportation, forced French Acadians to leave the territory, many migrating to the American colonies or to French Louisiana. This was viewed as the first major step in the British conquest of New France, followed by the French loss at the battle of the Plains of Abraham in Quebec in 1759 and ultimately culminating in the surrender of French territories in Canada to the British crown in 1763.

without having married on July 9, 1825 in Saint-Jacques.

Anne, born April 16, 1749, married Joseph Richard on February 4, 1771 and died on March 21, 1787 in Saint-Jacques.

Daniel, born in Sturbridge, Mass. on October 6, 1760, married to M. Louise Vaillant from L'Assomption, Québec Province, on August 13, 1782, and died on June 4, 1838 in Saint-Jacques.

Joseph, born in 1755 in Annapolis Royal and married to Marie Madeleine Vaillant on January 8, 1776, died in the same place as the others.

The ship that Claude and his family took was called "Hélèna." It was a boat that had a 166 ton capacity on which embarked fifty-two married men and women, 108 boys and 111 girls, for a total of 323 souls. The ship left "Goat Island," on Monday, December 8, 1755 at five o'clock in the morning, heading for Boston. This leads us to believe that very probably, and contrary to what our manuscript seems to show, the Dugas family was among the unhappy victims of the English barbarism which was protested and condemned in the fateful year of 1775 by the entire civilized world. The sole sentence brought against the Acadians was in fact pronounced, against the laws of humanity, by Belcher, an atrocious torturer, on July 28, 1755.

Supposing it is true, as the manuscript tells us, that the family of Claude Dugas left before the deportation of the poor Acadians, they would have soon shared the fate of their friends when they arrived in this country. Why was this family recognized as neutral, and why did they leave Acadia at the request of the Governor? So many unsolved enigmas[8].

We can, however, state that the Dugas family was one of the first families in Dugas Village, near Annapolis Royal, a village that is called Ryersonville today.

---

[8] Acadians are referred to in British documents as "the neutral French."

John Holden, first explorer in 1633.

A Canadian family arrives in Southbridge in 1832.

Site of the refuge of the first pioneer of Southbridge, James Denison.

As it is impossible to determine the exact nature of this family's situation, we can only affirm that they would have been expelled by the Governors, who were anxious to divide up the spoils of the poor exiles and to seize their rich lands and many flocks. For the English wished to be rid of the Acadians not because they had any real grievances against them, but rather to get rich at their expense. Oh! The traitors, they can try to justify their cruelty against our Acadian brothers and offer excuses that seem reasonable for the deportation, citing the Acadians' refusal to modify the oath they swore to the British crown in 1726 and in 1731 which exempted them from bearing arms against the French and the Natives in favor of one with no restrictions, but the real reason was their insatiable greed.

I'd rather believe that Claude Dugas followed the example of so many other good family men like our own forefathers who, with a large family, chose to leave his homeland with regret to go seek elsewhere the bread his children needed.

Whether he was driven out of Acadia or whether he left with the goal of finding calmer skies, it is no less true that he was harshly tested and treated much like the final exiles. We were revolted to read the following paragraph in volume XXV of the Archives of Massachusetts. On June 6th, the Committee chosen by the Court to discuss the division of the "Canadians" living in Worcester county, convened. Here is what was said of the Claude Dugas family:

Claude Dugas and his wife received an order to live in Sturbridge, but their children would be separated from them; Marguerite, Madeleine and Félécité were sent to Oxford. The two other daughters: Elizabeth (Cécile) and Hannah (Anne) were sent to Dudley, while the two sons, Charles and Joseph, left for Charlton. Charles Belliveau (Claude's son-in-law) and his wife and their young children received an order to go to Leicester, but the second child was sent to Spencer. In the spring or summer of 1767, however, despite anguish and misfortune, Claude Dugas succeeded in reaching the Province of Québec with the whole family, except for Charles.

We also have in our possession a document which proves that our valiant compatriot was in dire straits, a document in which we see that Moses Marcy demanded that the Municipality of Sturbridge refund a certain sum of money he paid to support the families of Claude Dugas and of Joseph Deblois; this document is signed by the Selectmen of the day, James and Joseph Cheney, and is dated October 6th, 1756.

We also possess all of the documents relating to this family from Miss K.L. Edwards. This young woman is linked to the Dugas family by the marriage of one of her ancestors, Martha, who married Firmin Dugas on March 21st, 1785.

We read with interest the following. The farm of Pierre Dugas was settled by his father Charles Dugas who was the son of Daniel Dugas, who emigrated to the United States and to the colony that is today Southbridge, from Louisbourg, Nova Scotia, a place he left because he did not want to join the wars that were occurring at that time between France and England.

Upon his arrival, he went to see Colonel Marcy, who procured lodging for him in a section of a saw mill that he owned at that time, and he lived there for several years. After the end of the war between France and England, Daniel Dugas took advantage of a government policy to provide land to those who remained neutral during the war and returned to Nova Scotia with his family, later moving to Saint-Jacques-de-l'Achigan in Montcalm County[9], leaving behind his son Charles who had fallen in love with an American named Sarah Chubb. They married in 1767.

Charles had bought and settled the farm that his son Pierre inherited after his death, which is today the property of Frank Shepard. He had to purchase this farm twice, as the first contracts were no longer valid; in that time, it seems, several colonists encountered this issue. Charles Dugas was very interested in work, was thrifty and was very generous; at his death, he was buried in the Oak-Ridge cemetery.

---

[9] Saint-Jacques was a settlement of Acadian refugees north of Montreal.

Today, there are commemorative marble statues dedicated to members of this family in the aforementioned cemetery. Descendants of the Dugas family continued to live in Southbridge until 1838; they returned to Canada at that time, to Montcalm County. We should note that this family was recognized by the Acadian people as one of their most distinguished families. The family was notable due to their wealth and also because of their sincere and loyal attachment to the Catholic religion. They were loved and blessed by God, and there were many with religious vocations. One of the nuns in the family became a Superior in the Putnam Convent, and as Canadian government documents show, several members of this family played important roles in Canadian politics, in the Québec government, and in the Federal Parliament. Monsignor Dugas, apostolic dignitary, is also descended from this family.

It is with great satisfaction and true joy that we have been able to share all the specific details that we were able to find regarding the Dugas family, the first family to settle the place in which we live and where today we find such an influential group of French-Canadians who are respected by all the other nationalities around them.

This family was Acadian, but to the best of our knowledge the first French-Canadian[10] family to arrive here was the family of Mr. Abraham Marois, who came to Southbridge in the fall of 1832. Mr. Marois, who had at first immigrated to Worcester, had heard that there was one lone Canadian living in Southbridge, so he set out to come pay him a visit. Upon arrival, he learned that the Canadian, or at least the only man known to speak French, lived in Westville, so he continued on there to see him.

The man was descended from a French family with the surname Lavallée and was married to an American woman; he was a carpenter workman, and as Mr. Marois himself was also a carpenter, the latter resolved to move here, for business seemed good and promising.

At that time, the "Globe Village" factory was being built, and it was there that Mr. Marois, who had brought his family with him, first found work.

Mr. Marois had emigrated from Saint-Ours, Québec Province to Worcester where, in 1906, Felix Marois, one of his sons then aged 78,

---

[10] Translator's note: Here, Gatineau makes a distinction between Acadians (generally from the Eastern provinces of Canada) and French-Canadians (generally from the Province of Québec). Although both descended from French settlers, Acadians and French-Canadians are considered two different groups.

was still living. Upon arrival in Southbridge, Mr. Marois and his family went to settle in Westville, near his friend Lavallée. Means of travel must have been quite primitive in those days, as according to Mr. Marois, it took nearly two days to move from Worcester to Westville.

In those days, there were certainly no streetcars or steam-engines; horses were a luxury, and money wasn't in everyone's pockets, so our first Canadians of Southbridge had to make do with oxen to move their belongings. That explains why it took two long days to make the trip.

Mr. Marois worked for a while on the construction of the Globe Village spinning mill, but the work was difficult given that the builders lacked all kinds of tools needed for working with large pieces of wood, and in short time our compatriot contracted a disease that would eventually send him to his grave. Mr. Marois died in Southbridge approximately ten years after his arrival, around 1842.

In 1837-38[11], a number of young people came to settle here, including David Potvin, Damase Potvin, Louis Girard and others, and they found work in the "African" factory, which is today Sandersdale.

Around that time, Mr. Joseph Bourassa arrived with his family, and shortly thereafter his wife died. She was the first female Canadian buried in the American "Oak-Ridge" cemetery, since there wasn't yet a Catholic cemetery in Southbridge.

Her mortal remains are still there, along with the bodies of several other Canadians who died after her. In 1838, more families came to enlarge the nascent colony, among them were Pierre Benoit, François Laflèche, Antoine Giard, Pierre Giard, and S. Larivée.

Several of these families came to live in Globe village, while others settled closer to the "Columbian" factory, which is today "Lensdale."

Shortly thereafter, in that same year, the Dumas, Mathieu and Dupré families arrived and went to live on "Paige Hill."

---

[11] Translator's note: This is an important era for French-Canadians, as it marks the time of the failed rebellions of the "Patriotes," a series of uprisings against British oppression of the French in Canada, which occurred in 1837-1838. During that time, a number of prominent French-Canadian rebels were publicly executed and others were exiled to Australia. Many others fled to the United States. Although most French-Canadian emigrants left for economic reasons, during this early period it is possible that emigrants were motivated by the political climate. Given the interest of Franco-American Southbridgers in the "Patriote" movement, evidenced in later chapters, it would not be surprising if this were the case for these early settlers.

The incorporation of the City of Southbridge was signed in the annex to the left of the main building.

In this house Governor Marcy was born. On this site the Notre-Dame Church stands today.

The village of Southbridge in 1835.

It's around this time that the first cluster of Canadians in Southbridge was formed. And today we still find among us many descendants of some of these first founding families.

Life was tough in the beginning, we must admit, because for the most part the Canadians coming here from the homeland were fairly poor and their families fairly large. Oh! How they were denigrated, these first compatriots, fleeing a country that could not provide for them. People hurled all sorts of insults at them, even saying that those leaving were the dregs of society and that it was best to let them leave; that their departure would not harm the country but rather purge it. And today, if we undertake to write the history of the Canadians of Southbridge, it's to show those slanderers that we are not the pariahs that they once believed us to be, for we must admit that today, people's eyes are starting to open and they have a more favorable view of us. Despite the defamation, immigration was in full swing.

CHAPTER III

Names of the First Canadian Families of Southbridge.

It is evident that the troubles in Canada in 1837-1838 were the real cause of the great emigration. At that time, numerous young people and entire families arrived from the homeland, particularly from St. Ours, and came to establish themselves in Southbridge. We thought it would be agreeable to our readers to publish the fairly long list below, giving the names of the pioneers who came to establish their homes and households in our dear village.

What we are publishing here is the fruit of arduous work and research in the registers of the municipality, and one can surely understand the nature of this work if one considers that a good number of the names are written in a way that is barely decipherable. The reason for this is that, during that time, our compatriots did not speak English, and it should be stated that some Canadians did not even know how to properly write their names. Further, it is easy to understand how the local officials, generally ignorant of the French language, mutilated the names to the point that we can no longer understand them. They settled for writing the names by sound. Finally, even in this early time there was an inclination for the inconceivable anglicizing of names, which a good number of our people chose to do.

We will provide a few examples which will help you understand the patience needed for this type of work. Thus, we find in the registers:

For	*For*
Bourassa...Burrows	Lafortune...Fortune
Giard...Shaw	Tessier...Tacy
Balthazar...Martin	Berthiaume...Buckham
Métivier...Marsh	Lapierre...Stone
Gélinas...Corey	Laroche...Stone
Benoit...Bennoy	Baril...Berry
Lataille...Dyos	Dupuis...Dupray
Brazeau...Barzo	Lafrance...Lafrince

Bessette...Bissent	Duval...Dover
Lusignan...Lovely	Daigle...Dake
Aucoin...Wedge	Thériault...Terrio
Pelletier...Pelky	Desgreniers...Greeny
Roy...King	Potvin...Porter
Dumas...Dermott	St. Martin...Martin
Beausoleil...Goodsun	Daviault...Davieo
Taupied...Toe Foot	Leblanc...White
Boisvert...Greenwood	Loranger...Wright
Moreau...Moro	Brindamour...Brown
Garriépy...Garrapy	Laporte...Door
Hêtu...Lichu	Petit...Little
Laflèche...Ritchie	Béfort...Belford
Mailloux...Mayo	Lemoine...Top
Rochette...Rusher	St. Onge...Mitchell
Simard...Seymour	Paquin...Paken
Lacroix...Cross	Ledoux...Ledort
Perron...Perry	Plouffe...Plufe
Forcier...Force	

Here, to the best of our knowledge, are the names of the first colonists to settle in Southbridge, along with the place the families came from.

1830 to 1832

Mailhot family, to Westville
Lavallée family, to Westville

1832

Abraham Marois from St. Ours, about whom we gave a lengthy account above.

1833

Pierre Benoit, St. Ours
David Pérus, Lotbinière

1837 to 1838

David Potvin, Norcisse Potvin, two unmarried brothers from St. Ours.
Louis Girard, Pierre Girard, two unmarried brothers from St. Ours.
Isaac Mathieu, St. Ours
Mr. Gentès, St. Ours
Pierre Larivière, St. Ours
Charles Daigle, St. Ours
François Dumas, St. Ours
Pierre Bourassa and family, St. Ours
Pierre Dumas and family, St. Ours
François Laflèche and family, St. Ours
Francis Daigle, St. Ours
Pierre Côté, Contrecoeur
Georges Dupré, Trois Rivières, Québec Province

1839

Augustin Benoit, St. Ours
Joseph Benoit, St. Ours
William Denis, St. Ours

1840

Henri Fontaine, St. Ours
Olivier Dupré, St. Ours
Prisque Larrivée, St. Ours
Felix Larivée, St. Ours

1841

George Lévesque, St. Ours
Jean Lazure, St. Ours
Felix Labrie, St. Ours

1842

Pierre Brazeau, St. Ours
Albert Giard, St. Ours
Pierre Pelletier, St. Ours
Norbert Giard, St. Ours
George Labrie, St. Ours
Olivier Lamothe, Sorel
Alexandre Lamothe, Sorel
Edouard Graton, Sorel

1843

Pierre Garand, St. Jude
Antoine Giard, St. Jude

1844

Olivier Bessette
Thomas Benoit, St. Ours
Thomas Devalley
Olivier Barrette

1845

Jean Roy, St. Jude
Narcisse Roy, St. Jude
Antoine Guilbert, St. Jude

In this year, fires in the "Columbian" factory, today "Lensdale," and the "African" factory, today "Sandersdale," resulted in a number of families moving to Webster, Milbury, and Worcester.

1846

André Benoit, St. Ours
André Bouvier, St. Ours
John Boulanger, St. Ours
Pierre Dupré, St. Ours
Charles Dupré, St. Ours
Pierre Dionne, St. Ours
Jean-Baptiste Larivière, known as « Batoche »
Jean-Baptiste Mailloux
Cyrille Myette
Cyrille Amyotte
Jean Legros, St. Ours
Pierre Lusignan, St. Ours
Frédéric Lacroix, St. Ours
Edouard Lacroix, St. Ours
Antoine Quevillion, St. Ours
Felix Roy
Mr. Bastien

1847

A. Ducharme, St. Ours
Joseph Béfort, St. Ours
François Bouthillette, St. Jude
James Benoit, St. Ours
Hercule Gaudette, Sorel
Pierre St. Martin, St. Victoire
André Arpin, St. Ours
Charles Gaudette, Sorel

Joseph Gaudette, Sorel
Joseph Bessette, Sorel
Charles Berthiaume
Laurent St. Martin, St. Victoire
Léandre Benoit, St. Ours
Robert St. Martin, St. Victoire
Toussaint Boisvert
Joseph Côté
Clément Benoit, St. Ours
Louis Bachand
Alexis Langevin
Pierre Palardy (blacksmith)

1848

Louis Lachapelle
John Lucier, Vermont
Pierre Lucier, Vermont
André Langevin, St. Ours
Pierre Langevin, St. Ours
Louis Langevin, St. Ours
Jean Langevin, St. Ours
Joseph Langevin, St. Ours
George Langevin, St. Ours
Jean-Baptiste Langevin, St. Ours
Alphonse Langevin, St. Ours
Antoine Quevillon, Coaticook
Herménégilde Charbonneau
Henri Balthazar, Vermont
Louis Larivière, St. Ours
Louis Racicot, St. Hilaire
Pierre Boucher, Sainte Madeleine
Louis Ricard, Sainte Madeleine
Gilbert Larivière, St. Ours
Ignace Langevin, St. Ours
Augustin Mathieu, St. Ours
Joseph Lataille, St. Victoire
Joseph Bourdeau, St. Victoire

1849

Louis Métivier, St. Ours
Paul Potvin, St. Ours
Pierre Gariépy, St. Ours
André Lapointe, St. Ours
Ambroise Lapointe, St. Ours

Alexandre Bouvier, St. Ours
Jean-Baptiste Potvin
Alexandre Potvin
Sylvestre Simard, Lacolle
Louis Boisvert, St. Aimé
Pierre Hêtu, Coaticook
Toussaint Duclos, Lacolle
Calixte Gélinas, St. Aimé
Joseph Chabot, St. Aimé

1850

Pierre Duval, Contrecoeur
Felix Bouvier, St. Ours
Jean Alexis Bouvier
Pierre Belleville, St. Ours
Pierre Potvin, St. Ours
Louis Plouffe, St. Victoire
Pierre Lambert, St. Aimé
Aimé Lambert, St. Aimé
François Lambert, St. Aimé
Dr. Provencher
François Delâges, Ste. Madeleine
Joseph Larivée, St. Ours
Abraham Chapdeleine, St. Ours
Ferdinand Fonrouge
Nicolas Lavoie
Joseph Plouffe
François Plouffe

In this year, a fire in the "Hamilton" factory caused several families to move elsewhere.

1851

Joseph Collette, St. Ours
Felix Lusignan, St. Victoire
Bruno Lusignan, St. Victoire
Pierre Lusignan, St. Victoire
Marcel Lusignan, St. Victoire
Clément Lusignan, St. Victoire
Joseph Malo, St. Victoire
Pierre Laroche, St. Aimé, he married a Native woman

1852

Joseph Lapierre, Lacolle
Prosper Godbout, St. Ours
Nicolas Lavoie, St. Ours
Joseph Ledoux, St. Ours
Joseph Moreau, St. Robert
Antoine Lamoureux, St. Ours
Pierre Martin, St. Denis
Charles Benoit, St. Denis
Wm. St. Pierre
Pierre Gadbois
Joseph Aucoin, St. Victoire
Jean Baril
John Pratte, St. Antoine
George Potvin

1853

Louis Lavallée, Sorel
Eugène Lacroix
Pierre Mailloux, Farnham
Louis Plante
Léonard Plante
Louis Potvin
Louis Duval, Contrecoeur
François Lapierre
David Lapierre
Pierre Giroux
Pierre Dionne, St. Césaire
Charles Dionne, St. Césaire
Louis Dionne, St. Césaire
Joseph Dionne, St. Césaire
Jean-B. Berthiaume, Lacolle
Augustin Sansoucy, St. Ours
Joseph Paquin
Marcel Sabourin, Ste. Marie
Louis Lavallée
Pierre Hévé, St. Ours

1855

Louis Baril
J.-B. Baril, fils
Adolphe Lacroix, St. Hyacinthe
Pascal Deslauriers, St. Hyacinthe
Louis Dupuis, Lacolle

Pierre Dupuis, Lacolle
Louis Surprenant, Lacolle
Moïse Chassé, Lacolle
Francis Simard, Lacolle
Pierre Thériault, Lacolle
Louis Perron
Pierre Fournier, St. Césaire
Louis Gendron, St. Ours
Pierre Lemoine, St. Victoire
J.-B. Lapierre, St. Victoire
Moïse Lagesse
Florence Plouffe
Widow of André Dumas, St. Victoire
Antoine Sabourin, St. Angèle
Etienne Richard, St. Denis
Joseph Lacroix, St. Ours
Augustin Beaudreau, St. Ours
Noël Fontaine, St. Césaire

1856

Athanase Gouin, St. Victoire
Pierre Gouin, St. Victoire
Joseph Gervais, St. Victoire
George Lagesse, St. Victoire
Joseph Chassé, St. Victoire
Fr. Aucoin, St. Victoire
Thomas Aucoin, St. Victoire
Thomas Potvin, St. Ours
Felix Leclair, St. Ours
Joseph Nault
Joseph Forcier
Alexis Bibeau, Sorel
Théophile Lamothe, St. Victoire
Michel Duchesneau, Lacolle
Charles Bazin, St. Ours
Gilbert Goddard

In 1856, because of the presidential election in which Buchanan was elected President of the United States, there was a great financial reaction, and in 1857, several mills were forced to close. This trying time negatively affected a great number of Canadian families who then had to leave Southbridge. Another fire occurred at the Hamilton factory, and several families left the area to go live elsewhere, some even returned to the homeland.

1857

John Bellerose
Isaac Dupuis
Pierre Daviault
Aubin Gamache
J.-B. Renaud, St. Césaire
Joseph Lemoine, St. Victoire
J.-B. Mandeville, Sorel
Antoine Mandeville, Sorel
Pierre Côté, St. Césaire
J.-B. Côté, St. Césaire

1858

Thomas Plouffe
Louis Simpson
Olivier Simpson
Louis Bessette, St. Valentin
A. Fontaine
Amable Gervais, Lacolle
James Gervais, Lacolle
Pierre Mathieu, St. Ours
J.-B. Nault, St. Ours
Paul Aucoin, St. Victoire
Pierre Aucoin, St. Victoire
Widow of Laurent Dupaul and family, Farnham
Adolphe Lacroix, St. Hyacinthe
Joseph M. Dupaul, Farnham
Théophile Lamothe, St. Victoire

1859

Jean-Baptiste Bachand
Jean-Baptiste Duquette
Albert Godbout, St. Ours
Pierre Joubert
George Gravel, St. Ours
Joseph Lavallée
Louis Renaud
Philibert Lacroix, St. Hyacinthe
J.-Bte. Martin, St. Denis
Paul Larochelle, St. Victoire
Olivier Lapierre, Lacolle
David Lagesse
Jean Roy, St. Jude

1860

Louis Bonnette
Charles Bibeau, Sorel
Lévi Désautel
Francis Lacroix
Frank Levitre
Pierre Raquier, Sorel
Léon Dupuis
Joseph Lachapelle
Elzéar Martin, Sorel
Edouard Tremblay, Lacolle
Richard Barrette
Arthur Côté
Louis Lavallée, St. Victoire
Ludger Leclair, St. Ours
Pierre Lafrance
Alfred Racicot
Joseph Simpson
Louis Berthiaume
Joseph Donais
Joseph Berthiaume

1861

Marcel Girard
Charles Giroux
Théodule Bélanger
Pierre Lavallée
George B. Langevin
Ludger Mïontminy
Charles Grenon
Joseph Laplante
Gilbert Chassé
Joseph Baril
Arthur Olivier
Joseph Nault
Pierre Grenon
Hyacinthe Roy
J.-B. Doucette
Moïse Leblanc
Narcisse Roy
Elzéar Martin
Michel Gélineau

1862

Charles Angers, St. Hughes

Salomon Lafaille
Charles Luc
Antoine Jalbert
François Beaudoin
Abel Gagnon
Pierre Gagnon
Henri Jalbert

1863

Pascal Sénecal, Boucherville
Joseph Girard, Roxton Falls
François Darche
Napoléon Leboeuf, St. Ours
Léon Cadotte
Joseph Cartier
J.-B. Gaudreau
Widow of Alexis Boyer, Lacolle
Joseph Brunelle
J.-B. St. Pierre
François Charron
Joseph Ouimet
Charles Nault

1864

Louis (Naflet) Larivière
Amable Doucette
Olivier Brousseau
Philippe Dupaul
Joseph Gaudette
Narcisse Lavallée
Widow of Augustin Ferron
Gilbert Forçier
Joseph Caouette
Léon Gaudette
Albert Gaudette
Louis Lavallée
David Boucher
Joseph Desgreniers
Médard Duquette
Louis Gaudette
Joseph (Felix) Peloquin
Louis Parent

1865

Joseph Lavoie

Moïse Monette
Charles Lacroix
Joseph Picotte
Antoine Pariseau
Gédéon Surprenant
Trefflé Tétreault
Narcisse Tessier
Clément Arnaud
Ambroise Abel
Albain Abel
Jacob Pinsonneault
Eugène Pinsonneault
Joseph Bertrand
David Bourque
Olivier Deblois
Pierre Gaudreau
Thomas Grégoire
Narcisse Vaillancourt
Edouard Vincelette
Joseph Bourdeau
François Tremblay
Toussaint Bourdeau
François Proulx
Joseph Goddu
Gédéon Pinsonneault

CHAPTER IV

Immigration—Hardships of the First Colonists—Their Faithful

Spirit—Canadian Gatherings

The first few years spent in this country were years of hardship for our forefathers. They were foreigners to the language and manners of those they encountered. Work was hard to find, and they were exploited in the most horrible ways. Often, they regretted leaving good old Canada, and often their eyes turned with anguish to that corner of the sky from whence they came. But their faith was as strong as their hardships were numerous; good Catholics, mostly from St. Ours, they arrived in a Protestant milieu where they risked losing the purity of their Canadian morals along with the religion of their fathers. Without priests, without churches, their strong faith was put to the test. It was a dark hour for these good souls, but God was watching over the cradle of this colony which, in time, would develop quite prodigiously.

From 1837 to 1850, religious services were rare and to compensate, people would gather at the home of one of the families, and there, kneeling at the foot of a makeshift altar, the first Canadians of Southbridge would say evening prayers together and would recite the rosary of the Virgin Mary. Perhaps they also sang some hymns, which would have most certainly provoked many tears by stirring up tender memories of the homeland and the loved ones left behind on the other side of the Canadian border. Most of the families who emigrated from Canada were not well educated, so when one of them received a letter from the old country, they would gather together to read it aloud.

Oh, how those Canadian gatherings must have been charming! They would play cards and smoke some good Canadian tobacco, for sure; the women would enjoy chatting away while knitting. These family gatherings were what kept the flame of patriotism alive, along with the torch of faith.

Thus by 1850, there were about thirty Canadian families and most of them lived in the "Globe," but there was a setback when a horrible fire destroyed the "Globe Village" factories. This conflagration sent the Canadian colony into disarray. However, no other important incidents befell this foreign population, outsiders to the manners and customs of this country.

In 1861, the Civil War was declared between the Northern and Southern states. Shortly thereafter, mills closed and money became scarce; these disastrous effects served to paralyze Canadian emigration for several years. Further, a certain number of families returned to Canada. But when the war ended, prosperity quickly spread across the country; the factories had to operate day and night in order to meet the demands of their clients.

In 1865, we see the number of Canadian families grow in the Eastern states.

God's Providence is great. The movement of our people towards the American coastline had as a happy consequence the enlarging God's realm and the propagation of the Catholic faith. Canadians were taking possession of Eastern America.

Southbridge had its throng of families newly arrived from the countryside and from the towns of Canada. As we know, among these families were day-laborers and ruined farmers whose worn-out lands, with no fertilizer or good crops, failed to give them what they needed to live.

Oh! I know, these unfortunate first families, driven out of their country by poverty, were shamelessly denigrated, hated, and considered to be rejects that Canada was proud to be rid of. I know that even men whose education would seem to preclude it dared to insult these people, people disinherited by fortune and fallen into poverty and destitution—I know that politicians went so far as to spit in the faces of these people who were far more honest than their detractors, saying these ignominious words: "Let them leave, it's only the vultures who are departing." But even in their tattered clothes, in all that poverty, there were good hearts, noble souls who painfully felt the insults slung at them.

Most left the homeland not because of ingratitude but because the land could not feed them; with a heart saddened by pain, tortured by the anguish of departure and by taking the path to the great unknown, the Canadian emigrant must have had proud courage in his soul. The hope of finding honest pay and of soon returning to the homeland with a bit of money to pay the mortgage, that's what pushed our forefathers to come work in the manufacturing centers of New England, that's the only crime that they can be found guilty of. Certainly, the great majority settled and stayed here, but we can not blame these Canadians who, after being jeered upon their departure, were seen as being lesser upon their return. Under the floating waves of the starred flag, there was enough room for our forefathers to breathe in the pure air of freedom. The motherland will always be dear to the Franco-American heart, but this heart will never forget the benevolent welcome that it received from its adoptive mother.

The reader will forgive us, we hope, for having inserted this topic, but we owe it to our ancestors; we want to rectify certain false beliefs that, happily, are starting to disappear among our Canadian brothers concerning their brothers in the United States.

We suggested earlier that the first Canadian colonists to settle in Southbridge were fervent Christians; well, we are going to prove it by telling you all that they accomplished for the Catholic faith in the chapter entitled "Religion."

CHAPTER V

Religion—First Catholic Parish—First Communion

As we previously indicated, from 1838 to 1850, we made do in terms of religion in Southbridge; we did not yet have a Canadian priest, and it was not unheard of to come across infants who were one year old or older who had not yet been baptized. The first marriages were celebrated by ministers of other religions or by justices of the peace. Happily, people hastened to the altar when the first occasion to bless these marriages by a Catholic priest occurred.

Some of the more fortunate among us, who had the means to afford it, would go to make their marriage vows in Worcester, the closest place where one could find Irish Catholic priests. It must be stated that the first Canadians of Southbridge to be struck down by death in these years of paucity had to leave this valley of tears without the consolations that our "Holy Religion" provides to the dying.

It was in 1840 that the first mass was celebrated in Southbridge, in a house directly across from the "Globe Village House." This house was the property of Mr. Leery, foreman at the "Hamilton" factory. The celebrant was Reverend James Fitton, and twelve people attended this first mass, including seven Irish people and the rest Canadian and German. Father Fitton came to say mass and administer the sacraments until 1843. For two years after that, it was either Father Williamson or Father Gibson, then there was Father Logan, who was the first priest to say mass in Southbridge on Sundays.

The first priest to come to Southbridge who spoke our language was Reverend Father Lévesque, from the "Holy Cross" college in Worcester, who celebrated mass for some time in a house owned by a Canadian family in "Globe Village."

Reverend L.O. Triganne, priest in the Notre-Dame parish.

The parish priest and vicars, 1873-1904: A. Lamy, J.M. Rioux, Monsignor G.E. Brochu, N. Rainville, J. Graton / Ed. Graton, Chas. Giroux / J.M.A. Genest, Alf. Langlois, J.H.

Reverend Fathers LeBreton and Barrette, first parish priests / Reverend Fathers Mignault and Levesque, first missionaries.

Monsignor Georges Elzéar Brochu

At this first mass Reverend Father Lévesque gave communion and baptized several children whose parents had not been able to baptize them earlier. One might easily imagine the happiness felt by these good Canadians when they were able to attend mass, to see and to hear priests of their own nationality, given that they had spent several years without a representative of their holy religion. Canadians like priests, and when circumstances deprive them of their faithful friend, they suffer. After much research on this topic, we are happy to provide our readers with some details about the life of Father Lévesque, who offered religious assistance to Canadians where they lived throughout New England. This Canadian apostolate was ordained into the priesthood on January 6, 1831 by Monsignor Bernard Claude Panet, second archbishop of Québec. After a ministry in Canada and one in France where he spent several years as a parish priest, he returned home and, having learned that a good number of his fellow citizens had crossed the border to live in the United States, he resolved to follow them and for "twenty-three years" he was a missionary. For twenty-three years, he devoted himself heart and soul to the Canadian emigrants from his homeland. He died in New Jersey on

February 13, 1862.

Father Lévesque, as we mentioned earlier, traveled around to various communities in New England, but he was particularly well known in Spencer, where he built the first Canadian church in honor of Our Lady of the Holy Rosary. Only those who saw him at work can understand the zeal that consumed this apostle of the Lord. Yes, for twenty-three years, this apostle was tireless; often obliged to celebrate the holy mysteries in private houses, to partake of the same lot as the poor parishioners, to travel throughout the year at a time when transportation was rudimentary, to share the meager fare of his flock, never having a stable home, it is easy to understand why this devoted priest died at a relatively young age.

First Communion

When Father Lévesque came to Southbridge in 1851, he prepared several children, even older young people, for first communion. Those who attended this very impressive ceremony cherish the memory of it. Not only did they have the thrill of seeing and hearing a priest who was Canadian like them, but to attend a first communion, to live a few of those intoxicating hours that remind us of the ever-comforting day when Jesus-Host came into our hearts for the first time and to remind us of the humble church or poor chapel where this great mystery occurred—oh, those dear Canadians must have shed tears of joy watching their children approach the Holy Table. They must have ravenously savored the words that Father Lévesque spoke during this solemn event!

It seems that even our good and devout missionary was very moved to see so many Canadians rushing over to him and above all to discover that the faith of their forefathers so strongly lived on in their souls. It was said that he was inspired to write a detailed report about it for the Archbishop of Boston. Monsignor Fitzpatrick thus established the first parish in Southbridge in 1852.

The first communion was held in the first white house located on West Street or "Pond Road"; this house still stands and was inhabited by Mr. Pierre Giard for thirty years. A good number of Canadians attended this religious ceremony, perhaps the first of its kind in Southbridge since the start of the emigration, which was twenty years earlier. Some people brought flowers, others rugs, chairs, candles, and other decorations; they say around forty children made their first communion that day, and we are happy to publish some of their names, which were difficult to procure.

The First Communicants:

Joseph Gélinas
Joseph Quevillon

Antoine Quevillon
Jean Hêtu
François Hêtu
Louis Métivier
Louis Potvin
Pierre Potvin
Pierre Lusignan
Charles Bouthillette
François Bouthillette
Joseph Langevin
Jean J. Legros
François Larivière
Israël Aucoin
Cyril Giard
Prudence Larivée
Julienne Langevin
Philomène Dumas
Edmire Larivière
William Laflèche
Marie Jeanne Legros
Délima St. Martin
Robert St. Martin
Marcelline St. Martin
Toussaint Boisvert
Louise Boisvert
Emélie Boisvert

In 1852, Reverend Father Lévesque came back to Southbridge, and the mass was celebrated in a hall in the city which, although quite spacious, was literally packed. Browsing through the registers of those first years, we see that Father Lévesque officiated at several marriages: in 1850, Paul Potvin married Désanges St. Martin. In 1852, Joseph Collette married Marie Larivée; Isaac Potvin wed Edwige St. Martin; Prisque Larivée wed Marie Daviault.

Names of the First Baptisms

We must first note that the Canadians of Southbridge who were baptized prior to April 10, 1852, had to go to the St. John parish in Worcester to get their baptismal certificates, for here are the excerpts that we have been able to procure thanks to the kindness of Reverend Father Mullin, priest of the Saint Mary church in that city:

a. *Rémi Balthazar*, son of Henri Balthazar and of Louise Gar, born on March 25, 1853, was baptized on April 3, 1853; godfather Fr. Delause,

godmother Madeleine Gar.
P.J. Blenkinsop, S.J.

b. *Jean-Baptiste Alphonse Lemoine*, son of Antonio Lemoine and
Elizabeth Mogie, born on May 17, 1853, baptized on June 5. Godfather
Godfroi Mogie; godmother Salina Langelier.
P.J. Blenkinsop, S.J.

c. *Eugène Lacroix*, son of Eugène Lacroix and Emélie Rivière, born July
9, 1853, baptized August 21; godfather Jean Chenille, godmother Julia
Longville.
P.J. Blenkinsop, S.J.

d. *Zilda Dupré*, daughter of Pierre Dupré and Julie Lacroix, born August
12, 1853, baptized on the 23rd. Godfather and godmother Herménégilde
Boutin and Sophie River.
P.J. Blenkinsop, S.J.

e. *François Aucoin*, son of Joseph Aucoin and Lucie Therrien, born on
October 5, 1853, and baptized on the 23rd. François Bouvier and
Rosanna Janelle.
P.J. Blenkinsop, S.J.

f. *Louis Lachapelle*, son of Louis Lachapelle and Carisse Longueville,
born December 14, 1853, baptized on the 25th.

Louis Roi, born January 30, 1854, baptized on February 5.

Joseph Collette, son of Joseph Collette and Marie DeRivière, born on
March 13, 1854, baptized March 19. Godfather Felix Larivière,
godmother Aramea Giguère. P.J. Blenkinsop, S.J.

CHAPTER VI

Second Apostle of Southbridge—Father Joseph Edward Napoléon

Migneault—Third, Fr. Barrette

The first Canadians of Southbridge were lucky to have known, other than Fr. Lévesque, another apostle of Christ who spared nothing for his flock, and this devoted priest was Reverend Father Nap. Migneault. Born in St. Denis sur Richelieu on September 17, 1826, Fr. Migneault was the son of the notary Joseph-Edouard. At the age of thirteen, he entered the St. Hyacinthe Seminary, and after completing his classical studies, he was admitted to the novitiate of the Oblates in 1844. He took his vows in that congregation and was ordained in Ottawa on December 24, 1849 by Monsignor Guigues. From 1845 to 1850, he was the director of students at the college recently opened in the Canadian capital, and from 1850 to 1851, he was the superior. When he left that position, he also left the community and became pastor of "L'Orignal," where he lived from June to September of that year; then, he left for Massachusetts in the United States. At first he tried to offer special services to the Canadians of Worcester. Despite two years of labor, he was not able to do it; in 1853, he became the pastor of Webster, and he served Spencer, Southbridge, Oxford, Charlton, Templeton, Barre, Warren and the Brookfields. He was succeeded by Rev. P. Quan on August 31, 1858.

Fr. Migneault left a lasting impression on the people of Webster and Southbridge, where his unfailing devotion and his warm and vibrant words won over everyone's hearts. Next, he spent four years as the chaplain in the 76th American regiment, which he followed on their campaigns during the Civil War. Afflicted by illnesses, the consequences of this difficult ministry, he worked no more. In the end, in recognition of his service, the United States government paid him a pension of $12 per month. He had spent only one year in retirement at the farm of the Grey Nuns of St. Hyacinthe when he died on December 15, 1895 at the age of 69, and two days later he was buried in the cemetery of his birth parish.

Fr. Angelus Barrette, D.D.

Up to this point, there had not yet been a resident priest in Southbridge, but on September 11, 1865, Fr. Barrette was named pastor of Southbridge and also served all of the Catholics of Charlton and

Sturbridge. Fr. Barrette lived in the parish until November 10, 1869, when he was named pastor to the newly founded parish in Grafton. Fr. Barrette came from a noble family in France and he was erudite.

Here is some information that we have been able to find here and there about him. First, it must be stated that his position was quite delicate because his name and his French origins must surely have been disagreeable to the Irish parishioners. According to some of the older parishioners who knew Fr. Barrette well, he was more or less pleased with his stay in Southbridge, though he had to reconcile many differences of opinion. Nonetheless, he was always held in high esteem. He had a remarkable eloquence, and people never tired of hearing him speak.

We read in *La Voix du Peuple* (*The Voice of the People*), Ferdinand Gagnon's Manchester newspaper, that during the big St. Jean Baptiste day[12] celebration in Worcester in 1869, Fr. Barrette from Southbridge gave the special sermon after the mass. We will quote in entirety. "The preacher, it is said, spoke of the text: *'Nisi Dominus aedificaverit domum, in vanum laboraverunt, qui aedificant eam.'* It was eloquent—he compared the St.-Jean-Baptiste Society of Worcester to a locomotive. The drops of water unite and under the influence of heat become steam. It is the same for the St. Jean Baptiste societies. They prosper, but if they are not supported by religion, they will fall. Returning to the Scriptures, he compared the first Canadian emigrants to the captives of Babylon. 'The Canadians were not respected; they were hated fifteen years ago and people told them: Go sing your national songs.' They responded, *'Quomodo cantabimus in terra aliena.'* Good-hearted people came together and exclaimed: *'Adhaereat lingua faucibus meis, si oblitus fuero Jerusalem'*—May my tongue stick to my palate if ever I forget you, Canada. And the St. Jean Baptiste societies were founded." This sermon made a strong impression on the listeners.

The party held that bright day, forever in the memories of the Canadians, was blessed with speeches and music. Fr. Barrette was still one of the favorite orators.

---

[12] Translator's note: Saint-Jean-Baptiste (Saint John the Baptist) is the patron saint of Québec. From the early days of French settlement in Canada, people celebrated the feast of St. Jean Baptiste, a religious holiday on June 24, as a way to give thanks for their lives in the New World. These celebrations later became patriotic, in addition to religious, a way of celebrating French-Canadian culture and heritage. Today, June 24 is the official "national holiday" of the Province of Québec.

CHAPTER VII

Founding of the First French-Canadian Catholic Parish in

Southbridge—Its First Pastor

Up to this point, we have been more or less working in the dark, being guided by details, sometimes obscure, that we were able to find here and there, but now we swing the doors wide open to work in the Lord's bright sunlight as we recount the most interesting part of our story. In this chapter, we will describe the humble beginnings of the first Canadian parish of Southbridge, Notre Dame parish, which is today one of the most flourishing and most beautiful parishes in New England. For half a century the French-Canadians of Southbridge have had their own church where, in their own way and with their own devotion, they are able to praise God with all their hearts and souls, to honor the One who has watched over them with such care and solicitude in this country where they are surrounded by all kinds and by so many dangers.

The year 1869 is consequently a year that will never be forgotten. It was the year in which the Notre Dame parish was founded, the year when the Canadians separated from the Irish with whom they had formed the first Catholic parish in Southbridge and with whom they had built the first church known as *"Eglise St. Pierre"* (St. Peter's Church). This first church was transformed into a parochial school for the children of the new Irish parish, Saint Mary's.

The dedication for the *St. Pierre* parish was held on May 1st, 1853 by Monsignor Fitzpatrick, and it was not until the fall of 1869, after the departure of Fr. Barrette for Grafton, that the Canadians obtained the right to organize and to establish a separate parish. Their first pastor was the Reverend M. F. LeBreton, of French origin, who was named by Monsignor Williams of Boston in October 1867. We know very little about this first pastor. His profound humility is the reason for the very few details we have. This is terribly regretful, for during the four years that Fr. LeBreton spent with us, he worked hard for his God and his compatriots, and we would have liked to have given you his full biography. At least he left a photograph, which we are happy to share with you. It's the only relic that he left behind, and we offer it to you.

Thus, the Canadians, free to work as they wished, immediately went to work under the direction of their parish priest whose zeal and devotion were surely equal to his position and circumstances. The land where today we find the old Notre Dame church, on Pine Street, was donated by the "Hamilton Woolen" company and a subscription from the Canadians soon raised $3,000 to build the church that was completed in 1870.

At that time, Canadians numbered 1,800 to 2,000 out of a population of 5,000 souls. The first mass for the Notre-Dame parish was celebrated on November 29, 1869 in Edwards hall.

The first church was built under the direction of the contractor Leonard Cutler and cost $17,000.

The First Baptisms in the Notre-Dame Parish

The first baptism held in the new parish was that of Marie-Jeanne Laplante, daughter of Olivier Laplante and Marie Leclerc. This baptism was held on November 21st, 1869, about a month after the arrival of Reverend Father LeBreton.

On the 28th of that month, the pastor baptized Edwige Lamoureux, daughter of Azarie Lamoureux and Hilda Nault.

First Marriages

On November 22, Fr. LeBreton celebrated the marriage of Narcisse Simon and Thaïse Ménard; on the 23rd, that of Jules Cartier and Marie St. Onge; and that of Pierre Lavallée and Julie Desgreniers; on the 26th, that of Jean-Baptiste Lussier and Louise Lusignan.

Monsignor G. Elz. Brochu, Second Pastor

After nearly four years, Fr. LeBreton left the parish in the spring of 1873 and Reverend Father P. Elz. Brochu, who was his vicar for some time, was named parish priest. Before his departure, Fr. LeBreton had put a mortgage on the rectory for a considerable sum of money in order to be able to reimburse the personal funds he had put into this building. A certain number of the parishioners were unhappy with this because they were under the false impression that the rectory had been paid for with parish funds. Our books show, however, that Fr. LeBreton had actually advanced the money, taking all the risks implied. In the spring of 1874, the Southbridge savings bank, who owned the mortgage, sold it at auction and the parish re-purchased it for the sum of $4,500.

In order to raise this amount, a subscription was launched and brought in $2,225.75. We are in a position to publish the complete list of those who, in this difficult circumstance, were able to open their purse-strings to avoid this disastrous shipwreck, but we will just publish the names of the primary donors:

Rev. G. Elz. Brochu...$100
Eugène Lescot (Lescault)...50
C. Edouard Houde...50

George Lamoureux...45
Victor Lamoureux...40
Victor Clément M.D....40
Alexandre Lataille...40
Abel Gagnon...30
Pierre Surprenant...30
Michel Cyriac...25
Marcel Girard...25
J. Felix Leclerc...25
Pascal Sénécal, junior...25
Narcisse Brodeur...25
Napoléon Métivier...25
Pierre Boucher...20
Xavier Aucoin...20
Léon Cadot, senior...20
Narcisse Champigny...20
Antoine Chapdelaine...20
Olivier Deblois...20
Joseph Dupaul...20
Joseph Goddu, senior...20
Wm. Gélineau...20
Pierre Larivière...20
Eugène Lacroix...20
Charles Lacroix...20
Gédéon Maurand...20
Gédéon Pinsonnault, senior...20
Pierre St. Martin...20
Jérémie Thériault...20
J.-B. Robillard, senior...20

Reverend Father Brochu took over in the parish, as he himself writes in the registers, on August 23, 1873. Upon his departure, Fr. LeBreton left a $10,000 mortgage on the Notre-Dame church. As you can imagine, this was a somber beginning for the second parish priest, who held nothing back in re-inspiring hope in the hearts of the parishioners who were a little discouraged at that time.

CHAPTER VIII

Fr. Brochu's Administration—First Schools—Nun's Convent

A priest knows from experience that a Catholic school in the parish is indispensable. He also knows that it is his commanding duty to establish one as soon as possible. Further, in this parochial school the Canadian priest wants to see that, after religion, the maternal language takes priority. In effect, without such a bastion for religion and patriotism, the abandonment of religious and national beliefs becomes all too frequent, for the priest has no reasonable assistance in his devotion and his efforts are in vain. Reverend Father LeBreton was not unaware of this truth; so as early as 1871, he built a house, that is today the residence of the Sisters, to use as a school. The pastor requested that Mrs. Louis Kasky, former Canadian school teacher, come teach the children in the new parish. In 1873, Mrs. Kasky left to live in Canada with her family and was replaced by Mr. Antoine Primeau; in 1874, she returned to Southbridge to regain her position as school teacher and stayed here until 1879 when she left to teach in Webster for two years and then in Spencer for a few more years.

At that time, Canadians felt the need for more education: an indispensable tool for employment in the commercial and industrial fields. It's for this precise reason that Reverend Father Brochu decided to expand the school, establish a convent, and have teaching nuns.

At that time and even earlier, the following people taught classes: Mrs. Fr. Bonin taught day and evening classes on and off from 1865 to 1870; Phélonise St. Onge from 1873 to 1874; Jacques Tétrault taught night school from 1876 to 1880; Joseph Park from 1879 to 1880 and Narcisse St. Germain taught evening classes almost continually from 1875 to 1880.

Mr. St. Germain, born in St. Dénis, was a notary and former teacher in Canada, which made him very well qualified for teaching. Also, several young people made great progress under his skillful direction and have excellent memories of him.

When Mrs. Kasky was teaching classes, the children also made rapid progress, for she had a remarkable way of teaching and several of her pupils here in Southbridge still praise her methods. Beyond the gift of teaching, Mrs. Kasky had a remarkable talent for organizing dramatic performances and entertaining shows, which were given at various times to benefit the school and the parish: this made her contribution even more precious. The shows also had the great effect of encouraging students to apply themselves to their studies and engaging the parents in the issue of education. So when Mrs. Kasky was leaving, the parishioners joined together with the pastor in thanking her for her devotion and congratulating her on her sublime work before God and man; they did not fail to express their regret in seeing her leave the parish. Indeed, it was a great loss for the parish, to witness the departure of someone so full of zeal who, with her two daughters Marie and Octavie as assistants, had done so much for Catholic and national endeavors in Southbridge.

In 1879, Pastor Brochu called a parish assembly and announced to the listeners that it was up to them to complete the convent, for, he said, he could no longer do anything else. Due to certain changes and reforms that he initiated in the parish, several people were very unhappy with him and no longer wished to contribute to that cause.

Committees were formed to go visit Canadians in their homes; Michel Surprenant, who was in business and who had a certain influence among his compatriots, was chosen as treasurer. The various committees soon got to work and encountered many obstacles and much bad will. Some did not want to give because they had issues with the pastor; they went so far as to demand his departure. Others, in their ignorance, did not see the need for a parochial school which would be a heavy burden to bear. They said that there were already good schools in Southbridge. Still others did not yet understand the need to send children to school, for at that time it was not obligatory and it was not uncommon for children of seven or eight years old to work in the mills. The parents said it was not necessary to be educated in order to make a living, *"that the more learn, the more dishonest you become."* Further, some of our compatriots gave the excuse that they were not planning to live in the United States for long, that as soon as they returned home their children would go to school, and that anyway it was not necessary for "farmers" to be that well educated. We insist on giving you these details so that you will understand the strange mindset of a certain group of Canadians from that time and the countless difficulties that Fr. Brochu had to overcome in achieving his goals. Despite the opposition, the various committees finally succeeded in raising a certain amount of funds.

In 1880, new obstacles emerged: some disagreements occurred between the pastor and the convent contractor, Alphonse Béford, a difference of opinion that led the contractor to stop work and demand a payment higher than his contract. He earned nothing however. New committees were formed to ensure the continuation of this work. In the fall of 1880, there was a great bazaar organized in this new building. Receipts totaled $5,000 and with this sum and other funds from similar events, work was completed and the convent was ready to welcome nuns from Saint Anne in Lachine, Québec when the school opened.

CHAPTER IX

1881—Arrival of the Sisters of St. Anne—Brochu Academy

Finally, the pastor's vow was fulfilled; he was going to have the strong support of the nuns in the work of his ministry. The Sisters of Saint Anne arrived in Southbridge on August 3, 1881. It was a real event in the parish, an event that was cause for much rejoicing in Southbridge.

The day of their arrival, a large delegation of parishioners awaited them at the train station; starting at 8am, a good number of people, many elderly women, hurried to get the best spots in order to be the first to greet the nuns who would do so much good for their children. We must admit that they had quite some time to anticipate and prepare for this honor, since the group did not arrive at the train station until 11:30am.

The Sisters of Saint Anne began work and assumed management of the school, a mission they continued religiously until 1889 when a regrettable misunderstanding led to their abandonment of the mission in July of that year.

This event distressed the entire parish because the good nuns were held in high esteem by the parishioners. During their time in Southbridge, they had earned the right to be admired and beloved by the population. Under their direction, the children were transformed; the nurturing influence of Christian education provided by the nuns was felt in even the most humble families. Many young girls had already entered the sisterhood, and thanks to their instruction, several young people already occupied enviable positions in commerce and in the mills, and still others had left to continue their studies in colleges in Canada.

In 1890, there were no longer any nuns and there were no public schools spacious enough to welcome the children from the convent school, so the pastor rented the convent to the municipal school committee for it to be run as a public school. This pastoral decision created a lot of emotion and significant discontent among a certain group of parishioners, especially among those to whom the sacraments had been refused precisely because they did not want to send their children to the parish school.

This act by the pastor was sorely misunderstood and as a result, for several years, a good number of parents no longer wished to send their children to the convent school, even after a permanent one had been established. Unfortunately, this prejudice still exists today among certain narrow-minded folks who held on to the deplorable compulsion to send their offspring to secular schools rather than the parochial schools, though their Catholic conscience requires it.

A law passed in the legislature in 1891 stated that in order for a parochial school to be exempt from municipal taxes, it must be placed under the direction of trustees and formed as a corporation. So, on October 11, 1891, Reverend Father Brochu named the following trustees: Clément Bégin, Amable Loiseau, Felix Gatineau, Horace Gravel, Joseph D. Blanchard, Camille Métras, Joseph M. Dupaul, Georges J. Lamoureux, Victor Lamoureux and Felix Leclair.

When the Sisters of Saint Anne took possession of the convent, there were nine of them and they had about 500 pupils. This convent, which was used both as their home and as a school, had cost the parish about $25,000.

When the Sisters of the Assumption of Nicolet replaced the Sisters of Saint Anne in 1891, there were about the same number of pupils, but since the parish was always growing, people started to feel the need to have a school separate from the convent. In 1899, there were twelve nuns who nourished the hearts and minds of seven hundred pupils.

The Pastor and the Vicars, 1904-1919. Back row: J.M. Marceau, P.L. D'Amour, G. Laverdière, A. Landry, S. Guillet, H. Rémy. Front row : Ph. Therrien, L.T. Rodier, L.O. Triganne, pastor, J.P. Bourassa, R. Laporte.

Reverend L.O. Triganne, Pastor" and "Notre Dame Church, Southbridge, Mass.

Notre Dame Church, Southbridge, Mass.: Interior of the Notre Dame Church

Interior of the Notre Dame Church. Photo taken from the Sanctuary.

The New School—Brochu Academy

Fr. Brochu wanted to give his parish a magnificent school, an institution that would make the parish proud and glorify the French Canadians living in New England, and his hopes were realized, for those who saw and visited this large and spacious school unanimously declare that it is a masterpiece of its kind. The work began in 1899. The land on which the building stands cost $5,000 and the building contract was $31,869. All in all, it cost around $40,000.

As for a description of this school, it is a vast brick edifice with three floors, ideally located at the corner of Pine Street and Edwards Street. On the first floor there are six classrooms, and the same on the second floor. The entire third floor is dedicated to a splendid chapel that can hold eight or nine hundred people. There's a sacristy and, in the chapel, they installed a superb organ that cost $1,000. In the rear of the chapel, there is a wonderful painting of Monsignor Brochu. For several years, every Sunday, a children's mass was celebrated in the chapel because, before the parish divided, the church was almost too small for worshiping. All of the children went to mass in the chapel so there would be enough seats for the adults in the church. Today, the Holy Sacrifice is only celebrated there under special circumstances, such as the opening or closing of the school year or on certain holidays. There are not many educational institutions, or even colleges here or in Canada, that have such a chapel.

Nothing was spared to make this school into a perfect model of its type; all modern improvements are there, light streams in as does God's fresh air.

They named the school *Brochu Academy*, in honor of Monsignor Brochu, who promised to pay for it out of his own pocket, a promise he kept, for by December 1899, at the start of the work, he did so. It was really "*his school,*" and as we saw earlier, it not only cost him a lot of money but also many setbacks, which led to many worries.

The second pastor of Notre-Dame was actually a great supporter of education, and he proved it by giving his parish this gem of a school and also by the force of his will.

Today, approximately 650 students attend this school. The children pay nothing to receive an education and Christian instruction. Despite all these advantages, it is deplorable to note that a certain number of parents are ignorant and blind to such a point that they refuse their children a Christian education, which is the only way to mold the human heart and mind so as to become a practicing Catholic and an honest and useful citizen. It's an illness that seems to have no remedy, and yet we must stamp out this prejudice which tends to cause so much harm to our youth.

What response will guilty parents have when they must account for their handling of their family affairs and the education of their children? Parents who are perhaps reading these lines, help us to achieve a total triumph for Catholic education in Southbridge. In another chapter, we will discuss the work of the Sisters of the Assumption.

CHAPTER X

Troubles in the Parish—1880-81-82—Consequences

Clearly, to run a parish like Notre Dame, one must have a great talent for tact and mediation. Fr. Brochu steered the ship, in spite of some fairly serious storms, without going off course. Although he was quite shy at first, he understood that a strong hand was needed at the helm, a hand that would not tremble no matter the danger, and nothing could stop him from accomplishing what he thought to be his duty. With a loyal, sincere, and open heart, he never wished to deviate from his first course of action.

A man of duty always encounters some obstacle in his path, and Fr. Brochu unfortunately encountered one; in his field of action, he found many useless plants and many barren trees; people chastised him for wanting to be rid of them in a way that was too brusque. As a consequence, he made enemies, and soon there were false prophets in the parish pews spreading seeds of conflict and discord by the handful.

Several Protestant ministers from Canada visited Southbridge around this time in order to establish a Protestant congregation. There were assemblies called by the ministers and in attendance were Chiniquy, Dorion, Leclair, Benoit and others. A few Canadians abandoned the church in which they were born, for a certain time, but finally the ministers realized that they had little chance of success in Southbridge and needed to go in a different direction, and then order was reestablished.

We should also say that Fr. Brochu was an eloquent man, and when he ascended to the pulpit, a religious silence reigned in the assembly. He had the gift of captivating his listeners, grabbing them and electrifying them. He was, however, often very vehement, becoming excessively carried away in certain circumstances and saying things that he later bitterly regretted. But since people knew his intense personality, they loved him and easily forgave him for any little mischief he might have gotten into during the heat of improvisation.

CHAPTER XI

Choirs—Their Formation

As soon as the Notre Dame Church was completed, the pastor's first thought was to form a choir. Narcisse Lavigne was the first choirmaster. The other cantors were: Flavien Laflamme, François Surprenant, Olivier Deblois, Romain Caron, Alcime Marchand, Eugène Marchand and Mr. Archambeault. For the most part, these gentlemen had been cantors in Canada and, following the custom reigning in the homeland at that time, were placed in the sanctuary, wearing cassocks and surplices. They sang plainchant for they had no organ to accompany them.

Among these cantors were several who were very skilled, and everything was to the highest satisfaction of the pastor and the parishioners who were reminded of the good years in Canada.

There were, however, a certain number of young people in the parish who had been involved in the choir at St. Mary's Church, and in that church there was usually regular singing with an organ, so plainchant was not too appealing. That is why, in 1873, there was a meeting of young people who wanted to form a choir like the ones we have in our parishes today.

They chose Clément Bégin as president and made immediate arrangements with Professor Baribeau from Worcester who, for several months, came each week to give singing lessons to the new choir of the Notre Dame parish. Joseph Bourque, who was a good musician, was chosen as director. Eléas Giard, Mrs. C.V. Clément and Miss Rosa Hefner were in turn the organists from 1873 to 1875.

The members of the first choir in 1873 were: Clément Bégin, Joseph and Alfred-Xavier Bourque, the four brothers George, Joseph, Edmond and Misael Goddu; Alexander and Alexis Sénécal, Remi Surprenant, Isaac St. Martin, Joseph and Alphonse Leclair, sons of Felix Leclair, Joseph Dionne, Edmond Hêtu, Damase Bourassa, Eléas Giard, Emélie and Pauline Giard, Delphine Caron, Alphonse Caron, Cédulie and Amanda Cadotte, Octavie Barrette, Exilda Bouthillette, Eugénie Bourdelais, Rosalie Chaput, Amanda Dionne, Victor W. Lamoureux.

Lectures to Benefit the Choir

Two lectures were organized to benefit the choir, in order to purchase the books needed and pay Professor Baribeau. The first lecture was given by Judge Joseph Leboeuf from Cohoes, N.Y., who engaged the audience by speaking on the topic of "education." The second lecturer was Reverend Father Primeau from Worcester who spoke on the subject of "fortune-tellers." A tidy sum was raised and in short time the "young" group was on solid footing. With their gradual progress, the "old choir disappeared little by little until it no longer existed."

The elders had looked unfavorably upon the work of the young people, and there was some anguish in seeing themselves replaced. Some found the singing of the new choir to be disconnected from the topics and spirit of the Church. These disagreements disappeared in time, and several members of the old choir even joined the new one and stayed on for several years.

Choirs—Next Episode

In 1875, Catherine Whitaker was chosen as organist to replace Rosa Hefner, and a certain number of new members joined the others. From 1875 to 1880, here are the names:

Marie Kasky
Octavie Kasky
Elise Kasky
Rosa Lafaille
Palmyre Lavoie
Felix Gatineau
Victor Gatineau
Camille Métras
Amanda Leclair
Dr. J.A. Robillard
Dr. Théophile Bélanger
Adelaide Girard
Henri Lavoie
Cordélie Lord
Miss. Remillard
Xyste Lescault
Odile Simpson
Marie Lavallée
Marie Donais
Séraphine Gravel
Sophie Lord
Marie Lord
Marie Richard

1880 to 1890

Ernest Decelles
Joseph M. Lareau
Arthur Sicotte
Jules Trudel

Raymond Dostaler
J.A. Caron
Arthur Riendeau
Joseph Pinsonneault
Marie Pinsonneault
Alexandre Montminy
Joseph Leclair
Horace Gravel
Joseph Gatineau
Alfred Potvin
Alfred Galipeau
Louis Delâges
Joseph Desrosiers, eldest son of Louis
Joseph Desrosiers, second son of Louis
Dr. L.O. Morasse
Maria Leroux
Olivine Leroux
Adéline Girard

1890 to 1900

Albina Surprenant
Maria Surprenant
Ida Surprenant
Felix Lavallée
George Cabana
Dr. Oswald Grégoire
Dr. J.E. Ferland
Dr. L.E. Dionne
Wilfrid Casavant
Sergius Gatineau
Ovila Paulin
De. Dr. J.A. Pontbriand
Olivier Lamothe
Pierre Peloquin

Miss Walker was the parish organist until 1889, when she was succeeded by Miss Emélie Surprenant. Miss Surprenant held this position until 1890 and was replaced by Albina Surprenant. Then there was Mrs. Alice Bardy-Dionne; Mrs. Louis Tétrault until 1905; Miss Joséphine Bonneau from 1905 to 1912; then Mrs. Ve. Joseph Tétrault from 1912 to 1916, and from 1916 through the present day, Prof. Eugène Tapin.

Choir Directors
Clément Bégin, Joseph Bourque, Catherine Whitaker, Ernest

Decelles, Horace Gravel, Oliva Palin, Dr. L.E. Dionne, Olivier Lamothe, Reverends J.A. Langlois, J.P. Chicoine, J. Fredette and Louis Delages, Rev. Pierre Bourassa, and the current organist Prof. Eugène Tapin.

Fr. Brochu's administration, like all administrations, was not perfect, but it is no less true that with his impetus the parish made rapid progress. From the founding of the parish in 1869 through the month of December 1898, there were more than 991 marriages and 4,728 baptisms.

CHAPTER XII

The Knights of St. Joseph

Fr. Brochu wanted to turn the Notre Dame parish into a perfectly organized parish, a parish where nothing was left to be desired. Not content with having built a model school to nourish his children's hearts and minds, he wanted to found a Catholic club which would have the goal of bringing together young people to give them good advice in order to guard against the influence of bad company.

This society founded by Fr. Brochu was known as the "Knights of St. Joseph." It was organized on May 15, 1881. There is no doubt that our readers will be happy to learn of the ultimate objective and goal of the group, as recounted by its founder. What follows is even more precious because it is pretty much the only writing from Fr. Brochu that we own. They say that "the style is the man," so judge the apostle from this glimpse:

Preface—"Knighthood"

"God having created social beings, it is natural that each individual should feel some need to establish or to join some kind of society. Unfortunately, the enemy of humanity learned to exploit this need to better achieve his goal of vice. It is through societies that, today in particular, the devil drags almost all nations of the universe behind this triumphal chariot.

"To rectify this evil, the Catholic Church has always believed in its duty to encourage and recommend the organization of Christian societies in order to counter balance the bad ones, which are the ruin of nations. Our goal in establishing the society called *The Knighthood of Saint Joseph* is, first and foremost, to divert our young people from bad societies by uniting them under the watch of the priest; second, to give them the means to acquire and improve their intellectual knowledge through reading and discussions.

"We give our society the name of Knighthood to signal to the members who will take part that they should be like the knights of the Middle Ages, men beyond reproach.

"The society is under the patronage of Saint Joseph, such that having chosen him as a model, they will attempt to imitate his virtues. As blasphemy and drunkenness are the two main heads of the hydra ravaging our population, and I can say in particular our nationality— blasphemy that offends and insults infinite mercy, drunkenness that brings misery and misfortune into the heart the family—the Knights of Saint Joseph will have to combat both, with fervor, at first in their homes, then in the homes of others.

"Since all societies need a code in order to maintain stability and their greatest strength depends on the observance of their rules, for its good government, we have decided to establish the following rules."

We will spare the reader from what follows. Suffice it to say that these rules, written largely by the pastor, are a model of their kind, and they were countersigned by the following members:

Felix Gatineau, Camille Métras, Joseph Métras, Anatole Caron, Jules Trudel, Louis Péloquin, Salomon Labonté and fifty others.

At the first assembly held on June 5th, 1881, the following officers were elected :

President, Felix Gatineau

Vice-President, Moïse Gagnon

Recording Secretary, Jules Trudel

Corresponding Secretary, Anatole Caron

Treasurer, Camille Métras

Collection Treasurer, Salomon Labonté

1st Commissioner, Joseph Bélanger

2nd Commissioner, Joseph Gamache

This association, which lasted for only three years since it no longer existed by the month of July 1884, did a lot of good; several of its members are considered today to be among the most well-known, the most honest and the most patriotic citizens of Southbridge. All the glory and all the honor stem from the zealous pastor.

CHAPTER XIII

The End of Fr. Brochu's Administration—Titles—His Death

In 1895, Fr. Brochu acquired the "Marcy" property which is without a doubt ideally located on one of the most beautiful sites in Southbridge. This property, on which we find the superb Notre Dame church today, was released to him for the sum of $10,000. We know that today it is worth over $25,000. Unfortunately, during the transaction, there was a clause that the pastor did not sufficiently take into account which prohibited him from immediately realizing his life's dream and desire: to give to the parish a church worthy of God and in line with the wishes of the devoted parishioners. The old man who had sold him the property, whether due to bigotry or stubbornness, insisted on remaining in his home until his death, and the parish had to wait until his end to realize the dream so long awaited. The poor old man was already quite elderly, but like all mortals, he loved his life and, like all others, would leave it only when God decided to end it. Later, in 1899, Fr. Brochu bought eighteen acres of land in a location above the village to turn into a cemetery which is today the magnificent "St. George" cemetery, named in honor of his patron saint. There was a need for it because the old Notre Dame cemetery could no longer accommodate the needs of the parish, which were constantly growing. Actually, upon its founding, the parish had about 3,000 parishioners, and in 1890 there were more than 6,000, including 3,500 communicants.

Monsignor Brochu's vicars, during his administration, were: Reverends Antoine Lamy, P.U. Brunelle, C. Giraut, Joseph M. Rioux, D. Daigneault, N. Rainville, Jules Graton, Edouard Graton, L.A. Langlois, J.H. Desrochers, J. Fredette, Joseph Chicoine, Pierre Bourassa and J.A. Landry. The last two were the ones who attended to Fr. Brochu in his final moments.

Fr. Brochu worked hard for the success of his parish, and needless to say, word of his success traveled as far as Rome. Thus, on July 11, 1887, the Holy Father bestowed upon him the title of Monsignor with the rank of Camerlengo of His Holiness, and on May 16, 1890, he was elevated to the highest function of Pronotary Apostolic *ad Instar*.

Biography of Monsignor Brochu

Monsignor Georges-Elzéar Brochu was born in St. Anselme, Dorchester County, Province of Québec on October 2nd, 1842. At the age of fourteen, he entered the seminary of Québec, and nine years later finished his classical studies in the Seminary of Montreal.

He was elevated to the dignity of the priesthood on August 9th, 1868 by Monsignor Ignace Bourget, and was named professor in the college at Terrebonne. In 1869, he was vicar at St. Polycarpe and two years later he moved to the diocese of Montreal where he was named chaplain of the "*Brothers of Charity*." In 1873, he was welcomed by the diocese of Springfield and, before being named pastor of Notre Dame, he was vicar in the same parish where Fr. LeBreton was pastor.

Monsignor Brochu had the gift of good health but was hard on his body, which resulted in the shortening of his days. He had absolute control over his people. Without a doubt, the road he had to travel in Southbridge was not always scattered with roses, for often he encountered thorns that painfully wounded the heart of this priest and apostle. But we can say that to his credit, during this battle, he never allowed any of his adversaries (and he had a few) to gain the upper hand. In his parish, there were ravenous wolves badly dressed in sheep's clothing; his strong and energetic will was able to stop them in their tracks, and they were never able to divert him when it came to accomplishing what he believed to be his duty.

Certainly, in the heat of the action, he did sometimes get carried away beyond limits, but after having reflected on the circumstances, and on the ill will of his adversaries, we easily forgave certain apparent errors. Those who lived during his time know that in the early days of the parish, there was a certain category of men in Southbridge who were far from being considered desirable citizens or exemplary Catholics.

He was the ruler, and he wanted to be! It is true that he even encountered violence; people went so far as to throw rocks at the rectory, which perhaps derived from bad education, but his unshakeable will prevailed above all, and little by little, the population came to realize that they had misjudged their pastor and that they had been sorely mistaken.

He wanted to be at the helm, and despite the storm, he steered the ship of his parish through all the perils, and death found him at his work. His charity and generosity prove to his people, even today, that he only chastised his parishioners because he loved them so much.

Monsignor Brochu came from a good and honest family; one of his brothers is a missionary with the Oblate Fathers in Manitoba, and three of his sisters are nuns with the Sisters of Charity. It was in the current rectory, at 27 Marcy Street, that Monsignor Brochu returned his soul to God on September 26, 1904, surrounded by members of his family and his vicars. His body lay for some time in the St. George cemetery, but later was moved to Saint-Anselme, his final resting place. In his will, he left $20,000 to the Assumptionist Fathers of Greendale, Massachusetts,

$40,000 to the Grey Nuns of Worcester, and quite a bit also to the Indian missions of Upper Canada.

CHAPTER XIV

Third Pastor—Rev. L.O. Triganne

The parishioners of Notre Dame mourned the loss of their late lamented pastor, departed to a better world, and their prayers followed him to the tomb and beyond. Nevertheless, they eagerly awaited his successor in order to continue the good work already underway with him.

In the meantime, things went on as usual under the direction of Monsignor Brochu's two devoted vicars, Mr. A. Landry and Mr. Pierre Bourassa.

At the end of November 1904, on the 24th, the Notre Dame parish welcomed its new pastor, namely the Reverend Father L.O. Triganne, current pastor, whose biography we will now provide.

Reverend Father Louis-Onésime Triganne was born in 1860 in Plessisville, Canada to Pierre Onésime Triganne and Ernestine A. Dubé. At a young age, he felt the burning desire to dedicate his entire life to God and to the salvation of souls; and after his preliminary studies, he entered the Nicolet Seminary where he studied Classics, Philosophy and Theology. He was ordained a priest by Monsignor Laflèche on December 20, 1884 in the chapel of the Seminary of Trois-Rivières. He was then vicar at Sainte Anne de la Pérade and in Saint-Justin, Canada.

Yet his zeal required a larger field of action, and so he decided to come to the United States to provide the support of his ministry to his compatriots who, by the thousands, were leaving the Canadian shores. Named vicar in Holyoke on December 8, 1886, then in Adams in 1893, it was, as stated earlier, on November 24, 1904 that Father L.O. Triganne took control of the parish of Notre Dame in Southbridge, to which he has just given one of the most beautiful churches in the diocese if not in the whole country.

The parishioners did not delay in getting to know their new pastor, and they learned that when there was work to do, the worker did not rest, and that he was up to the job.

In very little time, the parish returned to life, piety visibly permeated the entire congregation, and every Sunday, "Notre Dame" offered the most beautiful and most impressive spectacle to God, that of a large family coming together in His house to bless, thank, praise and adore their Master. It was the good old religious Canada tucked into a little corner of the country that is protected by the grand old flag.

The new pastor wanted to know his immense garden in order to be able to better cultivate the land, and since the best hope for the harvest is always in the seeds sown, this apostle first turned to the children.

School is the fulcrum on which is built the base of the entire organization of the parish, and when it is well under control, you can have the highest hopes for future success; Fr. Triganne understood this. Also, he wanted to visit the children often, and to have his vicars visit them, in order to encourage them and to invigorate their studies. Further, in Southbridge perhaps more than in any other place, children respect and love their priest; they do not run away nor do they have that awkwardness, that fear that you find among children in some of our Canadian towns; the priest is really a "father" to them!

Fr. Triganne, by nature active and devoted, quickly understood that there would be many occasions to test his zeal in this new field of action. He got to work straight away. Under his supervision, the parish took on such proportions that it was necessary to start thinking about dividing it, for the church could hardly hold everyone on Sundays. So a few years after his arrival, Southbridge created a new parish called Sacred Heart and Fr. Emile St. Onge became its first pastor. With this act, about five hundred families left Notre Dame to form the Sacred Heart parish. We will tell you more about this with ample details in a subsequent chapter, but for the moment will focus on the mother parish.

Rev. Ph.J. Therrien,
Notre Dame Parish

VicarRev. R.A. Laporte,
Vicar, Notre Dame Parish

Professor Eugène Tapin,
Organist at Notre Dame Church

H.U. Bail, Contractor for the
Notre Dame Church

First Notre Dame Church in Southbridge

Rectory of the Notre Dame Parish

First Convent, now home of the Sisters.

New Notre Dame Church—Construction—Dedication

The first Notre Dame church, erected in 1869, was a modest construction in wood and could hold around 1,200 people. It was an excellent example of its type. The old church is now used by Polish Catholics from Southbridge, and is still a comfortable building located on Pine Street, between the parish school and the residence of the Sisters. But as we said earlier, people dreamed of building, for the parishioners had long been making sacrifices and could already envision the magnificent palace that they wanted to construct for their God.

Finally, good old Wm. Marcy, despite his desires to live a long life, happily went to join his forefathers, and there were no more obstacles in the way.

So, after having taken the proper steps with the diocese, Fr. Triganne started construction on the new Notre Dame church on March 25, 1911, the day of the Annunciation of the Holy Virgin. No more perfect day could have been chosen for the construction of a church that would become one of the richest and most beautiful churches dedicated to the Mother of God in this part of the continent. And there was no better way to bestow the special benediction of God and the protective guardianship of the Virgin upon the venture and the construction work. We should also add that during the six years of work on the project, there were no accidents and no loss of life. Evidently, Mary presided over the erection of her temple, and She did not allow any obstacles to deter it.

The architect of this memorable temple is Mr. Joseph Venne of Montreal, who is in no need of a bolster to his reputation. Those who have admired his work can clearly see his talent and his genius. The same praise can be given to the contractor, Mr. Hormisdas Bail of Southbridge, the artistic designer Mr. Hugh Cairns, and the artistic painter Mr. Gunippo Raggi.

Notre Dame School

Group of priests – sons of Southbridge: A. Potvin, A.N. Carrier, N. Benoit, J.B. Lamothe, A. Robillard, E. Larochelle, P. Roy, P. Bourassa, S. Guillet

CHAPTER XV

Description of the Church

The Notre Dame Church is very well situated on an elevated plot that towers above Southbridge and its environs. No matter which way you enter the city, from several miles away you see the gleaming whiteness of the church's colossal tower, which reminds us of the purity of the Immaculate Virgin to whom it is consecrated. Yes, in our village, it is the "House of God" that holds this place of honor and any stranger who visits knows that this is a place where religion is strong and God is loved and served.

The church is made of white marble from the quarries of Lee, Massachusetts; the roof is made of red tiles that recall the old cathedrals of Europe; the lines are extraordinarily clean. The facade, which is on Main Street, is one of the best examples of architecture found in this country. The colossal church tower is unique, piercing the sky at a height of 180 feet and topped with an gigantic cross that is intricately carved and sculpted. The front entrances are very regal, and you approach on a true boulevard that extends from the sidewalk. You must see it in order to really grasp the idea. There are three entrances on the Main Street side and two at the other end in the transepts. The stained glass is exceptionally sophisticated.

Words fail us in describing such beauty and such sumptuousness, and anything we can say or imagine can only give a weak or imperfect idea of what our beautiful Notre Dame church looks like. The moment we enter the church is when we are overwhelmed with admiration and we feel obliged to cite the Holy Scripture, "*Non est hic alind, nisi domus Dei, et porta coeli.*" "This is indeed the house of God and the doorway to Heaven." The inside of the church is large and spacious with five naves able to seat 1,400 people. Further, there is space next to the organ for more than 200 people. The first impression that strikes the visitor who enters this church, especially one who knows a bit about art, is that it feels like entering one of the illustrious palaces of old France. There is not even one inch of carpet, as the whole floor is a mosaic with designs worthy of God's house. The arches are supported by a colonnade with marble at the base (*xagliola*). There are rich, artistically framed paintings representing the various stages in the life of the Virgin. These paintings are true artistic gems and are the skillful works of a famous Italian painter, Raggi. The exceptional Stations of the Cross, along with the magnificent painting representing the Holy Trinity, are also the work of this painter.

The pulpit is in stucco and richly decorated; it is located in the nave on the side of the Gospel and a superb Crucifix is hung from the column directly across from it with a life-sized figure of Christ. There are five altars, corresponding to the five naves, so that five priests can offer the holy Sacrifice of the Mass at the same time. Each altar is positioned so as to form a small chapel unto itself. The balustrade is finished in white marble and is ornately sculpted; nearly one hundred people at a time can gather before it. All of the woodwork is in red cherry wood, sculpted by "Thomas & Co." of Worcester. The stalls in the sanctuary can easily seat a choir of one hundred children.

The high altar sits between four columns that rise up to the triforium on which is situated the cross of Christ, and at the foot of each column are statues depicting the Mother of God and St. John, beloved apostle. Between the two columns, and immediately above the tabernacle, but a little further back, is a beautiful and elegant statue of Mary. This life-sized statue dominates the whole interior of the church; it really is "Our Lady."

The principal sacristy is one of a kind, and it alone has established the renown of this church, which is visited by people from all over. Do not forget to visit the famous statue of Good Saint Ann, a true masterpiece. Adding to all that has just been described, imagine this church illuminated by thousands of electric lightbulbs with waves of light intermingling with the music flowing through the air from the powerful Notre Dame organ; imagine further 2,000 people kneeling respectfully before God and waiting for the solemn moment when the priests dressed in the richest and most sumptuous vestments enter the sanctuary escorted by a choir of over one hundred children; imagine the incense wafting up towards the Divinity, a symbol of the prayers being said by all the souls; then you will have an idea of the beautiful and touching ceremonies that inspire in the hearts of "Southbridgers" a love of God and a love of Christ and of his beloved Mother!!!

Certainly, we can not give the reader a description of this church any more than we can give a description of Heaven, but we endeavored to give those who have not seen it at least a simple sketch of its ingenious beauty; and to top it off, this church that cost $266,030.81 was not one penny in debt on the day of its dedication.

The Bells

There is a great bell in the tower of the new church. Oh, sure, it is not one great bell as powerful as the one in Notre Dame in Montréal, but three bells by the name of *Jesus, Mary* and *Joseph* who were baptized on

May 13, 1915. Monsignor T.D. Beaven blessed them that forever memorable day in the parish of Southbridge. Those who attended the grandiose event—which, however, was meant only to have been a prelude or a small taste of the great unforgettable event for the Dedication of the Church that happened a year later—know the sheer joy that was in everyone's hearts on that day, a day so idyllically beautiful and serene. The sun spread its warm rays across the immense assembly gathered around the bells that would henceforth announce the hours of joy and the hours of extreme sadness in Southbridge; there was an air of joy and of satisfaction that curled everyone's lips into a triumphant smile. After the blessing of the bells, we began to look forward to the grand opening of the heavy doors to the new church. We hoped while living and lived with hope. These bells came from the Meneely Bells Company, Watervliet, West Troy, New York.

The Organ

One must hear the organ in order to fully comprehend it. Music lifts the soul towards God, inflating it, warming it, feeling the vibrations in unison with the Creator down to one's smallest capillary fibers. Music leads to piety, elevates the splendor of ceremonies, and inspires in the human soul all of the generous feelings God has placed there. The parishioners of Notre Dame love their church, and they love the organ as well.

This organ came from the "Casavant Brothers" company in St. Hyacinthe, Québec and is among the most beautiful and most expensive made by this important company. It cost close to $15,000. It should be noted that the parish organist, the renowned Prof. Eugène Tapin, knows how to make the most of this instrument and enchants us with many musical gifts.

CHAPTER XVI

Dedication of the Church—1916

The parishioners of Notre Dame heard their last mass in the old church on Sunday, June 25th, 1916. The anticipation of soon entering the recently completed sumptuous new church was mixed with regret at leaving forever the blessed sanctuary that had served as a gathering place for parishioners to adore and praise God for over half a century. It was still in great shape, even with age, this mother-church that sheltered her dear children of Southbridge under her roof for many years. Yes, this good old mother welcomed their pain on days of mourning and beheld their joy on happy days. The arch, darkened by the passage of time, darkened by the smoke of thousands of candles burned in the enclosure to honor God and his saints, darkened by the wafts of incense that floated up from the altar of God Almighty for fifty years, proved that the mother-church had served the people well. No, she was not jealous to see herself replaced by her daughter, the brilliant new church radiating youth, for it is she who had given her life and she was quite proud.

The farewells to the old church were very touching, and if today we were able to see into the hearts of our good old Canadian mothers and our dear old fathers, we might have seen that for them especially, the separation was painful and sad. What! Are you surprised? Many had been baptized in that church, many had taken the sacred vows of marriage there, and a good number said their last good-byes to their dearly departed in that church. The church's Stations of the Cross, worn by time, had been for some the silent witnesses to their tears and anguish! Oh, it was filled with tender memories, and it was time to leave it all behind!

But alas, that's the way of the world; we forget too quickly those who leave us and replace them too easily with those who arrive.

In Southbridge on Sunday, July 2nd, 1916, all worries were set aside, the tears of the previous day were wiped away, it was a great day, the day so long anticipated when we would take possession of the "New Jerusalem." It was a day of triumph for the Virgin, the Feast of the Visitation of Mary.

Beginning the day of the Annunciation, the church's doors were opened wide to its children for the Feast of the Visitation. A happy coincidence, the will of Mary, for we had to prepare for the dedication several weeks before this date.

Many hearts, and noble hearts at that, had yearned for this great day of the solemn opening of the Church, but Providence had called many to Her fold, but there is no doubt that from high in Heaven, they cheered with joy for those who stayed behind. During the last weeks leading up to the celebrations, many prayers were offered up for nice weather on the chosen day. There was some apprehension, for it often rained that year and often on Sundays.

The parishioners' wishes were fulfilled, and the day began with radiant sunshine. The Virgin willed this beautiful, great and glorious day, and those who were there know that it was just that and it was ideal! The celebrations, which coincided happily with those for the centenary of the city, were attended by an enormous crowd.

Never had Southbridge witnessed such profound religious solemnity. Two bishops, more than a hundred priests, and around a hundred nuns attended, as well as several thousand lay people from the city, from New England and from Canada.

Low Masses were held at the five altars on the hour, from six o'clock to ten o'clock, when the ceremony began. That's when the procession started. All sides of the church were filled with spectators, of all denominations. Monsignor T.D. Beaven, bishop of the diocese, officiated, assisted by Reverends P. Dinand, S.J., D.D., Superior of the College of the Holy Cross in Worcester, and Omer Rochain, A.A., Superior of Assumption College in Greendale.

A great pontifical mass was celebrated at 10:30am by Monsignor J.S.H. Bruneault, bishop of Nicolet in Québec. Fr. Jules Graton, pastor of the Church of the Nativity in Willimansett, was the assistant priest; Fr. Joseph E. Chicoine, pastor of Saint Cecile's in Leominster, Massachusetts and Fr. J.A. Langlois, pastor of St. Francis of Assisi in Fitchburg, held the positions of honored deacons, respectively. The officiating deacons were Rev. Pierre Plante, S.J., from Montréal, and Rev. Stanislas Guillet, two children of the parish. Master of ceremonies was Fr. Adélard Landry, ex-vicar of Notre Dame.

The homily was given by Rev. J.A. Bournival, S.J. of Saint Mary's College of Montréal in Québec. It was a judicious choice, and the preacher's anointed word made a strong impression on the immense audience. The eminent orator had chosen the following words from the Holy Scripture to guide his sermon: *"And the Word became flesh,"* a phrase that he elaborated upon with remarkable eloquence. The master of ceremonies at the mass was Fr. J. Tétreault, chancellor of the diocese of Nicolet, Québec.

The choir, led by Prof. Eugène Tapin, included the following people: Ulric Lareau, Raymond Richard, Fr. A. Sansoucy, Anatole

Caron, Richard Laron, Léon Gagnon, Alphonse Bertrand, Georges Guillemette, Edouard E. Leclair, Michel Moquin, Sergius Gatineau, Arthur A. Larochelle, Arthur Grégoire, A. Bertrand, Arthur Delâge, Omer E. Bonnette, Georges Bélanger, Henri Dumas, Eugène Lange, Oswald Laliberté, Georges and Roland Cabana, Felix T. Lavallée, Raymond Favreau, Ulric Surprenant, Henri Massé, Georges L. Dumas, Louis Chagnon, Joseph Fournier, Napoléon Chénier, Henri Dufault, Ovide Trahan, Armand Labossière, Omer Bélanger, Raoul Blanchette, J. Favreau.

Irène Allard, Cora Gatineau, Mrs. Michel P. O'Shaughnessy, Mrs. Arthur Grégoire, Natalie and Fabiola Lareau, Gertrude Allard, Yvonne Larochelle, Anna Bachand, Rosanna Dufault, Mina Leblanc, Léna Désaulniers, Olivia, Blanche and Olga Pagé, Blanche, Béatrice, Eva and Cécile Daigle, Alexina and Parmélia Ravenelle, Bernadette St. Onge, Ida Gatineau, Léontine Généreux, Florence Coderre, Aline Meunier, Orea St. Onge, etc.

The ushers at the mass were Arthur Lamoureux, Léo Lamoureux, Camille and David Blain, Joseph Plante, Felix Gatineau and Joseph Plouffe.

The collection at the solemn mass was taken up by Mr. and Mrs. Joseph Métras, Mr. and Mrs. Anatole Caron, Mr. Ronaldo Guillemette, Mrs. Dr. J.A. Généreux, Dr. Charles A. Tétrault, and Miss. Marie Laperle.

At four o'clock in the afternoon, the parishioners returned to the church to attend Pontifical Vespers. Monsignor J.S.H. Bruneault officiated. At eight o'clock in the evening, a holy concert was offered, under the direction of Prof. Eugène Tapin, the new church's organist. The Monsignor from Nicolet blessed the new organ and the statues, and the homily was given by Fr. Arthur Cayer, vicar of Saint Mary's church in Winchendon, Massachusetts and former vicar of Southbridge. Everyone listened intently; Fr. Cayer had the honor of being the first priest in the diocese of Springfield to give a homily in the new church. In addition, it was a masterpiece of eloquence. After the homily, there was the benediction of the blessed sacrament. At each service during the day, the church, which easily seats 1,400 people, was literally full and not sufficient to accommodate the crowd anxiously awaiting entry. An estimated 18,000 people took part in the grandiose celebrations which are now in the annals of the history of Southbridge.

The morning ceremonies were enhanced by a great parade, both municipal and religious. All of the Franco-American organizations of Southbridge participated, as well as the religious groups. Of note were the Société des Dames de Ste. Anne (St. Anne's Women's Society), the

Enfants de Marie (Children of Mary), the Council Brochu (Brochu Council), Triganne, the St.-Jean-Baptiste Rochambeau, the Jacques-Cartier, the Forestiers Catholiques (Catholic Foresters), the Cercle Canadien, the Artisans, etc. In all, there were over 2,000 people lined up starting at the rectory of the new church, following the procession of the children's choir, members of the clergy, ecclesiastical dignitaries, and the two officiating bishops. All was under the skilled direction of the vicars, Laporte and Therrien. The parishioners were proud, and rightly so, for their church, which cost over $266,000, was paid off from the day they entered it.

The dedication celebrations left an indelible mark on the memories of all who attended, especially the parishioners.

CHAPTER XVII

The Sisters of the Assumption—Fifteen Nuns—Current Mother

Superior Sr. Ste. Mathilde, 1919

It's a true pleasure for us to tell you about the good nuns who, since 1891, have been in charge of nurturing our dear children's hearts and minds; this task is enjoyable and a necessary recognition of their work. We regret that we can not express in more elegant terms the gratitude that overwhelms our hearts in regard to these devoted servants of Jesus Christ.

You need only see them at work, or contemplate the successes that have crowned their efforts despite the unheard of obstacles they have encountered, to have a true sense of the unfailing zeal and devotion that drives them. Many parents, obliged to work in the factories to earn their daily bread, totally neglect the education of their children and have little concern for it. And so, the task becomes difficult for the nuns, or I'd say even thankless. It is true that the priest is always there to support and encourage them, but the secret to their devotion lies in the heart of the Holy Father and the maternal heart of the Virgin to whom they have dedicated their lives! The reward for these daughters of God comes not from mere men, that would be a lost cause, but from Above! Do not think that we have forgotten what the Sisters of Saint Anne did for our children, for these first arrivals had to undertake the feat of clearing the fields and laying the groundwork, so to speak, but we are in a better position to speak about the works of the Sisters of the Assumption, because we know them better and because our children reflect the work they accomplished. We insist on offering this tribute of gratitude to them, before recounting the details of their work among us.

It was on August 22nd, 1891 that the Sisters of the Assumption arrived to establish themselves in Southbridge; there were seven of them and their superior was Sister St. Anselme. The welcome offered by Monsignor Brochu was, it seems, very warm. Upon their arrival, a succulent dinner was served, prepared by several women by the name of Gravel, Généreux, Desrosiers and Lapierre. The good nuns expressed their great appreciation, for as foreigners, they found this kindness quite touching.

That year, the school opened on September 1st; 650 children started that day, and that same number continued for the next nine years, until 1900.

In that year, the school became an academy, the royal gift of Monsignor Brochu, and the number of children increased to 800.

In 1904, with the arrival of our devoted pastor Fr. Triganne, former diocesan school inspector, an era of great progress began, for from that time through 1919, 206 children obtained their Institutional Diploma, gold medal, admission to the Upper School. 120 pupils obtained their Diocesan Diploma.

When, in 1917, the Union St. Jean Baptiste of America decided to start offering scholarships, in the amount of $1,000 each, to allow young Franco-Americans to pursue classical studies, students from Notre Dame entered the competition; the applicants included William Lavallée, son of George Lavallée, Arthur Bousquet, son of Louis, and Albert Langlais, son of Edouard. It was a success, and today Arthur Bousquet and Albert Langlais are studying at Assumption College in Greendale, Massachusetts.

This fact alone is sufficient to indicate the high level of instruction that the Sisters of the Assumption give to our children. Congratulations to the Nuns and to the Brochu Academy!! May these devout spouses of Christ forever benefit from strong support from the priests and families in our parish! In the Sacred Heart parish, the same nuns are devoted to the same work, and are seeing the same success. Here is the complete list of Notre Dame students who have obtained their institutional and diocesan diplomas.

Diplomas—Notre Dame School, Southbridge, Mass.

	Parish	Diocesan
1905		
1. Anna Bédard	X	
1906		
2. David Blain	X	
3. Georges Proulx	X	
4. Norma McDonald	X	
1907		
5. Emma Allard	X	
6. Clara Désaulniers	X	
7. Irène Allard	X	
8. Léo Sénécal	X	
9. Antonio Desloges	X	
10. Ovila Gagnon	X	
1908		
11. Alfred Péloquin	X	X
12. Wilfred Bonin	X	X
13. Napoléon Bachand	X	X

14. Camille Blain	X	X
15. Eulalie Deslages	X	X
16. Alma Proulx	X	X
17. Parmélia Desmarais	X	X
18. Rose Giroux	X	X
19. Laurentia Boyer	X	X
20. Alice Leclerc	X	
21. Lina Désaulniers	X	X
22. Camillia Laliberté	X	X
23. Alma Ouellette	X	X
24. Antoinette Délage	X	X
25. Cora Gatineau	X	X
26. Alice Langevin	X	X
1909		
27. Ernestine Ouelette	X	X
28. Léontine Robida	X	X
29. Gertrude Allard	X	X
30. Elméria Therrien	X	X
31. Armand Dupaul	X	X
1910		
32. Armand Caron	X	X
33. Ernest Coderre	X	X
34. Léo Allard	X	X
35. Homère Généreux	X	X
36. Alexina Ravenelle	X	X
37. Ozanna Larochelle	X	X
38. Rachel Leriche	X	X
39. Eva McDermott	X	X
1911		
40. Joseph Gervais	X	X
41. Léo Renaud	X	X
42. Philippe Larochelle	X	X
43. Hermas Bail	X	X
44. Josaphat Leclerc	X	X
45. Nelson Ravenelle	X	X
46. M. Louise Girard	X	X
47. Evangeline Roy	X	X
48. Dora Bédard	X	X
49. Oliva Pagé	X	X
50. Flore Lepain	X	X
1912		
51. Marguerite Bousquet	X	X

52. Cécile Surprenant	X	X
53. Adrienne St. Onge	X	X
54. Arthur Bertrand	X	
55. Zéphirin Plouffe	X	
56. Arthur Martin	X	X
57. Yvonne Bosvert	X	X
58. Evelina Leblanc	X	X
59. Annette Lamoureux	X	
60. Aimé Vary	X	X
61. Georgianna Castonguay	X	
62. Eva Cloutier	X	
63. Léo Giroux	X	
64. Clarinda Asselin	X	X
65. Elzébert Ouellette	X	X
66. Armand Gendreau	X	
67. Irèné Benoit	X	X

1913

68. Raoul Bail	X	X
69. Wilfred Renaud	X	X
70. Ulric Lareau	X	X
71. Georges Castonguay	X	X
72. Ulric Roy	X	
73. Hermas Lippé	X	
74. André Goyer	X	X
75. Hector Nolin	X	X
76. Irène Tétreault	X	
77. Exina Tremblay	X	X
78. Parmélia Ravenelle	X	X
79. Evélina Lavallée	X	X
80. Corinne Monette	X	
81. Olga Pagé	X	
82. Anna Dermers	X	X
83. Cécile Daigle	X	X
84. A. Marie Payant	X	
85. Alméria Robichaud	X	
86. Clara Desmanches	X	X
87. Ernest Coderre	X	X
88. Elzéar Tremblay	X	X
89. Ronald Dupaul	X	X
90. Armand Therrien	X	X
91. Lionel Plouffe	X	
92. Rosaire Giroux	X	X

93. Armand Langlais	X	
94. George Burlingame	X	X
95. Napoléon Désaulniers	X	X
96. Joseph Grégoire	X	
97. Alice Surprenant	X	X
98. Claudia Lamoureux	X	X
99. Evélina Petit	X	
100. Nelda Collette	X	
101. Lucile Hufault	X	X
102. Marie J. Blanchette	X	
103. Alberta Poulin	X	
104. Rose Leblanc	X	
105. Gertrude Grégoire	X	
106. Dora Lafortune	X	
107. Ida Leduc	X	

1915

108. Raymond Favreau	X	X
109. Adonilda Lavallée	X	X
110. Armand Labossière	X	X
111. Willie Richard	X	X
112. Henri Roy	X	X
113. Herman St. Onge	X	
114. Omer Duchesneau	X	X
115. Rosaire Farley	X	X
116. Hormidas Cloutier	X	
117. Adrien Bousquet	X	X
118. Raymond Richard	X	
119. Ernest Ravenelle	X	
120. Théodore Marchessault	X	
121. Stanislas Petit	X	X
122. Eddie Castonguay	X	X
123. Gertrude Gatineau	X	
124. Antoinette Dermers	X	
125. Rita Proulx	X	X
126. Ida Leblanc	X	
127. Sylvia Lafortune	X	
128. Orise Bélanger	X	
129. Albertina Leblanc	X	
130. Christine Allard	X	
131. Emélia Bachand	X	
132. Yvonne Larochelle	X	
133. Yvonne Proulx	X	

134. Valida Dufault   X
135. Mathilde Lepage   X
136. Alberta Lavallée   X
137. Rosetta Drolet   X
138. Imelda Gaumond   X

Plouffe Family: Nine brothers in the choir of the Notre Dame Church;
Adolphe, Etienne, Charles, Daniel, Georges, Alexandre, Ephrem, Zéphirin,
Lionel

Graduates of the Notre Dame School, 1919:D. Adams, L. Bourassa, L. Martin, H. Renaud, D. Ferron, G. Garceau / O. Tessier, N. Benoit, C. Brodeur, R. Allard, Y. Renaud, G. Proulx / Rev. R. Laporte, R. Huet, V. Bertrand, Rev. L.O. Triganne, A. Loiseau, Z. Duteau, Rev. P. Therrien

Sacred Heart Parish: Reverend Emile St. Onge, First Pastor / Reverend William H. Ducharme, Current Pastor

Group of pastors and vicars of the Sacred Heart Parish: Rev. W.H. Ducharme, current pastor; Rev. E. St. Onge, first pastor / Rev. J.B. Lamothe / Rev. L. Ruty, Rev. A. Cayer / Rev. A. Buisson

1916

139. Roméo Duclos	X	X
140. Alphonse Giroux	X	X
141. Omer Renaud	X	X
142. André Paulhus	X	X
143. Roméo Caron	X	X
144. Liliose Lamoureux	X	X
145. Yvonne Jourdenais	X	X
146. Dora Langevin	X	X
147. Mélina Huet	X	X
148. Lauretta Surprenant	X	X
149. Lauretta Roy	X	
150. Rita Paul	X	
151. Merilda Lepain	X	
152. Albina Lavallée	X	

1917

153. Albert Langlais	X	X
154. William Lavallée	X	X
155. Lionel Demers	X	X
156. Arthur Bosquet	X	X
157. Aline Benoit	X	X
158. Cécilia Proulx	X	X
159. Blanche Gauthier	X	X
160. Alberta Therrien	X	X
161. Amabilis Cloutier	X	X
162. Emma Bousquet	X	X
163. Irène Dumas	X	X
164. Lilianne Brodeur	X	X
165. Mélina Benoit	X	
166. Laura Langlois	X	

1918

167. Alphonse Dugas	X	X
168. Léo Martin	X	X
169. Sylvio Brodeur	X	X
170. Lionel Lataille	X	X
171. Alfred Marchessault	X	X
172. Ubald Larivière	X	X
173. Lionel Cabana	X	X
174. Aimé Girard	X	X
175. Ernest Allard	X	X

176. Béatrice Surprenant	X	X
177. Alvina Labossière	X	X
178. Laurette Désaulniers	X	X
179. Laura Taylor	X	X
180. Rita Richard	X	X
181. Lydia Raîches	X	X
182. Alice Dupaul	X	X
183. Florianne Délage	X	X
184. Adrienne Brodeur	X	X

1919

185. Candide Brodeur
186. Loretta Bourassa
187. Yvonne Renaud
188. Geraldine Gareau
189. Albert Loiseau
190. Dolorès Adam
191. Zéphirina Duteau
192. Odina Tessier
193. Dora Ferron
194. Gertrude Proulx
195. Norbert Benoit
196. Robertina Huet
197. Victor Bertrand
198. Léo Martin
199. Rolland Allard
200. Hector Renaud

The entire class earned their institutional and diocesan diplomas. Brilliant succcess!

CHAPTER XVIII

Religious Vocations—Men

Notre Dame parish, as it stands, is one of the most important and most prosperous in the Springfield diocese. Devotion there is intense, and frequent Communion treasured. It is not surprising if it pleased God from time to time to choose for himself some of these elite souls for service on the altar or for the education of children. Certainly, in these days, the paucity of vocations is lamentable nearly everywhere. The more a population ages, the more it becomes egotistical, the less it appreciates devotion, and the less it understands the value of sacrifice. Nonetheless, throughout the ages, we see certain young men and certain young women devote themselves to Him, from whom all derives. Blessed be the families of these young people.

Priests Originally from the Parish

Mr. Paul Roy, Mr. Stanislas Guillet, Mr. Alfred Carrier, Mr. Alfred Potvin, Mr. J.B. Lamothe, Mr. Elzéar Larochelle, Mr. Albert Robillard, Mr. Narcisse Benoit, Mr. Pierre Bourassa, Father I. Plante, S.J., Mr. Amédé Bonin, Jesuit brother; Mr. Camille Blain, ecclesiastic in Montréal.

We will give you their biographies, in as much as we can, without consideration of age or title.

Reverend Father Carrier

Reverend Father Alfred Carrier was born in Southbridge on December 24th, 1868 to Elzéar Carrier and Eléonore Falardeau. After his studies at the Seminary in Sainte-Marie-de-Monnoir and in the Seminary in Sherbrooke, Canada, he entered the Grand Seminary of Montréal to study theology. He was ordained into the priesthood on December 17, 1892 by Very Reverend Monsignor Fabre in the chapel of the Grand Seminary of Montreal. After his ministry as vicar in Centreville, R.I., Fall River, Providence and Taunton, he was named pastor in Taunton on October 11, 1904, where he still serves.

Reverend Father Alfred Potvin

Reverend Father Alfred Potvin was born on December 25, 1869 in St. Ours, Québec to the late George Potvin and Marie Dumas. He completed his early schooling in St. Ours and in Southbridge and did his classical studies in St. Laurent, near Montréal. He then studied philosophy and theology in Montréal, Baltimore and Rome, Italy; was ordained in Boston by Monsignor Williams on December 18, 1901. He was a vicar in Worcester (1902), in Willimansett (1902-03), at St. Mary's in Spencer (1903-1906), at the Immaculate Conception in Holyoke

(1906), and is currently vicar in South Fitchburg.

Reverend Father E. Larochelle

Reverend Father Joseph Elzéar Larochelle was born in Southbridge on June 8th, 1884 to Napoléon Larochelle and Marie Sénécal. After studying at the College of Sainte-Thérèse, Québec, he studied philosophy and theology at the Grand Seminary of Montréal. He was ordained as a priest at the hands of His Excellency Monsignor Paul Bruchési, bishop of Montréal, on December 18, 1909, in that city's cathedral. He is now vicar at Holy Name of Jesus, Worcester, Mass.

Reverend Father Pierre Bourassa

Reverend Father P. Bourassa, while born in St. Anselme, Québec, can be considered a native of the parish for he lived here for quite some time before becoming a priest. He also practiced the holy ministry here for more than ten years. He was born on December 2nd, 1866, to Joseph Bourassa and Philomène Morissette. He studied in Joliette and in the Seminary of Montréal, where he was ordained by Monsignor Bruchési on December 21, 1901. Vicar in Willimansett in 1902, at the Holy Name of Jesus, Worcester (1902-1903), in Southbridge, etc. He is now pastor in Easthampton, Mass.

Reverend Father Joseph Albert Robillard

Reverend Father J. Albert Robillard was born in Southbridge on July 24, 1879 to Joseph Arthur Robillard, M.D., and Joséphine Pagé. He did his early studies at the College of the Assumption, Canada and his classical studies at the College of the Assumption, Greendale, Mass. He studied philosophy at the Seminary of Nicolet, Québec, theology at St. Mary's Seminary, Baltimore, MD. Ordained on May 29, 1915 by His Eminence Cardinal James Gibbons, Baltimore. Fr. Robillard, who is currently vicar in Willimansett, has the honor of being the first priest to come out of the College of the Fathers of the Assumption in Greendale, Mass.

Reverend Father Stanislas Guillet

Reverend Father Stanislas Guillet was born in Saint-Charles-sur-Richelieu on February 27, 1871 to Michel Guillet and Louise Luissier. After attending parochial schools, he completed classical and philosophical studies at the College of Sainte-Thérèse. He took theology courses at the Grand Seminary of Montréal, and was ordained to the priesthood by the Very Reverend Monsignor Paul Bruchési on December 23rd, 1899 in the Cathedral of Montréal. After practicing the holy ministry in several locations, as vicar, he was named pastor of Fiskdale several years ago, and he is still there today.

Reverend Father Narcisse Benoit

Reverend Father Narcisse Benoit was born in Southbridge on

August 4th, 1884 to Pierre Benoit and Marie Proulx. He completed his early studies in Saint-Robert, Québec, then entered the College of St. Hyacinthe, where he did classical and philosophical studies. He studied theology at Saint Mary's Seminary in Baltimore, Maryland, and was ordained to the priesthood on June 1st, 1912 by Monsignor P. Bruchési, archbishop of Montréal, in that city's cathedral. After sharing his zeal in Holyoke, Springfield and Worcester, he is now vicar in this city, in the Notre Dame parish.

Reverend Father J.B. Lamothe

Reverend Father J.B. Lamothe was born in Southbridge on December 14th, 1880 to Narcisse Lamothe and Marie Nadeau. After spending several years in Spencer, where he went to school, he left for the Seminary of Saint-Hyacinthe, to round out his classical studies. He then went to study theology in the Seminary in Rochester, N.Y., where he was ordained. He was vicar in Southbridge, in the Sacred Heart parish, in Adams, Holyoke, North Adams, and currently in Springfield (1919).

Reverend Father Paul Roy

Reverend Father Paul Roy was born in Southbridge, Mass. on January 15th, 1869 from the marriage of Simon Roy and Marguerite Cormier. After attending parochial schools, he went to do his classical studies in the College of Saint-Thérèse. He took courses on theology at the Grand Seminary of Montréal. He was ordained a priest in the Cathedral on December 17th, 1898, by the Very Reverend Monsignor Bruchési for the diocese of Springfield. After his ordination, at the request of the bishop of Portland who at that time was in great need of French-speaking priests, and with the consent of his bishop, he went to minister in Augusta, Brunswick and Waterville, Maine, for about two years. Upon his return to the diocese, he was vicar in Leominster, Willimansett and Holyoke. He was the pastor in Fiskdale for several years; later in West Warren and Greendale, where he is at present.

Reverend J.B. Plante, S.J.

Reverend J.B. Plante, S.J., was born in Southbridge on March 17th, 1875. At age eleven, after the loss of his mother, he went to live with his grandparents in Saint-Ours, Richelieu county, where he attended parochial schools. At age sixteen, he entered the College of the Jesuits in Montréal and was admitted to the priesthood in 1908, and he currently lives in Montréal.

Religious Vocations—Girls

This list is as complete as we have been able to make it. We can tell from a glance that the good Lord found in our village many hearts who responded to his call. We hope that many will follow the example given by so many young girls who, despite the world and all its so-called charms, renounced all for their Master. But as we mentioned earlier, today people no longer know how to understand the grandeur and the sublimeness of a religious vocation. The more the vine of the Lord spreads its branches, the fewer workers he has, and yet, many hear the call but few respond to it. That's why today we see so many young people, so many young girls, who are unhappy, so many missed callings, so many poorly matched marriages. We should forget ourselves a little more often and to think more of the thousands of children, of poor elderly, of unfortunate people who await help from those who give themselves in life and death to their royal Spouse.

The young girls of Southbridge who now belong to the Congregation of the Sisters of the Assumption of Nicolet are:
1. Cordélia Bouthillette, "Sister Saint Isabelle," daughter of Herménégilde Bouthillette
2. Alphonsine Nadeau, "Sister Saint Honorine," daughter of Louis Nadeau
3. Emma Richard, "Sister St. Raymond," daughter of Arcade Richard
4. M. Jeanne Richard, "Sister St. Arcade," daughter of Arcade Richard
5. R.A. Trahan, "Sister St. Augustin," daughter of Jacques Trahan
6. Maria Laflèche, "Sister St. Jean du Calvaire"
7. Lucindy Girard, "Sister St. Anatole," daughter of Anatole Girard
8. Odina Robert, "Sister St. Armand"
9. Clara Désaulniers, "Sister St. Claude," daughter of Alexandre Désaulniers
10. Emma Allard, "Sister Saint Céline," daughter of Joseph Allard
11. Emma Renaud, "Sister Marie de la Passion," daughter of Edouard Renaud
12. Caroline Beaudoin, "Sister St. Aimé de Jésus"
13. Joséphine Lemay, "Sister Marie Adéline," daughter of Charles Lemay
14. Amabilis Cloutier, "Sister Aimé du Divin Coeur"
Novice
Laurentia Boyer, "St. Alexis of Rome," daughter of Alexis Boyer
Nuns Belonging to Other Communities
1. Anna Désaulniers, "Sister Désaulniers," daughter of Oscar Désaulniers
2. Anna Sansoucy, "Sister Sansoucy," daughter of François Sansoucy
3. Sophronie Sansoucy, "Sister St. Léon," daughter of François Sansoucy
4. Alma Proulx, "Sister Louis Elzéar," daughter of Elzéar Proulx
5. Alice Leclair, "Sister Leclair," daughter of P.N. Leclair
6. Marie-Louise Desrosiers, "Sister Hermogène," daughter of Octave Desrosiers

7. Georgianna Demers, "Sister Saint Philippe de Néri," daughter of Louis-Eusèbe Demers

8. Stella Thériault, "Sister Thériault," daughter of Emery Thériault

9. Ida Lorange, "Sister Aimé de Jésus," daughter of Louis Lorange

10. Délia Cabana, "Sister Marie Fabien"

11. M. Alb. Peck, "Sister Marie Roger," daughter of Napoléon Peck

12. Diana Chapdelaine, "Sister St. Michel," daughter of George Chapdelaine

13. Eulalie Blain, "Sister St. Benoit," daughter of Jules Blain

14. Irène Langevin, "Sister M. Anne de Jésus," daughter of Paul Langevin

15. Blandine Coderre, "Sister Palmina," daughter of Pierre Coderre

16. Alice Marchessault, "Sister M. Thérèse de Jésus," daughter of Bernard Marchessault

17. Eva Desrosiers, "Sister Maria," daughter of Onésime Desrosiers

18. Delvina Desrosiers, "Sister Marie Constance," daughter of Onésime Desrosiers

19. Eugénie Desrosiers, "Sister St.-J. Baptiste," (deceased), daughter of Onésime Desrosiers

The two daughters of Jean St. Onge and Léonore Potvin: Phélonise "Sister Angeline," Amabelis, "Sister Joanna," from the community of the Presentation of Saint-Hyacinthe, both entered before 1880.

CHAPTER XIX

The Sacred Heart Parish

The Canadians of Southbridge were growing in number with each passing day to the point where the old Notre Dame church could barely hold them all on Sundays. That was the problem that should have been foreseen but that was important to resolve. Steps had already been taken with the goal of founding a new parish in the part of the city generally known as the "Flat." The Ordinary of the diocese, Monsignor Beaven, deigned to agree to the requests of the parishioners, who found the old church a bit too far away, especially for those who had settled down in Fairlawn.

On Sunday, December 15, 1908, Rev. Fr. Triganne, from high on the pulpit, announced to his parishioners there was to be a division of the parish, a division which should take place on December 1st, 1908, according to the episcopal order. The new pastor of the parish who was dedicated to Sacred Heart would be Rev. Fr. Emile St. Onge.

On November 28, the pastor announced that the following Sunday, December 6th, the parishioners of Fr. St. Onge should attend mass at their Arsenal (Armory) chapel, on the corner of Central and Hook streets, then he defined the boundaries of the new parish. It is unnecessary to revisit that. Starting December 1st, those who no longer belonged to the Notre Dame parish had to go to their pastor for illnesses, baptisms, marriages, etc.

The new pastor went right to work, and he was supported by his flock, who were proud to contribute to the success of the new endeavor. Of course, separations are always cruel; many families missed the old church which spoke so eloquently to their hearts; above all, they were leaving a pastor who was so devout and so compassionate.

There was a whole collection of tender and cherished memories associated with the old church, but the founding of a new establishment was necessary! God's Providence willed it so; the daughter had to leave the mother, and after ten years of separation, or rather eleven, the Sacred Heart parish is solidly established and in a period of great prosperity; it has a superb school-chapel, which is a model of its kind; it has a magnificent rectory and residence for nuns.

The properties are situated in a picturesque and enchanting location. At the time of the division, there were around 550 families in the parish, which is more or less the current number of families. However, we can say that there are at least 600 families today, if not more.

Fr. St. Onge was an active man, and his efforts were always successful. We should also add that he found sincerely devoted hearts in his parish; furthermore, the pastor of Notre Dame, Rev. Fr. P. Triganne, was as friendly as could be with him. The mere fact that the old parish gave the new parish the plump sum of $70,000 at the start, is enough to convince us that the pastor had many reasons to be encouraged.

The parish school, just like Notre Dame's, is under the care of the Sisters of the Assumption of Nicolet; currently at the school there are four hundred children with eleven nuns teaching them.

When Fr. St. Onge arrived in Southbridge, he came from Fiskdale where he had been pastor since 1903.

He was born in Saint-Césaire, Rouville county, on March 20th, 1861 to J.B. St. Onge, farmer, and Euphémie Chicoyne. He studied at the Seminary in Saint-Hyacinthe and was ordained a priest in 1891. Vicar at St. Mary's in Spencer from 1891 to 1892, in Ware (1892-1894), in Chicopee Falls (1894-1899), in North Adams (1899-1901); pastor in East Longmeadow (1901-1903), in Fiskdale 1903, and in Southbridge 1908.

An apostle filled with zeal, his career in Southbridge was short. He had devised many projects, but soon illness brought him down and rendered him powerless. He had to abandon his post about five years ago to go for treatment in Saint-Hyacinthe, where he died on June 2nd, 1918. During his absence, the new parish was administered by Rev. Wm. Ducharme, who still occupies this position. The latter has walked nobly in the footsteps of his predecessor, and thanks to his skillful administration, the Sacred Heart parish of Southbridge is now out of debt.

From the founding of the new parish, the vicars were Reverends H. Pelletier, Edouard Lussier, Arthur Cayer, J.B. Lamothe, Léon Ruty. The current vicar, Rev. Ambroise Buisson.

The parishioners of Sacred Heart opened their chapel-school in 1910; the nuns, after spending some time in the residence of Mr. Victor Pelletier, settled into their new home a little later. Fr. St. Onge, before moving into the rectory, lived in the house of Mr. Pascal Sénécal, very close to the parish properties.

CHAPTER XX

Vicars of Rev. Fr. Triganne

Since his arrival here, that is to say since 1904, the vicars of Rev. Fr. Triganne have been: Fr. Ad. Landry, today pastor in Brightwood; Pierre Bourassa, pastor in Easthampton; L.T. Rodier, D.D., pastor of Ludlow; J.O. Marceau, vicar in Spencer; Arthur Cayer and Hormisdas Rémi, now chaplains for the American army in France; Rosaire Caron, vicar in Canada; Paul D'Amours, vicar in Holyoke; Lévi Pagé, deceased in 1913. The two current vicars are: Reverends Raoul A. Laporte and Philibert Therrien. We would love to provide their full biographies, but do not have enough space; we will settle for giving you those of the vicars who, at the time of penning this work, are faithfully collaborating with our devoted pastor.

Rev. R.A. Laporte

Fr. Raoul A. Laporte was born in Woonsocket, R.I., on August 8th, 1885 to Gilbert Laporte, shopkeeper, and Marie Gouger. He attended parochial schools first, then went to study business at Sacred Heart College in that city. He then left for the Seminary in Joliette where he did his classical studies, including philosophy, and a year of teaching in that institution. With a Bachelor's of Arts and Sciences from Laval University in Québec, Fr. Laporte did his theological studies at the Grand Seminary of Montréal, Québec, and in the Saint Bernard Seminary in Rochester, NY. On June 24th, 1912, he was ordained to the priesthood by Monsignor T.D. Beaven in St. Michael's cathedral in Springfield, Mass. He was named vicar in Linwood, Mass where he remained until June 14, 1915, the date of his nomination to the vicariate in the Notre Dame parish of Southbridge.

Fr. Ph. J. Therrien

Fr. Philibert J. Therrien was born in St. Lin des Laurentides to Calixte Therrien and Marie Courtemanche. He did his primary schooling in the St. Joseph's parish school in Worcester, and pursued classical and philosophical studies at the College of the Assumption in Québec (1902-1910). He completed his theological studies at the St. Bernard Seminary in Rochester, NY (1910-1914), and was ordained to the priesthood on June 6th, 1914 by His Eminence Monsignor Thomas Hickey, bishop of Rochester. After several weeks of rest, he was named vicar in the Notre Dame parish, Southbridge.

Rev. Fr. Lévi Pagé (Deceased)

Rev. Fr. Pagé

Of all the vicars of Fr. Triganne, there is one who left us for the celestial homeland; we used to call him good Fr. Pagé, and God knows that he merited this name. Always working day and night, always ready at the first call, he was respected and loved by all. Children, especially, would go to him with full confidence, "he loved the youth." But they always say that the softest flowers are the first to be picked. Fr. Pagé was to soon receive his reward. It is with sorrow that we saw him leave, but we submit to the divine end. Here are some details, which will certainly interest our readers.

Death of Rev. Lévi N. Pagé—Impressive Funeral

Friday morning, on March 28, 1913, in Granby, Mass., Rev. Lévi N. Pagé, former vicar of the Notre Dame church in Southbridge, expired in the Lord's peace at the age of 33. The deceased received all the last consolations from the church, to which he had generously devoted his too brief existence, and his death was that of a saint.

His funeral service was held in the Our Lady of Perpetual Help church, Holyoke, the parish where he was raised and where he completed his early schooling. Thanks to the cordial and benevolent hospitality of Rev. Pastor Marchand, on Saturday the body of the deceased was put on view in the parish rectory from whence the transfer was made to the church on Sunday afternoon at 3 o'clock. The ceremonial procession was presided over by Rev. J.B. Sullivan of South Hadley Falls, with Rev. Camille Triquet, pastor of Immaculate Conception, as deacon and Rev. J.M. Bissonnette, pastor of Springfield, as assistant deacon.

The funeral service was held Monday morning, at 10 o'clock. A great crowd of clergymen attended, as well as a considerable number of relatives and friends of the dearly departed. The Office for the Dead was sung by members of the clergy and presided over by Monsignor John T.

Madden, vicar-general of the diocese of Springfield, assisted by Rev. W.J. Choquette of Chicopee Falls as deacon and Rev. J.B. Lamothe of North Adams as assistant deacon.

The burial was held in the Notre Dame cemetery, on the family plot, and Rev. Pastor Joseph Marchand said the final prayers over the body.

The porters were Ryno Bibeau, Joseph Drapeau, Odilon Bergeron, Charles Hamel, Narcisse Bouchard and Dr. W. Rouillard, all classmates of the deceased, and the ushers were also classmates Théophile Guertin, Gérald Meunier, Frank Hamel and Georges Coderre.

The eulogy for the dearly departed was given by Rev. Pastor Triganne of Southbridge, to whom Mr. Pagé had served as assistant for the better part of his brief career. We are extremely pleased to reprint here this superbly eloquent piece which will be a precious memento for the many relatives and friends of the late Lévi Pagé:

"In the introit to the mass of the feast of St. Stanislas de Koska, we read these words: *Consummatus in brevi, explevit tempora multa. Placita enim erat Deo anima illius propter hoc properavit educere illum de medio iniquitatum.*

Having come to perfection so soon, he lived a long life; his soul being pleasing to the Lord, he has hurried away from the wickedness around him. (C. IV. V. 13-4 from the Book of Wisdom).
My venerable fellow brothers in the priesthood, My very dear brothers: - -

Allow me to apply what the Holy Spirit said in the Book of Wisdom to the one to whom this funeral ceremony is dedicated:

That, though he came to perfection so soon, he lived a long life.

Yes, my Brothers, we can say this truthfully of the one we mourn today. He lived a short life, if we only measure his life by the number of years spent among us; but if we measure it by the work that he accomplished with each step, by the good deeds that the spread all around us, what a great long career he had!

You know, you, parishioners of Perpetual Help, you witnessed his early days when he was a child in this parish; you know, you, fellow brothers in the priesthood, there was not a single instant in his whole life as a seminarian and as a priest that he did not spend usefully and following the expression of the prophet: there, we find only full days; days devoted to his works of charity towards others and to his own sanctification.

Born in the heart of a sincerely religious family, to parents who were careful to fulfill all of the duties that nature and religion impose upon Christian families, he had the good fortune of extracting the seed of all of his virtues from his Christian education.

Residence of the Revered Sisters—Residence of the pastor, Sacred
Heart Parish / Convent and Chapel of Sacred Heart / First church
built in Southbridge

Graduates of the Sacred Heart School in 1912: A. Cloutier, E. Pelletier, R. Robillard, G. Langevin, H. Larochelle, A. Robert, D. Denatte / N. Savage, Rev. Pastor Emile St. Onge, Fr. Léon Ruty, G. Cloutier

Graduates of the Sacred Heart School in 1919: R. Tremblay, B. Leboeuf, A. Lataille, A. Payant, A. Métras, R. McGrath, Rev. W. Ducharme

Officers of the Order of the Knights of St. Joseph, Photographed in 1881: J. Métras, P. Roy, E. Robillard, J.F. Larivière / A. Robillard, J.A. Caron, C. Métras, F. Gatineau, L. Péloquin / S. Labonté, P. Métras, J.B. Poirier, E. Gagnon, R. Boucher

Sent to the parish school, in this very location, under the sage direction of a zealous pastor and the maternal watch of the good sisters of the Presentation of Mary, it was here in the Perpetual Help school, in this blessed chapel where he often knelt down to pray to God at the end of the school day, that the young Pagé heard for the first time the call from his God to the function of the priesthood. After a solid preparation in the college of Nicolet, where he was recognized for his talents and virtues, he studied theology in the Grand Seminary of Rochester, under the skilled direction of Monsignor McQuaid, fondly remembered, whom he often spoke about with praise. On March 19, 1905, he had the happy honor to receive from his hands the sacerdotal anointment, the object of his vow and the fulfillment of his desires.

It was then that he left to practice the holy ministry, to take up the post assigned by his bishop, His Eminence Monsignor Beaven, as vicar of the Notre Dame parish of Southbridge.

It was there that the young Levite distinguished himself, not by showy actions, but by a peaceful and devout ministry, doing good quietly and without ostentation. I can attest to this more than any other, Father Pagé was a veritable model of a priest of God, with his humility, his consistency, his zeal and this: all done with the most amiable joy. We did not know him as a close friend, someone said, because everyone was his friend and he was a friend to all.

Just a few months into his ministry, they were already calling him Good Father Pagé. The children, the youth used to run to greet him. His confessional was frequented by the elderly and the young, for all found sage direction there.

Like his Divine Master in Nazareth, he led a life hidden in a humble country vicariate, he passed doing good, and his name will forever be engraved in the memories and in the hearts of those who knew him.

When we learned of his death, people repeated from one to another, the Good Father Pagé is dead, he was a saint, if he is not yet in Heaven, we shouldn't even aim for it. *Vox populi. Vox Dei.* These are the sincere testimonies that show us what this good priest accomplished in so little time for the good of his neighbors and the sanctification of others. Thus, it was deservedly so that I quoted these words of Wisdom at the beginning: *Consommatus in brevi, explevit tempora multa*: Having come to perfection so soon, he lived a long life.

But being a wise man, he understood that the foremost and only thing necessary was to sanctify himself. He understood it, this truth; and we can say without exaggeration that his life as a priest was a long preparation for his death. He saw it coming without fear, with calm and resignation. He requested that his funeral take place in the Perpetual Help church and that his remains be buried in the family plot, favors granted with good grace and the pastor of Perpetual Help, whose hospitality is not limited to the living, opened the doors to his heart and his home to the Good Father Pagé by generously and royally giving this good priest, this dear friend, all the honor of a sacerdotal burial.

Having disappeared from our view for the field of rest, waiting for the great awakening of the resurrection, he seems to be telling us from his casket: *hodie mihi, cras tibi.* Today, my turn, tomorrow yours. Let's learn our lesson and follow his example.

And you, Christian family, join your natural feelings with religious feelings, and bless the secret design of the Good Lord.

If God took him so soon from your loving arms, it is because he was ready for Heaven. This is the consoling thought of our faith which should soften the bitterness of our sadness and our regrets.

However, my Brothers, as holy as his life was, as edifying as his death was, let us not pray to God in the fear that a few minor errors will close for a time the entrance to the resting place of glory, where nothing tarnished may cross the threshold. Let's join our prayers with those of the Church and ask the Lord to give him eternal peace. *Requiem aeternam dona ei, Domine, et lux perpetua luceat ei. Amen.*"

As the requiem of the High Mass would not be sung on Monday, the day of the feast of the Annunciation was celebrated Tuesday morning at 9 o'clock in the Our Lady of Perpetual Help church by Rev. L. Geoffroy, pastor of Three Rivers, Mass., assisted by Rev. M.W. Ducharme of Southbridge as deacon, and Rev. M.W.J. Choquette of Chicopee Falls as assistant deacon. At these various ceremonies, there was great attendance, both from clergy and the faithful.

"Justice" joins the family and friends of the dearly departed in mourning.

PART TWO

CHAPTER I

First Citizens

In the first years of emigration, our compatriots were not very concerned about becoming American citizens, primarily because it was with regret that they left Canada to come settle in the United States. Further, their sole ambition was to save money and to return as soon as possible to the homeland because a great number of them had left land there, half cleared and half paid off.

They spent the winter in this country to make some money and left in the spring to go farm in Canada. It was truly a vagabond emigration at that time, and several of our compatriots would spend all of their money on their travels. Not to mention that this situation was quite inconvenient for the older relatives who, when they took the road back to Canada, were forced to leave behind several members of their family. It was also a source of discontent among the younger ones, who easily adopted the manners and customs of this country, absolutely refusing to return to the land of their ancestors.

As for those who wished to stay here, they found a thousand reasons not to "naturalize," first because very few knew how to read and understand English, also because the majority of our influential Canadians did not approve of the idea of renouncing Canada to become American citizens.

In our big rallies, our conventions, the speakers often openly condemned naturalization and saw those who chose to "naturalize" as traitors. Of course at that time, as there are today, there were Canadian agents who used to urge our people to return to the good old homeland, using all means within their power.

These were enough obstacles to inhibit our people from becoming citizens of "Free America." In 1875, for example, there were at least 3,000 French-Canadians in Southbridge, and fewer than 25 voters. As there were several shopkeepers and building owners among our Canadians, they soon felt the need to become voters so as to be able to take an active part in municipal affairs and especially to protect their interests. So in 1875, a committee of citizens was named to work on naturalizing the others. They established a night school, to familiarize people with the English language. The work progressed slowly for the task was difficult and arduous; and they each also had other occupations, which inhibited them from giving themselves heart and soul to this enterprise. But perseverance overcame the obstacles; thanks to the "Cercle Canadien" contest, in 1877 there were 40 Canadian voters on the electoral list. In the spring of 1879, when the first Canadian was elected to a municipal post, the number of voters was 70. We are happy to mention that this first Canadian elevated to a position of confidence was Mr. Clément Bégin, who had been named "officer of the poor."

From one year to the next, the number of American citizens grew; in 1890, there were 265 who had the right to vote; in 1895, 331, and in 1900, over 500. Today, there are over 1,200, which means that voters of French-Canadian ethnicity constitute the majority of the electorate in the municipality of Southbridge.

First Voters

The first French-Canadian who had the right to vote in Southbridge was Jean Lussier, in 1850. Because he was born in Vermont, which he left in order to settle here with his family in 1848, he did not have to go through the formalities of naturalization.

The second voter was Mr. Etienne Richard, who enjoyed this privilege beginning in 1865. Mr. Richard, who was the first Canadian to establish a factory in Southbridge, wanted at that time to apply to the government for a patent for the manufacturing of knives, and since one needed to be a citizen to do so, he wasted no time in taking the necessary steps to become one.

In 1870, we find in the electoral lists the names of Régis and Herménégilde Bouthillette.

In 1871, Azarie F. Lamoureux and his brother Victor W. Lamoureux.

In 1872, Godfroi Petit, Alexandre Pagé, Thomas Lucier.

In 1873, Joseph Jacques, Alexandre Lataille, Felix Laverdière, Georges J. Lamoureux.

In 1874, Salomon Blanchard, Joseph D. Blanchard, Clément Bégin, Alexis Boyer, Sr., François X. Casavant, Paul Denis, Joseph Gélineau, Fr. O. Hêtu, Jean Langevin, Pierre Surprenant, Michel Surprenant.

In 1875, Joseph Bourque, Joseph Bibeau, Georges Bouthillette.

In 1876, Norbert Duval, Joseph M. Dupaul, Jacques Gaumond, Samuel Boisvert, Adolphe Lusignan, Jean-Baptiste Loranger, Flavien Laflamme, Alphonse Leclair, Zotique Leclair, Alphonse Lavallée,

Alexandre C. Lavallée, Alexandre St. Martin, Charles St. Pierre and J.B. Plante.

In 1877, David Patenaude, Augustin Roy, Alex. Sénécal, Pascal Sénécal, Rémi Surprenant, Albert Tisdel, François Tremblay, Trefflé Tremblay.

In 1878, Dr. Théophile Bélanger, François Bonnette, Dr. Jos. A. Robillard, Felix Quevillon, Ed. Deslauriers, Joseph Bouvier, Antoine Farland, Denis Fortier, Henri Gervais, George Laverdière, Henri Lamothe, Dr. Franklin Gauthier, Louis Langevin, Antoine F. Lamoureux, Charles Martel, Napoléon Plante.

According to the annual municipal reports, we observe that the first Canadians of Southbridge named by council members to municipal functions were, in 1878, V.W. Lamoureux, who was named inspector and measurer of firewood. Paul H. Leclair, truant officer and George Lamoureux, constable.

In the spring of 1879, Clément Bégin was the first Canadian elected to a municipal post, *by a majority of voters*. As we stated earlier, he was named "officer of the poor," an important position especially at that time when business was reasonably stagnant in the country. A number of families were forced to rely on public charity, and as our compatriot was a conservative, he did not like his position and did not want to accept a second term.

In 1885, he was named to the committee that dealt with the public library, a post he occupied for three years. This position allowed him to garner favor from many of his compatriots, for through his efforts, the library purchased a certain number of French books that are still much appreciated by the Canadians of Southbridge.

In 1888, he was part of the school commission, and for three years, in as much as possible, supported the children from the parish who attended municipal schools.

In 1896, he had another three year term on the committee of the public library.

Joseph D. Blanchard was the first Canadian elected to the council (selectman) and that was in 1888.

Joseph Ouimette was elected auditor and reelected in 1890; selectman in 1899, reelected in 1900-1901.

Horace J. Gravel was elected commissioner of the poor in 1890. Victor Lamoureux, assessor in 1891, selectman in 1892; reelected assessor in 1894, he occupied that position until 1902; named deputy judge by Governor Russell in 1893, a post he occupied until his death on June 2nd, 1919.

Mr. Paul Leclair was named to the commission of the poor by the selectmen in 1891; he occupied that post until 1892. In that same year, François X. Tétreault was elected member of the school commission, a position he occupied with distinction for twelve years.

Mr. Camille Métras was also elected in 1892 to be part of the library committee for a term of three years.

Mr. Felix Gatineau was elected as municipal selectman in 1893, and commissioner of the poor in 1895, a post he occupied until 1904.

Joseph A. Allard was on the library commission in 1893, and after 1900 was assessor for several years; he fulfilled his duties with honor. Like his predecessor, V.W. Lamoureux, he did his utmost to write French names correctly.

Georges J. Lamoureux, after occupying the post of chief engineer for the fire department, was elected commissioner of the poor in 1898. Reelected in 1899, he held this esteemed position until 1904.

In 1898, Alexis Boyer, Jr., was part of the library committee, and that was for three years. He was auditor in 1900 and 1901. Elected as selectman in 1903, he made his compatriots proud as he protected them in every way and edified them with his good example. He held that post for thirteen years.

CHAPTER II

Our Politicians—"Municipal Positions"

We would need not just one chapter but a whole volume to provide a dignified account of the achievements of our people in the political and municipal arenas. Nevertheless, the frame that we have selected will just allow us to provide a sweeping overview. The classification that follows, though dry and monotonous, will give the reader a glimpse sufficient enough to convey how active a role our men, full of energy and initiative, have always played in civic affairs! They have proven their worth in these positions, so much so that in this year of our Lord, we can say that almost all of the most important positions are in the hands of our fellow citizens. No matter the department, our people hold all the power and impose their will everywhere. Further, they live in perfect harmony with citizens of other foreign ethnicities and satisfy them all fully, so great is their faithfulness to the principles of full equity and justice. We do not say this to boast and to retreat into a sense of false security; we do not say this to rest on our laurels either; on the contrary, our goal is to show our people the path that was taken, in a true light, in order to further inspire them to engage in work yet to be completed.

Religion admirably prepares citizens to faithfully accomplish their duties, and in Southbridge like elsewhere, Canadians have only attained the highest positions and are only able to serve their country because they also serve their God. When you give to God what belongs to him, you are better positioned to give to Cesar what is his, and it's through their honesty that our compatriots have done so, as well as by the perfect union of the two. Certainly, in any camp there are disagreements, and among Canadians especially some jealousy, but combat makes the soldier stronger and skirmishes make the fighter more vigilant and more valiant. We beg the reader to forgive the long list that follows, but we are sure that it will be of interest even though its preparation cost us endless hours of thankless and difficult work. In creating this work, we have not tried to create a masterpiece or write a novel, but we rather wanted to assemble into one document all that relates to the Canadians in our city, which is so dear to our hearts. Facts, we have always believed, are better proof than words; we pray that our esteemed readers will understand.

Here is the List of Selectmen

Joseph D. Blanchard, 1890
Victor W. Lamoureux, 1892
Felix Gatineau, 1893
Joseph Ouimette, 1899-1900-1901

Antoine Farland, 1902-2903
Alexis Boyer, Jr., 1903-1916
Dr. Jos. G.E. Pagé, 1909-1910
J. Anatole Caron, 1910
Charles Proulx, 1911-1912 and 1915
Wilfrid J. Lamoureux, 1914-1919
Alexandre Désaulniers, 1914-1918
P.H. Hébert, 1917
François Sansoucy, 1919

Commissioners of the Poor

Horace Gravel, 1890
Felix Gatineau, 1895-1906
George J. Lamoureux, 1899-1902-03
Antoine Farland, 1900-1901
Alexandre Lataille, Jr., 1903-1908
Honoré Dorval, 1906
Wilfrid P. Gendreau, 1907-1908
Alex L. Désaulniers, 1909-1910
Napoléon Giroux, 1909-1913
Gédéon Pinsonneault, Jr., 1910-1916
Eugène Matte, 1914, 1915-1919
Narcisse Peloquin, 1916, 1918-1919
Oscar F. Gatineau, 1917
Philibert E. Quevillon, 1917

Assessors

Victor W. Lamoureux, 1891, 1894-95, 96-97 to 1902
Joseph A. Allard, 1903-1911
Joseph Gagnon, 1903-1909, 1912-1916
Antoine Farland, 1910-1919
Philias Casavant, 1917-1919

We can state that it is thanks to the assessors, Lamoureux, Allard, Gagnon, Farland and Casavant, that French names are written correctly in municipal registers. In passing, we should also congratulate the Canadians who, in Southbridge at least, have had enough resolve to write their names correctly.

Auditors

Joseph Ouimette, 1889-90
Wilfred J. Lamoureux, 1898-99
Alexis Boyer, Jr., 1900-01
J. Anatole Caron, 1903-04
Joseph T. Blanchard, 1905-08
Arthur Cabana, 1909-12

Philias X. Casavant, 1909-11
Joseph Métras, 1910-12
Joseph Laflèche, 1912-14
Joseph Tremblay, 1913-1914
George Dumas, 1914
    Joseph Laflèche was named municipal accountant in 1914-18.
    Valmore P. Tétreault, municipal accountant, 1919.

School Commission

Clément Bégin, 1889
Fr. X. Tétreault, 1890-1901
J.A. Caron, 1900-1902
Salomon E. Blanchard, 1902-1911
P.H. Hébert, 1903-1905, 1910-1919
Albéric Thibeault, 1911-1916
Dr. J.A. Généreux, 1906-1911
Dr. Chas. A. Tétreault, 1912-20
Dr. J.G.E. Pagé, 1915-16-17
Hector Leclair, 1918-19-20

Bureau of Health or of Hygiene

Dr. J.A. Généreux, 1900-1913
Dr. J.G.E. Pagé, 1903-1905
J.A. Caron, 1906-1917
Dr. Jos. E. Donais, 1911-1919
Philias Caron, 1918-20

Library

Clément Bégin, 1885-86-87, 1896-97-98
Joseph Bessette, 1889-90
Camille Métras, 1890-92
Joseph A. Allard, 1893-94-95, 1915-16-17
Alexis Boyer, 1897-98-99
J.H. Caron, 1899-1904
W.J. Lamoureux, 1900-02
Rev. J.A. Fredette, 1901-02
P.H. Hébert, 1902-1910, 1914-15-16
Albéric Thibeault, 1903-1908
Joseph T. Blanchard, 1904-05
Origène J. Paquette, 1909-1914
Henri Tétrault, 1910-1912
Théophile Houle, 1912-14
Isidore Leblanc, 1912-14
Hector Leclair, 1913-15
Alfred M. Blanchard, 1914-16

Hector L. Peloquin, 1914-1916

Managers named by the selectmen, Alexis Boyer and Louis O. Rieutard.

Sewer Committee

Jos. Ouimette, 1899-1900-1901
W.J. Lamoureux, 1903-1915
H.W. Bail, 1910-12, 1917-19
Fred Lamoureux, 1913-1916
Alfred M. Blanchard, 1915-16-17
Joseph A. Allard, 1919-20-21
Goerges Dumas, [no dates]
Philippe Dagenais, 1919-1921

CHAPTER III

Other Municipal Positions—Sinking Fund Committee

Salomon E. Blanchard, 1903-1904-05
Edouard Lareau, 1902
P.H. Hébert, 1900-1903, 1906-08
Oswald Grégoire, 1904-06
Joseph Métras, 1905-07
H. Bail, 1907-1910
Fred J. Adam, 1908-1911
Isidore Leblanc, 1909-1914
Hector Leclair, 1910-1912
Joseph Laflèche, 1911-1913
Ephrem Chicoine, 1913-1919
Louis Dupuis, 1914-1920
Edouard Leclair, 1915-1921

"Engineers," Fire Department

Geo. J. Lamoureux, 1893-1898
Paul N. Leclair, 1899, chief in 1900
Louis N. Duquette, 1899-02, chief in 1903
Alfred Allard, 1902-1905, chief 1904-1905
Basile J. Proulx, chief 1906-1911
Antoine Farland, 1906-1908
Charles Proulx, 1909-1910, chief in 1912
Joseph Leclair, 1910
Louis Lamothe, 1911-1918
Joseph Duchesneau, 1911-1912, chief in 1913-1919

Constables Elected by Voters

George Goddu, 1885
Alexandre Sénécal, 1886-87
Alexandre Lataille, 1888
Horace Gravel, 1889
Moïse Gagnon, 1890
Pierre Caplette, 1890-1919
Jos. P. Larivière, 1900-03, 1906-07-08
Zotique Leclair, 1901-1909
Felix St. George, 1909
Pierre Cormier, 1902-1906
Basile J. Proulx, 1906-1907

Joseph Paulhus, 1906-1909
Pierre Leclair, 1906-1907
Louis Lamothe, 1907-1914
Pierre Benoit, 1908-09-10
Georges Graveline, 1909
Joseph Paquin, 1908-1914
Louis Langevin, 1914

Regular Uniformed Officers

Zotique N. Leclair, 1900-1903
Pierre Cormier, 1900-1919
Joseph Paulhus, 1904-1909
Olivier Paul, Jr., 1909-1919
Georges A. Graveline, 1909
Joseph Paquin, 1910-1919
Honoré St. Martin, 1913-1919
Hormisdas Duplessis, 1915-1919
Ulric Breault, 1915-1918, at which time he left for the army
Eusèbe Laliberté, 1917-1918

Mr. Paul N. Leclair was chosen as chief of the police department for the year 1904; Mr. Napoléon Giroux, chosen in 1913, still holds this prestigious post.

Cemetery Committee

Jos. T. Larivière, 1903-1908
Adolphe Péloquin, 1911-1916
Jos. Desrosiers, 1912, 1913 and 1914

Lawyer to the City Council

Louis O. Rieutard from 1908 to 1917

Treasurers

Edouard Desrosiers in 1909
Salomon Blanchard, 1910-1915
Felix Bouvier, 1919

City Arborist

Pierre Benoit from 1910 to 1919

Tax Collectors

Victor W. Lamoureux, 1905
Edouard Desrosiers, 1906-1910
François-Xavier Tétreault, 1911-1912
Joseph Métras, 1913
Eugène Gabrie, 1914-1919

Public Works Manager—Aimé Langevin, 1906 through 1919

Mr. Honoré Dorval was named caretaker of the poor farm in 1907 and he held this position until 1912. He was replaced by Mr. Joseph

Payant, who current occupies this post.

Mr. Moïse Gagnon, appointed to be part of the registration bureau in 1901, has occupied this position ever since.

Mr. Pierre Caplette, elected constable in 1890, was reelected each year from that time on for 28 consecutive years. Mr. Caplette was named caretaker of city hall in 1893, a post he occupied for 25 years, that is to say until 1918; this allowed him, according to state laws, to obtain a pension of half of his regular salary for the remainder of his lifetime. He is the only citizen of Southbridge to occupy a municipal post for a quarter of a century. He died in 1919.

A great number of our compatriots have long occupied and continue to occupy different civic posts to which they are annually appointed by the selectmen, but it is impossible for us to list them all in this work. We mean jobs like prison guard, weights and measures inspector, special police, inspector of goods. Several of our fellow Canadians have also been part of important committees for the construction of public buildings, etc.

CHAPTER IV

Capitation and Property Owners

Long before the date of the incorporation of the city of Southbridge, we believe that there were French names on the assessors list in the municipalities of Dudley, Charlton and Sturbridge, which would later form the municipality of Southbridge. Here are the names that can be found: Allard, Daigle, Dugar, Gérauld, Lévesque, Lazure and others; some were Huguenots from the colony of Oxford, others were Acadians deported to New England in 1755.

Before the year 1800, Charles Dugas, son of Acadian Daniel Dugas, purchased a 139 acre farm located at the end of Pleasant Street, a farm known at the time as "Barefoot."

This farm was considered as having great value and was one of the most advantageous in the budding colony. However, as the first French descendant to acquire property, Mr. Dugas was not happy, for the titles were not clear and after his death, his son Pierre was forced to pay for it a second time. It goes without saying that the latter was not at all discouraged by this, and after several years he became one of the most wealthy farmers in the area.

In 1838, he sold his properties to go live in Saint-Jacques-de-l'Achignan, Canada with his family, and today this farm is divided into two properties, one belonging to Mr. Alfred McKinstry and the other to Frank Shephard.

"Capitation"

According to the municipal registers, the first Canadians to pay a capitation (poll tax) were Joseph Bourassa, Pierre Benoit, Antoine Benoit, François Daigle, François Laflèche, Pierre Dumas, Fr. Dumas, Albert Giard, Victor Brazeau and Pierre Pelletier.

In 1844, Henri Fontaine paid a tax of $100 on a blacksmith shop; in 1847, brothers Frédéric and Edouard N. Lacroix were taxed a sum of $300.00 for merchandise (stock in trade). It seems that these compatriots were carpenters, and after a short stay in Southbridge, went to live elsewhere. They say that one of them, Edouard N. Lacroix, went to live in Detroit, Michigan, where he played an important role among our compatriots; he died there in 1885.

In 1847, Pierre Palardy was taxed a sum of $300.00 on a blacksmith shop. Mr. Jean Roy was perhaps the first Canadian to become the owner of a house, located on Mill Street, and that was in 1851. That property was located on the land where today we find Mr. Rémi Surprenant's old house.

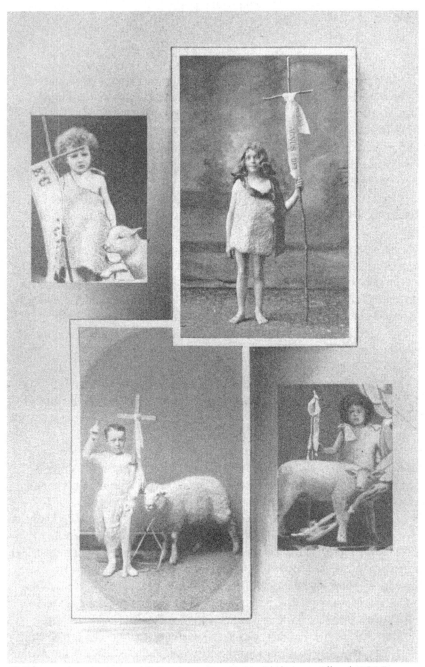

Children who portrayed Saint Jean-Baptiste: Alphonse Allard, 1917 –
Henri Dumas, 1918 / W.J. Lamoureux, 1875 – Omer Généreux, 1898

Triumphal Arch, during the Feast of St-Jean-Baptiste in 1881

Officers of the St. Jean Baptiste Society in 1891: J.E. Proulx, J. Chagnon, L. Bachand, O. Robidoux, J.D. Proulx, C. Bégin, B. Proulx / J.D. Blanchard, A. Potvin, Dr. J.A. Généreux, F. Gatineau, V.W. Lamoureux

Officers of the St.-Jean-Baptiste Society, 1919

In 1864, Napoléon Leboeuf became owner of an inn in "Globe Village"; in 1865 and 1866, Pierre Berthiaume and Alexis Bibeau also became owners.

From 1865 to 1870, our compatriots arrived in Southbridge in great numbers, and several bought properties, such as Albert Duval, François X. Casavant, Joseph P. Nault, E.F. Girard, Joseph Berthiaume, Isaac Fontaine, Herménégilde Bouthillette, Alex. Lataille, Charles Bouthillette, Louis Berthiaume, Amable Gervais, Louis Langevin, Louis Lavallée, Philippe Lussier, Joseph Béford, Olivier Deblois, George Lamoureux, Mr. Lachapelle, Etienne Richard, Joseph Chassé, Pierre Mathieu, Pierre Dionne, Edouard Papillon, Joseph Péloquin, Théophile Tremblay and others.

In 1872, Rev. Fr. LeBreton, then pastor of the Notre Dame parish, bought a property to become the rectory, and it is still today the residence of the parish's pastor.

From that time through the present day, Canadian property owners became quite numerous, for according to the municipal assessment of 1915, we have 572 owners, assessed at a total value of $1,488,950.

Taxes paid by them were $33,490.99. Add to those figures the lands that are owned by the Notre Dame and Sacred Heart parishes, which are not subject to taxation, and several other properties handed down to our people, and you arrive at the conclusion that from 1915 to 1919, we can, without exaggeration, estimate the value of the properties owned by Franco-Americans in Southbridge at being over $2,000,000.

The Presidents of the Cercle Canadien from 1876 to 1916 presented by Felix Gatineau, March 6, 1916. According to the old rules, elections were held every 6 months. (See Appendix for enlarged images)

CHAPTER V

Our Canadian Doctors

With the waves of French-Canadian emigration to Southbridge, there came a respectable contingent of doctors of all sorts. Some did not stay long in our vicinity; others practiced their profession here for years. Some of them held degrees, others were seeking funds to complete their studies; still others were nothing more than fervent charlatans, and Southbridge was not spared on this account.

According to the information that we have been able to obtain, Dr. Provencher, originally from Chambly River, was the first French-Canadian doctor to settle in Southbridge in 1850. He married a Miss Migneault, cousin of Rev. Fr. Migneault, who had come to our city during that time as a missionary.

As there was a sizeable group of Canadians here at that time, we can only think that it was at the instigation of the good father Migneault, as the parishioners called him, that this first doctor came to settle among us; but since the Canadians of Southbridge were not yet numerous enough to provide a living wage for a doctor of their nationality, Dr. Provencher left the area in 1852 to find his fortune elsewhere.

Around the year 1855, Dr. Edmond Dorion, a native of Saint-Ours, practiced the medical arts in Southbridge, but he did not stay here long. He went to live in northern New York State, where he was both doctor and journalist, especially in Ogdensburg and in Syracuse, where he was residing when he died several years ago.

Towards 1860, there was a young French doctor who practiced here, but since people did not know his name, they called him Dr. French; his stay here was short.

In 1862, a young doctor by the surname of Roy came to Southbridge where, after a time, he married a Miss Vinton of Dudley. Shortly thereafter, he changed his name from Roy to King and then quickly disappeared from the colony.

From 1865 to 1870, as more and more Canadian families were arriving from Canada, several doctors or so-called doctors visited Southbridge with the goal of moving here; such as Doctors Cotrel, Ousé, Trudeau, Dudevoir, Douray, Duverger and others, but they only spent a short time with us.

In 1869, Dr. M.G. Fontaine, originally from St. Hugues, Canada, a young doctor, came to settle here; it was around the beginnings of the

Notre Dame parish for which he showed a zeal worthy of mention. He was also the first president of the St. Jean Baptiste Society. In 1871, he went to live in Millbury, Mass., where he had already resided, and later returned to St.-Guillaume, Canada where, after several years of practice, he died.

In 1870, Dr. Laciserais came to settle in Southbridge and moved to Union Street, in the old rectory, and was Rev. Fr. LeBreton's neighbor; he lived in Southbridge for a little over a year.

Also in 1870, Dr. Fr. X. Gauthier arrived to live in Southbridge. Our compatriot was always well respected here, for in all kinds of circumstances, he devoted himself in every way to the well-being of his fellow citizens. In the year 1879 and in 1881, small pox afflicted several of our Canadian families, and it was above all during this epidemic that Dr. Gauthier devoted himself, body and soul, to the population of Southbridge. He died on February 13, 1913, after having practiced in Southbridge for forty-three years.

Dr. C.V. Clément—Dr. Dutrisac

In 1872, Dr. C.V. Clément, coming from Montréal, came to settle among us; he stayed about two years and left in 1874 to return to Montréal. In 1873, Dr. Dutrisac, born in Québec but having practiced in Meriden, Conn., arrived in Southbridge, probably with the goal of replacing Dr. Clément. He received a warm welcome from Rev. Fr. Brochu, for the two had been classmates in college, but his stay was short.

Dr. Théophile Bélanger

Dr. Théophile Bélanger was born in Murray Bay, Québec.[13] A young and gifted doctor, he arrived here around 1875 and during his stay in Southbridge, he acquired a most enviable reputation. He took an active part in the national movement; a good doctor, good speaker, consummate actor, and of a limitless devotion. In 1876, he assisted in the formation of the "Cercle Canadien." He supported national societies and also the naturalization of our people. However, the illness that afflicted him for a long time led him to his grave on February 7th, 1883.

Dr. J.A. Letourneau

Dr. J.A. Letourneau was born in St. Sébastien, Québec and arrived here in the year 1883. He established a pharmacy at the corner of Main Street and Chapin. Several years later, he left for Montréal and Farnham, where he died on February 23rd, 1894.

---

[13] Translator's note: Today, La Malbaie.

Dr. Joseph A. Robillard

In 1874, Dr. Joseph A. Robillard, whose family lived in Southbridge, was admitted to the practice of medicine. He was the founder of the "Cercle Canadien" and its first secretary. He was also its dramatic director until his death, which occurred on December 7th, 1884. He was only 31 years old. This was a sad shock for the Canadians of Southbridge, who had great respect for this devoted man. With his death, the parishioners of Notre Dame lost one of their most devoted leaders who was always interested in the advancement of his compatriots, devoting his time and his health to their well-being and striving to procure positions for them. His career was really too short; we will not attempt to eulogize our illustrious brother, but we will settle for the words of one of his dear friends, written in an article at the time of his death:

"The Death of a Patriot, December 7, 1884"

"The Canadian population of Southbridge has just been plunged into mourning and grief by a terrible incident. Dr. J.A. Robillard died suddenly on Saturday at five o'clock in the afternoon, leaving behind a tearful widow, four young children, and all of his family, that is to say all of us here, without exception, all those who call themselves Canadians by birth or by name.

"This blow was so unexpected that, having only been aware that he was bedridden for two days and thinking he had some minor indisposition, we had just barely heard this news about him. 'The doctor is better, said some; a cold, a chill, he will be totally better in a few days.' And suddenly, the sound of an atrocious, unbelievable tragedy began to spread. The doctor is dead!

"It is not my intention here to write a eulogy or to devote a long article to the memory of the one who has departed. The timing would be bad. Great sorrow is mute. It is almost impossible to describe the consternation that looms here. The show that is being offered in Southbridge by the Cercle Canadien, this show, we say, is upsetting. The members arrive, greet each other, shake hands and cry. It is here, especially, that his loss is and will be felt in the worst way. He was not only one of the founders, one of the members, he was the soul, the life of the group. It was not self-interest but rather devotion that he always showed us. How many times did we see him, after having spent day and night with the sick, arriving here tired, drained, and yet always smiling, offering advice and assisting with the rehearsals he was directing. Friendly to all, always ready to lend a hand, never knowing how to say no, his goodness and his selflessness carried him along.

"The instability of human life! Unfathomable mysteries! Eight days ago, the rehearsal hall of the group was animated, we were working on a show that will—what am I saying? that should have opened soon. The doctor was there, guiding, encouraging with his words and deeds. 'Fine sirs,' he used to say to us, 'we must open on the 24th. The Canadians are waiting, let's be worthy of them, let's be worthy of us.' Today, in this same hall, we rehearse: it's no longer about a scene or an act, it's a song. Grave voices are heard, it's not French, it's Latin, as the group's chorus rehearses the Requiem Mass and Mr. Ernest Decelles, the director, says with tears in his eyes: 'My friends, let's work, this mass must be sung, let's follow his example, let's muster all of our strength, all of our souls, let's be worthy of him.' Again, the profound emotion we feel in this moment is preventing us from writing more.

"The funeral service for our dear friend will take place this morning, Tuesday, at 9 o'clock." December 7th.

CHAPTER VI

Dr. V. St. Germain—Dr. Ovide Morasse

Dr. Valmore St. Germain came to live in Southbridge in the month of December 1884. The Canadians of this place were very happy to welcome him here, for he had remarkable qualities as a doctor, writer, cantor and musician. Later, he left to settle in West Warren and Fall River.

Dr. O. Morasse, coming from Sorel, his home parish, arrived in Southbridge in the month of February 1885. A good doctor, he quickly developed a quite enviable clientele; he was very involved in national issues. [14] An active member of the Cercle Canadien, on different occasions he gave interviews, discussions, and lectures on various current events topics. When Riel[15] was hung in 1885, he had the Cercle Canadien adopt protest resolutions against the Canadian government. These protests caused an uproar and were commented on by several Canadian newspapers. Later, he had a few quarrels with Monsignor Brochu, which caused troublesome feelings among the parishioners. These disagreements with the pastor did not serve him well, and he had to leave for Putnam, Conn., where he died in 1918.

Dr. A. Buissière—Dr. Joseph Albéric Généreux

In 1885, Dr. A. Buissière came to live among us; he had a record of brilliant studies, had practiced medicine in different hospitals, and was known as a skilled surgeon, but he did not stay here for long.

Dr. Joseph A. Généreux, born in Drummondville, Québec in 1860, went to the college in Trois-Rivières, the Normal school in Montréal and Bowdoin College in Brunswick, ME, where he obtained his medical degree, before coming to live here in 1886.

During the twenty-five years that he spent in Southbridge, he took

---

[14] Translator's note: When Gatineau speaks here of "national issues," he is referring to the concerns of French-speaking Canadians and the "Patriote" rebel movement in Québec.

[15] Translator's note: Louis Riel was an important political figure who fought to preserve the rights of the "Métis" (biracial French/Indigenous people) in Canada's western territories. He led two rebellions against the Anglophone Canadian government, was convicted of treason and executed in 1885. He became a folk hero to French-Canadians, as they saw in him someone who took a stand against Anglophone oppression of Francophones.

an active part in the political affairs of this village and was a fervent supporter of naturalization. He held a number of important posts, on the board of hygiene and the school commission, for several years. He devoted himself to the advancement of our national societies, was one of the founding members of the Chevaliers St. Pierre, the Rochambeau Council, and a delegate from Southbridge to the first conference of the Union St-Jean-Baptiste in the month of March 1900. He declined the honor of being the official physician of that society. He died on December 25th, 1911, mourned by all.

Dr. Alfred Gagnon—Dr. J.A. Pontbriand—Dr. J.E. Farland

Dr. Alfred Gagnon, born in Trois-Rivières, Canada, after having lived in Woonsocket, R.I., arrived in Southbridge in 1887. He only lived here for six months.

Dr. J.A. Pontbriand, born in Sorel, came to Southbridge in 1890. This young man, who had completed excellent studies, did not lack in popularity here. In 1893, he left for Canada with his family; he currently lives in Sorel, where he practices medicine.

Dr. J.S.E. Farland was born in Lanoraie, Québec, and arrived to settle here in 1891. As many of the families coming to Southbridge at that time were from Berthier county, and as the new doctor found relatives and friends living here, in short time he developed a robust and solid clientele. During his stay here, given his talent for instrumental music, he organized an orchestra and a brass band. For some time, he also directed the choir of the Notre Dame parish. It was with sadness that his friends saw him leave, in 1901, for Lanoraie, where he currently lives.

Dr. L.E. Dionne—Dr. Louis Elzéar Leriche—Dr. Joseph G.E. Pagé

Coming from North Brookfield on the invitation of several friends, Dr. Dionne established a medical office in Southbridge in 1892. A skilled physician and also a good musician, he soon had a large circle of friends. Dr. Dionne was director of the choir and his wife, Mrs. Alice Bardy, was the organist of the parish for two years. After that, Dr. Dionne returned to North Brookfield, then moved to Ware, where he still lives and has a robust clientele. His fellow citizens, who on several occasions elected him to various municipal posts, also hold him in high esteem.

In 1897, Dr. Louis Elzéar Leriche, born in Montréal, arrived to settle among us. He had a good clientele, but left us the following year to return to the homeland.

Dr. Joseph G.E. Pagé, born in Sorel, Québec, studied at the college in St. Hyacinthe and did medical studies in Montréal. He arrived in Southbridge in 1898. His skill as a physician soon earned him a place of honor among his fellow citizens, who proved their admiration by electing him to several important posts. He was a city selectman, member of the school commission, the library committee, etc. Dr. Pagé still has a robust clientele today and is generally held in high esteem; given his affable manner and his characteristic smile, he easily made many friends.

Dr. Oswald Grégoire—Dr. Joseph Chagnon

Dr. O. Grégoire was born in Joliette, Québec. In 1898, this young dentist moved here; he had studied in the college of his hometown, and then went to live in Pawtucket, R.I., Holyoke and Fall River. He completed his studies of dentistry at the University of Maryland, where he graduated with high honors. On July 8, 1912, the doctor, although still quite young, was taken from his family and his many friends and admirers.

In 1899, Dr. Joseph Chagnon, originally from St. Hyacinthe, arrived here after having practiced in Fall River, Mass. and in other New England towns. His stay was relatively short, for in 1901, he left for New Bedford and then lived in Willimantic, where he died in 1917.

CHAPTER VII

Doctors (continued)

Dr. Rodolphe Goyer—C.J. Bisaillon—Dr. Arthur Chaussée

Dr. Rodolphe Goyer, born in St. Rémi, Canada, came here in 1900; during the few years he spent in Southbridge, he was entirely devoted to the advancement of our national societies. A good orator, he never refused a chance to speak up in defense of our institutions and in favor of the advancement of our people, and he generously dispensed both health and dedication. In 1905, he went to pursue specialist studies in Paris and upon return settled in Springfield, then two years later he left for the Canadian metropolis.

Dr. C.J. Bisaillon was born in Stafford Springs, Conn., and came here in 1901. He soon left for Athol.

In 1903, Dr. Arthur Chaussé, born in New Bedford, opened an office on Chapin Street, in the building of the St. Onge pharmacy, but returned to New Bedford after several weeks of practice.

Dr. Pomerat—Dr. Edgar Smith—Dr. J.A. Robinson

In that same year of 1903, Dr. C.M. Pomerat moved to Southbridge, and lived for some time on Mechanic Street, where he opened a dispensary. A member of the Cercle Canadien, at various times he gave interesting lectures on current events topics. He left for Spencer in 1910.

Dr. Edgar Smith opened an office here in 1906 on Mechanic Street. He was only here for a few months.

In 1908, Dr. J.A. Robinson, born in Champlain, NY, arrived in Southbridge; several years later, he was in Fiskdale and he died in Indian Orchard in 1918.

Dr. Joseph Donais—Dr. S.J. Benoit—Dr. E. Robillard

After his medical studies at Laval University in Montréal, our compatriot Dr. J. Donais came to practice in our city where he garnered an excellent reputation and an enviable clientele. On several occasions, he was elected a member of the board of health, a position he still occupies. He was also the doctor to the poor in Southbridge.

In 1908, Dr. Benoit came to live here from Holyoke; in 1910, he went to live in Lowell, then in 1914 he opened a temporary hospital here on Chestnut Street. It was a great idea, but unfortunately, he was not supported in this effort; people did not understand his thinking. In the spring of 1915, he left to live in Worcester then in 1917 in Gardner. Shortly thereafter, he enrolled in the army with the title of chief surgeon and went to France. He was wounded several times and has made his family and fellow citizens very proud. He is now in Gardner.

In 1908, Dr. Robillard, dentist, moved to Southbridge; he soon left for North Adams and then went to Lowell, where he currently lives.

Dr. Chas. Tétreault—Dr. Chas. Simpson—Dr. Eug. Tétreault

Dr. Charles Tétreault was born in Danielson, Conn. on September 17, 1876 to François X. Tétreault and Célina St. Onge. He first attended municipal schools, then took courses at Brown University, Providence. He did his medical studies at Yale University and received his degree in 1906. For several years, he practiced in various hospitals then enrolled in the American army and was sent to the Philippine Islands where he held the rank of major-surgeon. After his years of service, he went to take a specialty course in Vienna, Austria. Upon his return in 1911, he opened a medical office in Southbridge. In 1918, he reenlisted in the army, with the rank of captain. He was discharged in December of that same year and returned to his office where he has enjoyed an enviable clientele ever since.

Dr. Charles Simpson was born in Millbury on September 4, 1877 to Joseph Simpson and Rose Huard. At a young age, he came to Southbridge; later he left for the college of Sainte-Thérèse, then entered Laval University in Montréal to study medicine. After having completed his degree in 1904, he practiced for several years at the Notre Dame hospital and at the Hôtel-Dieu in Montréal, as well as at hospitals in Worcester and Boston. He opened an office here in 1911, and thanks to his experience and his cosmopolitanism, he gained an excellent reputation as both a citizen and a doctor.

Dr. Eugène Tétreault was born in Southbridge on March 27, 1887. After his preliminary studies here, he took courses at Harvard University and received his diploma in 1917. He opened an office in Southbridge and several months later enrolled in the American army in the medical corps. Service was not good to him, for he contracted an illness in the camp that sent him to his grave on January 11, 1919. We salute him for so generously sacrificing his life for the country!

Dr. Roch Lepage was born in Montréal on August 16, 1886 to J.Z. Lepage and Anna Charest. Student of the Marist Brothers in New York, then in the college of Ste-Marie-de-Monnoir, Canada, he went to the university of dental medicine in Baltimore where he received his diploma in 1908. He opened an office in Rumford Falls, Maine in 1912, then came here, where he has a top-notch office.

M.P. Tétreault was born in Southbridge on September 6, 1890 to

F.X. Tétreault and Célina St. Onge. He attended Clark University in Worcester, where he received his degree in 1912, and in that year accepted the position of Professor of Biology at Lafayette University, Indiana, where he now teaches.

M.H. Tétreault, brother of Charles, Eugène and Philippe Tétreault, was born in Danielson, Conn. on January 1, 1881. A college graduate, he went to study law at "Boston Law School" and was admitted to the bar in 1917.

Mr. Arthur Gravel was born in Southbridge on December 10, 1884 to Horace Gravel and M. Louise Lord. After attending parochial schools, he was a student at the College of Ste.-Thérèse, Canada. He took classes at the University of Maryland and obtained his diploma in dentistry in June 1909. He moved to New Bedford and had an office in New York for six years. On March 1, 1917, he opened an office in Southbridge where he currently resides.

Dr. H.L. Desmarais was born in Millbury on February 9, 1886 to L.F. Desmarais and M. Louise Lussier. He studied dentistry at the University of Philadelphia and in Baltimore. He earned his diploma in 1909 and, after practicing in Providence and Worcester, opened an office in Southbridge in September 1915.

Dr. H. Péloquin was born in Southbridge on August 24, 1883 to Adolphe Péloquin and Clara Lord. He attended parochial schools, the Seminary in Trois-Rivières, Canada, the Mont St. Louis College in Montréal, and the College of the Holy Cross, Worcester. He then studied dental medicine at the University of Maryland and received his diploma in 1910. The following year, he took specialist courses in dental medicine; he then practiced in Lowell, Mass. and moved here in 1913.

Irène Céleste Thresher, D.M.D., daughter of W.S. Thresher and Hermine Leclair, was born in Brookfield on September 14, 1895; after attending municipal schools, she entered Tufts University of Boston, where she studied dentistry and obtained her degree in the month of June 1919. Her office is in the Whitford building.

CHAPTER VIII

Newspapers in Southbridge

From 1838 to the present day, a great number of French magazines and newspapers were founded in the United States; some are still quite successful today, but the majority only had a brief day in the sun, despite the unheard of sacrifices of some of our compatriots. Southbridge also experienced this. In the month of August 1872, Clément Desmarais, originally from Montréal, where he had done his studies, was employed in a store in our city and founded a weekly newspaper that he dubbed *L'Étoile de l'Est* (*The Star of the East*). But in the space of a few weeks, "the star soared towards the east" and never reappeared. The editor himself left for Woonsocket, where he endeavored to publish another newspaper called *La Guêpe* (*The Wasp*) which also soon disappeared.

In 1881-82 and 83, the *Southbridge Journal*, owned by George Whitaker, published several excerpts in French written by Dr. J.A. Robillard, Arthur Sicotte, and several others. This innovation was immensely appreciated by our fellow citizens and contributed quite a bit to the increase in circulation of this local paper.

In 1896, M.C. Daoust founded *Le Patriote* (*The Patriot*) in Southbridge, which invited a great number of our compatriots in the village to support the movement by having announcements or advertisements published. But alas! such a wonderful enterprise could not last long, for after several weeks, we learned that the owner has gone off to seek his fortune elsewhere, leaving behind the memory of announcements and subscriptions paid in advance. He also published *La Patrie Nouvelle* (*The New Homeland*) and in 1897, *Le Citoyen* (*The Citizen*).

In 1903, J.B. Bélisle, born in St.-Aimé, Richelieu county, where he did his studies, arrived in Southbridge after having lived for a time in Rhode Island, and shortly thereafter, founded the newspaper *L'Ouvrier* (*The Laborer*), which soon became popular due to its interesting news items and editorials.

Mr. Bélisle had been a brilliant student and he had a skillful pen, for he really loved literature. Several months after the founding of his newspaper, Mr. Bélisle was called back to Canada by his family and the newspaper disappeared.

From the earliest days in Southbridge, we mostly received newspapers from Canada. But starting in 1870, some Canadians were getting *La Voix du Peuple* (*The Voice of the People*) from Manchester, a voice that soon disappeared. Later, the *Foyer Canadien* (*Canadian Home*), the *Travailleur* (the *Worker*), the *Jean-Baptiste* and for many years *L'Opinion Publique* (*Public Opinion*), were among the papers supported by our compatriots. Today, *L'Opinion Publique*, which has always presented our municipal interests and which prints a significant number of papers, is recognized as the official voice of Franco-Americans in Southbridge.

Officers of the Cercle Canadian 1919: L. Martel, A. Robillard, J.A. Martin, P. Dagenais, F. Gatineau, J.B. Demers, L. Girard, H. Tétreault, A. Guillmette / Ph. Casavant, J. Coderre, V. Tétreault, H. Bastien, E. Ouellette

Officers of the Cour Jacques-Cartier, F.F.A, in 1907

Founding Officers of the Succursale des Artisans, founded in 1902

Officers of the Council Jacquest-Cartier, U.S.J.B. D'A., 1919: A. Trahand, A. Durocher, E. Dupaul / T. Poirier, J. Casubon, J. Larivière, J. Tremblay, H. L'Homme, N. Robidoux / N. Duquette, Dr. J.G.E. Pagé, Rev. L.O. Triganne, H. Robida, S. Martel

Officers of the Artisans Canadiens-Francais, 1919: P. Bachand, M. Duhamel, H. Matte, H. Ravenelle, T. Duquette, A. Lapierre, L. Cloutier, E. Demers / B.J. Proulx, Rev. L.O. Triganne, W. Richard, L. Meunier

CHAPTER IX

Patriotism—Our Soldiers

Those who would label French-Canadians as weak or cowardly will see in reading the following that they are severely mistaken. There is certainly a wonderful chapter that could be written about the selflessness, the devotion, the spirit of sacrifice and the patriotism of "Southbridgers." When the country needed people to defend it, when dark clouds began to gather on the horizon signaling a coming storm, when there was a possible threat against the great flag that shelters us, our compatriots did not turn a deaf ear. At the first call, at the first cry of alarm, they promptly jumped in to assist the country, and a good number of them died protecting our rights and in so doing covered their names, their families and their fellow citizens with glory.

During the Civil War in 1861, there was already a sizeable contingent of French-Canadians in the United States. However, they had not been here long enough to have been forced into taking up arms by law. Since those who voluntarily enrolled were offered very tempting bonuses, a number of them hastened to don military uniforms, not only because of the bonuses but also due to their patriotism. It is estimated that at least 40,000 French-Canadians enlisted in the army of the North.[16] There were even some who came from Canada specifically for that reason. In Southbridge, although there were relatively few Canadians, several fellow citizens made the sacrifice of leaving their homes to defend the nation's honor. Through painstaking research, we were able to procure a partial list of names of those who left, including those from Woodstock, Conn. who were related to families from Southbridge.

Here it is: Augustin Benoit, Co. D, 8th Infantry Regiment; Pierre Benoit, Co. D, 8th Infantry Regiment; Frank Benoit, Co. G., 60th Infantry Regiment; Joseph Bourassa, Charles and Edouard Bourassa (three brothers), Joseph Bouvier, Charles Bouthillette, Louis Bolduc, Antoine Dionne, Cyrille Giard, Louis Giard, Gabriel Hêtu, François and Jean Hêtu (three brothers), Louis B. Larivière, Co. G, 24th Infantry Regiment.

Pierre Larivière, André Langevin (Co. G, 36th Inf. Reg.), Jules Lambert (6th Battery), Fabien Lescarbeau, Israël Ledoux, Victor Leveillé (enlisted in Vermont), Adolphe Lapierre, Joseph Lapierre, Olivier Lapierre, Pierre Giroux (enlisted in Connecticut), John M. Lucier (Co. D,

---

[16] Translator's note: We know today that this estimate is too high. Jean Lamarre says fewer than 20,000, based on the enlistment paper in the National Archives. (see footnote in Introduction)

4th Regiment), Philippe Lucier, Pierre Aucoin, Thomas Aucoin, P. Palardy, Paul, Isaac and Pierre Potvin (three brothers), Charles Provost, Salomon Paul, Paul Sabourin (Co. A, 24th Inf. Reg.), Antoine Sabourin, Robert St. Martin.

Emma Riendeau[17] enrolled in the army as a telephone operator and a nurse in June 1918 and went over to France that same month with a group of around twenty French-Canadian women who enrolled at the same time as her. She was the sister of Sargent A.J. Riendeau, the first soldier from Southbridge to be killed in action on June 7, 1917, after having received the Medal of Honor from General Pershing for bravery and distinction on the battlefield.

The Spanish-American War

When the Spanish-American war broke out in 1898, the 6th Regiment of Massachusetts, which included Co. K from Southbridge, was called to action, and since there were a great number of Franco-Americans from Southbridge who belonged to that company, they took part in various battles in Cuba, Puerto Rico. In San Juan, the battalion that Company K belonged to was on the front lines of the battle, and a young Canadian from Southbridge had the honor of being the standard-bearer during that battle, which was a true victory for the soldiers of the North. That young Canadian who garnered so much glory was Alexandre Montminy. Additionally, several other Canadians from this village held places of honor.

Here are their names:

W.P. Lacroix, Lieutenant, Co. K, 6th Regiment

Frank Bonnette, Emery Rhéaume, Naopléon Phaneuf, Sergeants, Co. K, 6th Regiment

Alexandre Montminy, Standard-Bearer

Co. K, 6th Regiment

Albert J. Martin, musician

Joseph Ducharme

Narcisse Allard

Antoine Bélanger

James Benoit

---

[17] Translator's note: Emma Riendeau was one of the "Hello Girls," a group of 223 bilingual women hired by the U.S. Army to operate telephones in France during WWI. Read more about the Army Signal Corps women in Elizabeth Cobb's recent book *The Hello Girls: America's First Women Soldiers* (Harvard University Press, 2017). Her photo is in this book. It is unclear why this paragraph is here and not included in the later section on WWI soldiers from Southbridge.

George E. Bouthillette
John B. Caplette
Albert Chapdelaine
Philippe Duhamel
Omer Galipeau
Napoléon Garceau
Fred. N. Gélineau
Pierre Laplante
Henri Laprade
George G. Loiseau
Alexandre Paquin
Pierre Péloquin
Paul Pelletier

World War—1914-1918

Long before the United States declared war against Germany and its allies, thousands of French-Canadians had gone to enroll in the Allied armies to champion freedom, rights and justice. They did so not only to make liars out of our detractors and slanderers, but because of the noble French blood running through their veins, pushing them to come to the aid of the old motherland that was in danger.

But when Germany's insolence required us, in turn, to declare war against them, the number of volunteers rose even higher. The Canadians of Southbridge were no less generous than their brothers across New England. Without waiting to be called, a number voluntarily offered themselves to their country. Many families were tested, many mothers regretfully saw one or two of their sons leave home. Never, no never, had there been such a war, blood flowing in surges, turning the soil of Old Europe red. The draft later tore sons, brothers and even husbands from their families.

Our youth rose to the challenge and not a single one tried to evade the law. They left behind everything, relatives, friends, life's comforts; but they never thought of looking back, for God and their country, they marched forward. Nearly 500 of our compatriots either enrolled or were drafted. Sixteen gave the ultimate sacrifice and died on the battlefield or in different concentration camps, in the country or in Europe.

We are sure you will be interested to read this list:

Adam, Hervé	Beaudry, Hector	Berthiaume, Arthur E.
Allard, Arthur	Beaudry, Jean-B. M.	Berthiaume, Joseph N.
Allard, Félix	Beaudry, Napoléon M.	Bertrand, Alphonse L.
Allard, Léo W.	Beaupré, Rudolphe H.	Bertrand, Arthur A.
Allard, Napoléon	Bélanger, Arthur	Bibeau, Adélard
Allaire, Charles E.	Bélanger, Edgar	Bibeau, Adélard E.
Anger, Louis F.	Bélanger, Joseph E.	Bibeau, Georges
Arcoite, Roméo	Bélanger, Hector	Bibeau, Léo
Arpin, Charles	Bélanger, Henri	Biron, Georges A.
Asselin, Deus	Bélanger, Henry L.	Blain, Aloysius J.
Asselin, Joséphat A.	Bélanger, Wilfrid J.	Blain, Josaphat C.
Bachand, Arthur	Bell, Louis A.	Blais, Hector
Bachand, Arthur H.	Benoit, Aimé	Boisvert, Stanislas
Bachand, Frank	Benoit, Arthur R.	Boiteau, Joseph E.
Bachand, Isaïe	Benoit, Ferdina	Bombardier, Joseph A.
Bachand, Léo J.	Benoit, George B.	Bombard, Joseph
Bail, Hermas	Benoit, Irène	Bonneau, Georges
Bail, Walter	Benoit, Joseph	Bonneau, P. Vitalis
Bartelette, Edouard	Benoit, Joseph P.	Bonnette, Antonio
Basilières, Armand	Benoit, Osias	Bonnette, Omer N.
Bastien, Arthur J.	Benoit, Raymond L.	Bonin, Henry J.
Beaudry, Alfred	Benoit, Wilfrid	Bonin, Wilfrid A.
Beaudry, Ernest T.	Bernard, Edouard	Boucher, Joseph A.

Boucher, Henry F.
Boucher, Victor
Boudreau, Joseph H.
Boudriault, Israël
Bourdelais, Charles A.
Bouthillier, Arthur
Bouthillier, Ed. R.
Bouthillier, Léon D.
Breault, Joseph A.
Breault, Ulric
Breault, Sylvia
Brière, Henry
Brodeur, Arthur
Brodeur, Jean-B.
Brodeur, Joseph B.
Brousseau, Adolphe
Brousseau, Frank
Brousseau, John E.
Brousseau, Chas. M.
Brouillette, Alfred
Brunelle, Edouard J.
Cadorette, Noé S.
Capistrand, Joseph
Capistrand, Mau., Jr.
Cardinal, Albert
Careau, Arthur
Carmel, Albert A.
Caron, Armand L.
Caron, Camille
Caron, Charles A.
Caron, Harry H.
Carrette, William J.
Castonguay, Alphonse
Castonguay, Geo. E.
Chagnon, Joseph A.
Champagne, Alfred

Champagne, Fr. M.
Champagne, F. Earl
Champagne, Ovila
Champeau, Amos
Champigny, Henry
Chartier, Hormisdas
Charron, Wilfrid
Chouinard, Joseph R.
Cloutier, Edouard
Coderre, Ernest
Coderre, Joseph C.
Coderre, Oscar J.
Coderre, Télesphore
Collette, Hector
Corriveau, Archie
Cournoyer, Dorila
Couture, Patrick
Craite, Herménégilde
Craite, Peirre
Daigle, George
Daigneault, Ernest
Daigneault, Joseph
Daigneault, René
Daniels, Charles
Dansereau, Albert
Dauphinais, Adélard
D'Aoust, William
Delâge, Antonio
Demers, Anatole
Demers, Placide
Demers, Hector
Demers, Joseph
Demers, Omer
Demers, Léo A.
Denault, Joseph
Désaulniers, Clovis

Désaulniers, Egile
Désaulniers, Léo J.
Désaulniers, Napoléon
Désaulniers, Nap. T.
Désautels, Adélard
Desmarais, Joseph
Desmarais, John
Desmarais, Samuel
Desmarais, Vaslas
Desplaines, Odilon
Desrosiers, Joseph E.
Desrosiers, Ernest A.
Desourdy, Joseph A.
Dion, Albert
Donais, Adélard
Donais, Ernest
Donais, Fred
Donais, Joseph R.
Donais, Parmelius
Dubé, Adélard
Dubé, Alfred
Dubé, Arthur
Dubé, Joseph C.
Ducharme, Napoléon
Duclos, Léo A.
Dufault, Alphonse
Duhamel, Adélard
Duhamel, Napoléon
Dumas, Félix
Dumas, Léo O.
Dumas, Wilfrid
Dumas, William
Dupaul, Armand M.
Dupaul, Henry
Dupré, Alcide
Duquette, Adélard

Duquette, Alonzo
Duquette, David H.
Duquette, Elie
Duquette, Léo L.
Durocher, Rosario
Duteau, John H.
Farland, Albert L.
Favreau, Gilbert N.
Ferron, Adélard M.
Fontaine, Alfred
Fontaine, M. Arthur
Fontaine, Georges J.
Fontaine, Joseph
Fontaine, Léo J.
Fontaine, Paul
Forgues, Georges J.
Fore, Léo J.
Fortier, Napoléon
Fournier, Alfred J.
Frenier, Basile
Gagnon, Wilfrid
Galipeau, Lionel
Gallant, Léo J.
Gamache, Léo
Garceau, Charles E.
Garceau, Léo
Garceau, Wilfred J.
Gaumond, Edward
Gatineau, Georges
Gaudette, Agénard
Gaudette, Albert
Gaumond, Armand L.
Gaumond, Lionel
Gauthier, Joseph
Gendreau, Armand
Généreux, J. Arthur

Généreux, Omer
Germain, François X.
Gervais, Joseph T.
Gibeault, Henri
Girard, Alphonse
Girard, Ernest
Girard, Georges
Girard, Louis
Girard, Wilbrod
Girouard, Frank
Girouard, Jean-Bte. 1
Girouard, Jean-Bte. 2
Girouard, Joseph
Girouard, Pierre
Girouard, Wilfrid
Giroux, Joseph
Grandmaison, René
Grégoire, Henri J.
Grégoire, Joseph
Grégoire, Roméo
Grégoire, Ubald
Grégoire, Wilfred
Guertin, Renaldo W.
Guillette, Léo M.
Guilmette, J. Alphonse
Hébert, Raoul
Hébert, W. G.
Hêtu, Georges O.
Houle, Ovila
Houle, Wilfrid
Hufault, Joseph
Jalbert, Alexandre N.
Julien, Wilfred
Keroack, Eugène A.
Kinic, Joseph A.
Labelle, Arthur

Labelle, Rudolphe
Lachapelle, Daniel J.
Lacroix, William C.
Laflamme, Ephraim
Laflèche, Alfred
Laflèche, Arthur
Lajoie, Joseph
Laliberté, Arthur J.
Laliberté, Cyrille
Laliberté, Louis
Lambert, Frank
Lambert, Henry
Lamontagne, James
Lamontagne, Israël N.
Lamothe, Léo G.
Lamothe, Frank
Lamothe, Nazaire
Lamothe, Wilfred
Lamoureux, Léo A. G.
Langlais, Andronic
Langlais, Napoléon
Langlais, Paul
Langevin, Edmond
Langevin, Hector
Langevin, Joseph Z.
Langevin, Léo
Langevin, Roméo
Lapierre, Alphérie
Lapierre, Léo N.
Lapierre, Onésiphore
Lapierre, Roméo
Laporte, Alexis
LaReau, Archille
LaReau, Armand J.
Lareau, Richard
Larichelière, Charles

Larichelière, Geo. V.
Larivière, Alfred E.
Larivière, Joseph A.
Larivière, Rodolphe
Larivière, Walter E.
Laroche, Joseph N.
LaRochelle, Arthur I.
Larochelle, Philip H.
Larochelle, Léo
Latraverse, Donat
Lataille, Albert
Lavallée, Arthur
Lavallée, Cyrille O.
Lavallée, Euclide
Lavallée, Georges
Lavallée, Joseph
Lavallée, Narcisse
Lavallée, Ovila A.
Lavigne, Aimé
Lavigne, Euclide
Lavigne, René J.
Lavoie, Armand H.
Lavoie, Wilfrid
Lazure, William
Lebœuf, Roméo
Leblanc, Arthur
Leblanc, Edgar
Leblanc, Joseph A.
Leblanc, Emile N.
Leblanc, Henry
Leblanc, Ovila L.
Leclair, Edouard E.
Ledoux, Alfred
Leduc, Télesphore
Leduc, Rosario
Lefebvre, John B.

Lemire, Alfred
Lemire, Antoine J.
Lemmelin, Edmond E.
Lemmelin, Léopold H.
Lemmelin, Raymond
Lemoine, Léo
Lemoine, Victor
Lepain, Arthur
Lepain, Joseph D.
Lepain, Louis G.
Lepain, Ovila
Lescault, Eugène
Lescarbeau, Arthur
Lescarbeau, Henry
Lescarbeau, Francis
L'Heureux, Alfred
L'Heureux, Wm. T.
L'Homme, Rudolphe
Lippé, Oswald
Livernois, Alfred
Livernois, Amédée
Livernois, Edmond
Lizotte, Armand
Lizotte, Joseph
Lizotte, Philippe
Loranger, Arthur
Loranger, Léo
Lorange, Henri
Lucier, Arthur
Mailhotte, Arcade
Malo, Laurent C.
Mandeville, Ernest
Marchesseault, Geo.
Marchesseault, Nap.
Marcil, Archie
Martel, Napoléon, Jr.

Martin, Albert
Martin, Alfred
Martin, Arthur M.
Martin, Joseph
Matte, Archille
Matte, Léo H.
Maynard, Lionel
Métras, Louis R.
Métras, Paul E.
Meunier, Arthur L.
Morrisseault, Louis
Montigny, Alfred
Montville, Joseph S.
Maure, Charles
Maure, Joseph
Morin, Alfred
Morin, Henry
Nadeau, Rosario
Noël, Clarence
Noël, David
Ouellette, Elzébert J.
Pagé, Ernest R.
Pagé, Régis C.
Paquette, Dom. S.
Paquin, William
Paradis, Joseph
Parent, Emile J.
Patenaude, Georges E.
Paul, Napoléon A.
Paulhus, Joseph Bte.
Paulhus, Wilfrid
Peck, Léo A.
Pelletier, Alphonse
Pelletier, Eugène J.
Pelletier, John
Péloquin, Alfred

Péloquin, Aimé
Péloquin, Edouard L.
Péloquin, Joseph M.
Péloquin, Léo V. A.
Péloquin, Narcisse
Péloquin, Romain
Perron, Omer
Phaneuf, Rémi
Pinsonneault, Elzéar
Plante, Rosario
Pleau, Claudio
Ploude, Joseph
Plouffe, Albéric
Plouffe, Lionel
Poirier, Louis
Poirier, Stanley
Pontbriand, Arthur D.
Potvin, Alfred
Potvin, Henry V.
Potvin, William
Poulin, Albert
Poulin, Omer S.
Prince, Georges
Proulx, Anatole F.
Proulx, Antonio J.
Proulx, Armand
Proulx, Edgar
Proulx, Herménégilde
Proulx, Honorius J.
Proulx, Joseph T.
Proulx, Ovila
Proulx, René J.
Proulx, Roméo M.
Proulx, Olivier
Proulx, Théodore

Proulx, Théodore F.X.
Proulx, Théophile
Provost, Edmond
Provost, Wilfrid
Riendeau, Arthur J.
Roy, Léo
Roy, Arthur A.
Rochon, Joseph
Robidoux, William
Robidoux, Victor
Robert, Reginald
Robert, George B.
Riopel, Wilfrid
Richard, Théodore
Richard, Raymond
Rhéaume, Amos
Renaud, Orino
Renaud, Léo
Renaud, Georges E.
Ravenelle, Nelson T.
Ravenelle, Arthur
Rajotte, Horace
Racine, Emery
Racicot, Rodolphe J.
Riendeau, Arthur
Savage, Euclide
Savarie, Henry
Simpson, Eugène
Staves, Arthur
Staves, Frank O.
St. Onge, Joseph
St. Onge, Philip T.
St. Pierre, Hervé
St. Pierre, Joseph E.

St. Pierre, Rosario J.
Surprenant, Ed. H.
Talbot, Hervé
Talbot, Joseph H.
Talbot, Pierre
Tétreault, Charles A.
Tétreault, L. Eugène
Tétreault, Eugène
Tétreault, Valmore P.
Thériault, Eugène
Therrien, Valmore D.
Therrien, Fred
Therrien, Edward
Therrien, Léon J.
Thibault, Alphonse
Thibault, Joseph H.
Thibault, Victor
Trahan, Ovide B.
Trahan, Ovila
Tremblay, Albert
Tremblay, Alphonse
Tremblay, Isidore
Tremblay, Léo J.
Tremblay, Wilfrid
Tremblay, Wilfred R.
Trudeau, Charles
Trudel, Alphonse
Vaillancourt, Albert A.
Vary, Paul J.
Vary, Isidore G.
Varin, Raymond
Vincelette, Albert A.
Votour, Joseph
Weeks, Albert S.

Reflections

After reading this long list, it is not difficult be convinced that the Canadians of Southbridge wholeheartedly did their duty in this monster of a war, the bloodiest ever recorded in the annals of history.

It was the elite of our youth who sacrificed themselves thusly. At this time, most of these young people have returned to their homes and to their daily routines without having had any negative experiences other than that of having tasted a bit of military discipline. This has had the effect of making those who had been a little too lighthearted and had known nothing of the seriousness of life a little more serious.

Others have come back from farther away, from the heroic and bloodied country of France; several took part in the most bitter battles of the war, in Soissons, Château-Thierry, St. Mihiel and Verdun. They came close to death, they saw the flow of blood, and all are unanimous in saying that their return safe and sound to their families is nothing short of a miracle. There are some who will continue to suffer until their last breath, who will always feel the Machiavellian barbarity of the Germans in their bodies for as long as they live. Disabled, or continuously feeling the nefarious effects of German gas in all of their limbs, these poor souls deserve our reverence and our charity. For them, hats off!

And above all, standing before the tombs of our courageous ones who gave the most precious gift of life in order to save us, to protect our wives, our daughters, our homes, our churches and our institutions, let us bow down with profound respect! Young Canadians, our brothers and our sons, thank you! Thank you in the name of our fathers who admired you through the day of your death! Thanks on behalf of your mothers who watched you leave with tears in their eyes and who still cry for you silently day and night. Thank you in the name of your brothers and sisters, and your friends, who would have loved to have felt your heart beating next to theirs one day! To your mothers, who waited in vain, since your bodies will forever rest in lands abroad, we offer our warmest sympathy and the tribute of our most sincere admiration.

May Southbridge forever glorify you, honor you, and follow the example of your brave and noble hearts! To all those who did their duty, in this critical phase for our country and the entire world, "Thank You!".

Franco-American soldiers from Southbridge who died on the battlefield:

Bibeau, Léo
Bibeau, Adélard
Boisvert, Stanislas
Desmarais, Samuel
Donais, Parmélius
Dufault, Alphonse
Fontaine, Paul
Girard, Georges
Girouard, Wilfred

Girouard, Joseph B.
Laflèche, Arthur
Proulx, Théodore
Proulx, Théophile
Talbot, Pierre
Riendeau, Arthur
Tétreault, Dr. Eugène

Soldiers—Veterans of the Civil War—Four Survivors

Mr. Victor Léveillée

Mr. V. Léveillée was born on April 8, 1837 in Montréal. At the age of 18, he emigrated to St. Albans, VT, where he found work on a farm. On June 17, 1864, he enrolled in Company E, 9th Regiment of New Hampshire. He was discharged in the month of July 1865 and has been living in Southbridge for thirty-five years.

Mr. Pierre Giroux

Mr. P. Giroux, age 78, was born in Lacolle, Canada; at the age of fourteen, he emigrated to Woodstock, CT. In 1862, he enrolled in the 18th Regiment of Connecticut; after being wounded and having spent several months in the hospital, he was discharged in 1864 and moved to Southbridge several years after.

Mr. Israël Ledoux

Mr. Israël Ledoux was born in St.-Denis, Québec, on August 14, 1842; at the age of ten, he was in Spencer, Mass. On February 14, 1862, he enrolled in the Northern army and served in the cavalry. He was discharged after the war, in December 1865, and has been living in Southbridge for twenty years.

Mr. Charles Provost

Mr. C. Provost was born in Plattsburg, NY in 1844; he enrolled in the Northern army, Company G, 5th Infantry Regiment, was discharged in 1865, and has been living in Southbridge for over thirty years.

CHAPTER X

Our National Societies—The Saint-Jean-Baptiste

In 1869, when the Notre Dame parish was founded, French-Canadians, who were quite numerous at that time, felt the need to join together in society in order to get to know each other better, to mutually support each other, and to care for each other in illness and when death came to knock on their families' doors.

On January 1, 1870, after several preliminary meetings held earlier, the St-Jean-Baptiste Society of Southbridge was born.

Preface

"Among the harsh tests the Canadian emigrant must endure are isolation and the absence of the homeland. Strangers to each other, coming from different parts of the Province of Québec, Canadians in the United States, surrounded by a foreign culture, find themselves shoulder to shoulder with other individuals who often do not share their habits, their customs, their faith or their aspirations. By this fact alone, they are at risk of rapidly losing their national character, of completely forgetting their mother tongue, and mostly of not conserving the treasure of their faith, their religion. However, there is an efficient way to protect our people from this misfortune and to ensure that their sacred warehouse of ancestral traditions remains intact. This solution, this lifeline, it is simply the idea of Canadians uniting, it is the assembly of our people under one banner that represents religion, fraternity and patriotism. Only this will keep the French-Canadian nationality safe, both in Canada and abroad."

The Canadians of Southbridge, having understood the importance and the necessity of this call to assemble under one banner, founded the St-Jean-Baptiste Society in this city on January 1, [1870].

The grand ideas that gave birth to this society are essentially these: to aid members who are sick, to support each other in misfortune, to preserve, in a word, all that constitutes the soul of a people—language, customs and religion.

Founding Officers of the Society—January 1870

President, Dr. M.M.G. Fontaine
Vice-President, Georges J. Lamoureux
Secretary, Michel Surprenant
Treasurer, Herménégilde Bouthillette
Corresponding Secretary, Alex. Lataille
Commissioner, Azarie Lamoureux

Director, J.B. L'Homme
Director, Treflé Tétreault
Director, Louis Dion
Director, Gilbert Dupuis
Safety Committee, Herménégilde Bouthillette
Safety Committee, Norbert Duval
Safety Committee, Marc Lachapelle

According to the registers, eighty-one members enrolled during the year 1870 and it was Mr. J.B. L'Homme, one of the members of the committee that organized the event for the signing of the constitution, was the first to sign on.

In that first year, on June 24,[18] the members showed up in droves to attend the high mass at which Rev. Fr. LeBreton gave the homily. There was also a very nice ceremony during the mass. There was blessed bread which was distributed to all of the members.

After a parade through the main streets of the city, everyone went to a picnic area. There, there was a whole schedule of amusements. There were speeches, songs, etc. The financial outcome, which seems quite modest, satisfied the organizers: after all expenses were paid, there remained a profit of $8.65! This seems fairly ridiculous looking back in time. But, for all things, there must be a beginning.

In short time, this society became quite large and contributed greatly to maintaining the national character of Canadians.

By 1872, St. Jean Baptiste day was celebrated with extraordinary pomp; there was a high mass, blessed bread, homily and grand parade in which a great number of other societies were invited to participate. Of particular note was the St. Jean Baptiste Society of Woonsocket, which came in a special convoy. In the afternoon, there was a picnic on the grounds of the Hamilton Woolen Company (Pine Grove), where several patriotic speeches were given by Mr. Boudreau, Mr. Clément, Mr. Bégin, Mr. Charles Desmarais and Mr. William Proulx, lead orator. Mr. Antoine Lamoureux was president and the principal organizer of the program. In the evening, crowds of Canadians showed up at the Edwards Hall to hear Rev. Fr. Barrette, then pastor in Grafton, Mass, who had been the first French-speaking pastor in Southbridge. Fr. Barrette, who was well-respected here and whose departure was sad for many, was listened to attentively. Also, it should be noted that he was a distinguished orator.

[18] Translator's note: June 24 is the feast of Saint John the Baptist, the patron saint of French-Canadians and of the St.-Jean-Baptiste Society. It was celebrated first as a religious holiday and later as a national holiday by French-Canadians in Canada. Franco-Americans in the U.S. continued this tradition.

This event, which was a great success, was designed with the principal goal of recruiting new members to the society. After the evening lecture, there was a "Dramatic Performance" entitled *"Proscrit"* ("Exile") directed by Mr. Edouard Parent, C. Desmarais and others. Its success was worth the effort put into it, for after expenses, a sum of $176.00 was made, and the funds were used to purchase a banner for the society.

In 1873, the national holiday was celebrated with enthusiasm and had even better results. In church, Mr. André Loiseau, Mr. Clément Desmarais, Mr. Napoléon St. Onge and their wives did the collection. The blessed bread was distributed by Mr. Ignace Hêvé, Fr. Tremblay, Joseph Béford, Norbert Duval and Léon Cadotte.

In 1874, representatives of the society attended the grand celebration of St.-Jean-Baptiste, which was held in Montréal that year. With great fanfare and a brass band, fifty members took part in the immense parade held on that occasion. They were accompanied by a crowd of Canadians from this city who took advantage of reduced fares offered by the railroad companies to return to visit their homeland and the loved ones they had left behind.

However, there was such high volume that this excursion was full of misery; several special convoys were a full day late arriving in Montréal, and many of the travelers had to make the trip without eating and without being able to purchase provisions anywhere.

While it is true that the celebration was spectacular, nonetheless, most of the travelers in turn swore later on that they would never again be duped into that type of excursion.

Upon his return, Mr. Alexandre Lataille, the president of the society who had accompanied the delegation to Montréal, presented the members with a superb portrait of Saint-Jean-Baptiste as a souvenir of the event; this portrait is carefully preserved and considered by the group to represent a great memory that will never fade.

In 1875, the society again celebrated the feast of their patron saint with a solemn high mass, song and music under the direction of Prof. J.O. Bourque, blessed bread, etc. The young Jean-Baptiste was played by young Wilfrid Lamoureux, son of Mr. George J. Lamoureux, who was then treasurer of the society.

The St. Jean Baptiste society of North Grosvenordale, the Hibernians of Southbridge, as well as several other foreign societies participated in that event. After the parade, people gathered on the grounds of the Hamilton Company, an ideal location for this party, and there was a great picnic. In the afternoon, there was a lovely musical program. Speeches were given by Rev. George Elz. Brochu, Louis P.

Lamoureux, president of the St.-Jean-Baptiste society of Grosvenordale, Clément Bégin and others. In the evening, at Edwards Hall, a dramatic performance: *"La Malédiction d'un Père"* ("A Father's Curse") directed by Edouard Parent. All was a success, however the financial outcome left something to be desired since there was a certain deficit that had to be paid off.

In 1877, under the leadership of president Alexandre Lataille, the society attended the "Feast of the Patron" in Spencer, Mass. A great number of members attended, with brass bands, banners and flags, and were accompanied by a certain group of fellow citizens of Southbridge who took advantage of the occasion to take a trip to Spencer to see relatives and friends who used to live in our city. It was a grandiose event and truly unforgettable because of the excellent welcome extended to all who attended.

In 1880, a grand celebration of our national holiday was held in Québec City, and several delegations from New England attended.

Southbridge also wanted to organize a great patriotic celebration, and this project was initiated in 1881. A committee was formed and started work with much enthusiasm. They were determined to organize the most magnificent party to ever be held in Southbridge. Invitations were sent to all of the sister organizations, and many accepted. Good subcommittees were formed and each had its job: all signs promised an immense success. The general committee made arrangements with Pastor Brochu to have a solemn high mass on the day of the celebration, the July 4th holiday, with an invited preacher. Enthusiasm was in the air, and all ardently awaited this most memorable day!

Unfortunately, despite their devotion, the Canadians in that time lacked experience and in such an undertaking there is always some gaffe. That's exactly what happened. The committee had invited young men with their dates to take up a collection in the church the day of the event; preparations had been made, and the collection would go to the one who wore the most beautiful outfit that day. But, the Sunday before the event, the pastor spoke of the event and announced from the altar that he noticed that the committee had invited young people to take up a collection in the church without consulting him; he made it clear to the committee that among those named were some who were not worthy of taking up a collection in the church and that he, the pastor, had selected Dr. J.A. Robillard, Mr. Michel Surprenant, and Mr. Charles St. Pierre and their wives, and that furthermore, the collection would be made to support the new parish school. This caused a great upheaval among the parishioners, a commotion never before seen. Some wanted to abandon the idea of the party and notify all of the invited groups; others wanted to make arrangements to attend mass at the Irish church. Still others no longer wanted any mass, and to complicate matters further, the president of the society, Mr. G. Lamoureux, who had a lot of influence with the pastor, was retained at home for serious reasons. All of these troubles with the mass came from the fact that the pastor had said to follow his recommendations or there would be no mass on the celebration day. But there was no time to waste, for the event was the next day and visitors were already arriving to attend it. The organization committee— composed of Joseph Blanchard, Dr. J.A. Robillard, Alexandre Sénécal, Alfred Marceau, André Blanchard—met in the afternoon, and after serious reflection, although they were still divided, the majority of the committee decided to go to the pastor and inform him that they would conform to his decision. The next day, early in the morning, everyone was up and ready; several neighboring societies with large memberships from Spencer, Webster and Putnam arrived with great brass bands. The Woonsocket society arrived by special convoy with at least 500 members and an allegorical float for the little Saint-Jean-Baptiste, flags and banners, and a well-made beaver carried aloft triumphantly! The convoy was an hour late, and the celebrant, who was fasting for good reason, found the trip quite long. Finally, all arrived at the church and the ceremony began. The preacher, Fr. Crevier from Holyoke, who was aware of the delicate situation, calmed people down and lifted up their hearts, bringing great enthusiasm to the event.

Officers of the Cour St. Georges, F.C. 1919: H. Robida, L. St. Martin / J. Larivière, L. Boiteau, P. Gauthier, F. Tétreault, A. Langlois, J. Duquette, A. St. Martin / T. Poirier, N. Robidoux, A. Paradis, A. Montminie

The St.-Jean-Baptiste Society, photographed on the occasion of the celebration of the patron saint on June 27, 1893, in front of the Gatineau and Proulx store on Elm Street.

Delegates of the Convention of French-Canadians from the States of Massachusetts and Rhode Island in Southbridge on the 9th, 10th, and 11th of August, 1887. Photographed in front of the J.D. Blanchard store, Hamilton Street.

A Group of Delegates to the Convention of the Union St.-Jean-Baptiste d'Amérique in Southbridge in 1902, with banner saying "Welcome."

The singing, with an orchestra, under the direction of Prof. Joseph O. Bourque, was splendid, and of course the ladies and gentlemen selected by the pastor took up the collection with great "dignity." However, given the little chill that had spread among the parishioners due to the pastor having upset the committee, and due to some having decided to go to church with foreigners, the consequence was a very slim collection, much to the regret of the pastor this time, who did not forget to tell the Canadians of Southbridge what he thought of them the following Sunday.

Though the committee thought it best to submit to the will of the pastor, they did not want the event to go by without some thoughtful recognition of the young people who had originally been invited to take up the collection in the church. These young people were: Joseph Lacroix, who was to accompany Mary Richard, Josua Blanchard and Marie Sénécal, Felix Gatineau and Odile Giard. A first-class carriage was put at their disposal, along with a place of honor in the procession, complimentary tickets, etc. The day was lovely, and people spoke for ages about this event. It was a lesson, and all knew to learn from it. After the mass, the procession started and the parade lasted at least two hours. The little St.-Jean-Baptiste was played by the young Amédée Lamoureux, son of Mr. Théophile Lamoureux who was then an active officer in the society.

Never before had Southbridge seen such a beautiful and impressive demonstration. It was a truly magical spectacle to see so many society members lined up, so many flags and banners of all shapes and all colors floating in the soft breeze.

But there had been a few clouds on the horizon the night before, which people would be subjected to on the day of the event, for at the moment when the parade arrived at the clearing on Oakes Street, thunder could be heard and the lightning was blinding. You would have thought it was the end of the world. In less than five minutes, the skies opened up. It was some kind of torrential downpour, battering down on the crowd. This deluge lasted for an hour. The picnic preparations were more or less destroyed by this shower. Everyone had run off, some took shelter in restaurants, others in the homes of friends or acquaintances. As it was late in the afternoon and stomachs were rumbling, the hotels and restaurants were quickly besieged by crowds of people and the provisions that had been prepared for the picnic went out the window. Around three o'clock in the afternoon, the sun peeked out from the clouds and was resplendent, and the visitors who had gone elsewhere, attracted by the old "Land," arrived on the picnic grounds. The most courageous of the committee members got to work to carry out, to the extent possible, the rest of the day's program. First were the speeches. Rev. Fr. George Elz. Brochu spoke first, then Léon Rheims, and the lawyer Odilon Desmarais from St. Hyacinthe who had been invited to give the main speech. He undertook the task with a rare happiness. As a matter of fact, he was certainly one of the best orators that we have ever heard in Southbridge. After the speeches, it was already late and the crowd started to disperse. Everyone went home to get ready to attend the play, directed by Dr. J.A. Robillard, at Edwards Hall in the evening. The play was entitled "*Les Pirates de la Savanne*" ("The Pirates of the Savannah"). It goes without saying that the crowd did not hold back their applause for the actors, who were marvelous in their roles. Thus ended one of the most beautiful days in the history of the Canadians of Southbridge.

When the final reports of the various committees were presented, the expenses exceeded the revenue by at least $600; the society had to pay the deficit, even though so much work and trouble went into making this party a success! It was all attributed to a lack of experience, but also to the weather which was particularly inclement.

When everything went back to normal, many stories were told at the expense of certain committees, and in particular, a certain committee was teased and the members dubbed it "the pie committee." Due to a misunderstanding, two members of the committee had each ordered *six hundred pies*, and since there was no bakery in Southbridge able to accommodate such an avalanche of pies, the orders were made in a bakery in Webster, and on the Saturday, two days before the event, the baker arrived in Southbridge with two wagons loaded with *great stretchers*, to ensure safe arrival of the pies. Loading up that many pies was no small feat! It was hard to find someone to take care of the pies, so fragile is the human spirit! It was even harder to guard this precious treasure the day of the party, for everyone wanted to take part in the celebration. Finally, with much difficulty and many woes, the committee succeeded in successfully transporting the precious cargo to the picnic grounds on the day of the event. Just when you start to breathe a little easier, there is always something that troubles your peace, something that spoils even the best made sauce! We do not know, in fact, if the pies had become a bit dry during their long pilgrimage to Southbridge, but the heavens, in their mercy, watered them anyway!

The visitors had not yet even had the privilege of gazing longingly at the first offerings when the storm, that ruthless storm, intervened and destroyed at least half of them. Oh, *our cherished St. Jean Baptiste pies*, what a cruel fate awaited you! For at least a full week, they marched around the streets Southbridge, and everyone had the sweet duty of welcoming one or two of the poor orphans, victims of chance, into their homes! The following week, the committee had to go from door to door selling the rest of the pies. They were sold for the original price paid. Were they any less delicious, these cherished pies from Webster? History has been silent on the matter. Doctors tell us, however, that there were several rather serious cases of indigestion in the community around that time.

As our dear readers can surmise, the "pie committee" was an honorable group, and in recognition of their service to the national cause, all of the committee's members were given the honorific title of "Pie Buyers" by their compatriots and fellow brothers, a title they each held with dignity until their death!

CHAPTER XI

Our Societies—The St. Jean Baptiste (continued)

On October 12, 1892, for the 400th anniversary of the discovery of America by Christopher Columbus, there were great festivities across the country. In Southbridge, the St.-Jean-Baptiste Society wanted to take the initiative to organize a patriotic event to coincide with the holiday. There was a high mass celebrated by Rev. George Elzéar Brochu, assisted by a deacon and assistant deacon, songs and music under the direction of Mr. Ernest Decelles, a suitable homily, special decorations, etc. The ceremony was very impressive. After the mass, the procession began; several societies with bands, horses, banners, flags, and allegorical floats depicting "Christopher Columbus discovering America," marched in the parade, which was a great success thanks to the president of the committee, Mr. Camille Métras.

After the parade, everyone went to city hall to hear patriotic speeches related to the holiday. Rev. G. Elzéar Brochu spoke, as well as Clément Bégin and L.A. Boudreault, a lawyer from Trois-Rivières, Canada who was invited to give the main speech. The listeners were disappointed, for the orator had not prepared his talk and was not up to the task.

After the debacle of 1881, the society had somewhat lost its interest in organizing patriotic events; however, in 1893, another celebration was organized on June 24, the feast day of the patron saint. There was a high mass, special songs, a parade and a picnic in Hillsdale park. This time, the weather was ideal and everything went much more smoothly.

In the afternoon, many people descended upon the amusement grounds. There was a band concert and speeches in French and in English given by local selectmen. The president of the society, Mr. Georges Goddu, welcomed the crowd and introduced the selectmen Joseph M. Olney, Albert Martin and Felix Gatineau. The main speeches were given by Rev. Mr. Genest, vicar of the parish, and Mr. F.X. Tétreault.

On July 4th, 1899, the society celebrated the patron saint feast day again with a great patriotic event. The temperature was favorable for a party, and our compatriots from neighboring villages came out in great numbers to celebrate with us. The St.-Jean-Baptiste society of Webster, especially, arrived with a special convoy full of visitors. There was a high mass, singing and music by the Notre Dame choir. The young Omer

Généreux, son of Dr. J.A. Généreux who was one of the organizers of the event, gave a fine portrayal of the "little St.-Jean-Baptiste." The parade, composed of several sister societies with bands, banners and flags flying, was most impressive. The little "Jean-Baptiste" was placed in a well-decorated carriage pulled by four white horses.

After this part of the program, the crowd went over to "Morse Grove" where they all enjoyed a succulent meal. In the afternoon, Mr. Moïse Moreau and Mr. Arthur Parent from Webster gave patriotic speeches, as well as Dr. Oswald Grégoire, Felix Gatineau and Dr. Omer Larue from Putnam, who gave the main speech. After the speeches, there was a tug-of-war competition between a team from the St.-Jean-Baptiste Society of Webster and one from here. Our kind visitors from Webster were well prepared for victory: they had chosen blacksmiths, masons, etc.; the president alone weighed 300 pounds. The fight was on, for Southbridge also had Homeric champions, but in the end, our visitors proved that they were stronger and they won the prize, which was a flag that they carried in triumph all the way to the train station and most certainly through the main streets of Webster upon their return.

And they never miss an opportunity to reminisce about the festivities in Southbridge in 1899, an event that was the last big celebration in the history of the society.

On different occasions, however, from 1872 to 1900, the society members attended various events in other Franco-American communities in New England. They attended the funeral of Ferdinand Gagnon[19] in Worcester in 1884. The members had great respect for the deceased who had come to visit the Canadians in Southbridge several times and had contributed quite a bit to the development of the St.-Jean-Baptiste Society.

The society was also very generous in supporting the parish, both the school and the church; as early as 1873, they gifted $25 to the school for exam prizes. They did the same thing the next year, and for several consecutive years they supported the school and the church bazaars. They donated the chandeliers over the main altar in the Notre Dame church.

Sometimes, the St.-Jean-Baptiste Society would organize recreational activities for the members and their friends.

---

[19] Translator's note: Ferdinand Gagnon was a Canadian-born journalist who established a French-language newspaper in Worcester. Like Gatineau, he was a strong supporter of French Canada and nationalist causes, and also an advocate for the growth and prosperity of the Franco-American community within the U.S. He actually died in Worcester in 1886.

On December 31, 1878, the society celebrated its eighth anniversary with a great banquet; there were no flaws in the program, and everyone who attended was enchanted, vowing that these kinds of family parties should happen more often. That is precisely what happened in 1889, 1890, 1892 and above all in 1909 for the fortieth anniversary of the society.

For fifty years, the society never failed to attend mass together as a group on June 24, the feast of its patron saint; and often it organized patriotic activities for the general public in the evenings. It was this very society that took the initiative to organize a party on the occasion of the elevation of Monsignor Brochu to the Roman Prelacy.

In 1886, on January 27, our society organized a big concert to benefit the family of Louis Riel who was sent to the executioner's platform for having supported the Métis people and the Indians of the Northwest, accused of having rebelled against the Canadian government.

The profit of $100 was sent to his widow and his children; this concert was a resounding success, for the top artists from New England were on the program and had offered their services for free. These artists were: Calixa Lavallée, famous pianist from Boston,[20] also Mr. E.N. L'Africain from Marlboro, Mrs. J. Lespérance from Worcester, and Miss Antonia Barolet from Putnam, Conn., who at that time had an enviable reputation as a singer. We must not forget a charming little twelve year old girl, Miss Diana Plouffe from Webster, a remarkable artist for her age.

---

[20] Translator's note: Calixa Lavallée was the composer of *O Canada*.

CHAPTER XII

St. Jean Baptiste Society—Charitable Works

The society offered assistance on numerous occasions to the Canadians of Southbridge and especially to its members, to the sick, to widows and to orphans.

From 1870 to 1908, the society paid the sick and orphans	$57,983.36
It paid insurance to widows and heirs	$23,169.97
Donations and administration	$13,361.66
Total during this time period	$94,514.99

More than 1,000 French-Canadians joined the society in Southbridge, but since there were some who traveled back to Canada and elsewhere, especially in the early days, some of them were not members for a long time. However, at one point during its history, the society had over 500 members and was considered one of the most important French-Canadian groups in New England.

Unfortunately, like many mutual aid societies in those early days, its rules required payment of too many benefits for its revenue, for beginning in those first years, each member had to pay monthly dues of 25 cents and collected $4.00 per week when sick, for as long as the illness lasted, and the consequence of this was that several members received considerable sums. Just one member who had had an accident collected the incredible sum of $3,300.00, and had not paid $100.00 in dues; after a few years, the dues went up to 50 cents a month, with a limit on how much a person could collect in case of illness, which improved the question of benefits for the sick. During the first years of the society's existence, the insurance system was very advantageous for the members, for upon his death, the family of the deceased received as many dollars as there were members in the society, that is to say, a proportional amount. The first member who died received just over $100; even though he had paid nothing for insurance.

From 1870 to 1890, nineteen members died, which is at least one member per year; the reason was that most of the members joined when they were young and old age was not yet a worry, so when a member died 20 to 25 years later after the founding of the society, he had barely paid $20 for insurance, while his family received over $400.00 upon his death. The society at that time had over 400 members. It is easy to see now how advantageous the society was and how many benefits the Canadian citizens of Southbridge obtained from it.

After thirty years of existence, however, the society began to feel the effects of a certain commotion capable of endangering its future; the deaths were becoming more frequent, for a good number of the members were already over sixty. Further, this special contribution of one dollar per member upon the death of each member began to worry the younger people who predicted that the number of deaths would increase each year, and when the Union St.-Jean-Baptiste was formed in 1900, there was a strong movement to promote joining this society with others in order to change the insurance system and better secure the interests of members. However, several of the older members did not approve of this idea, and by a vote that won a strong majority, the society rejected the idea of affiliation. This last project was renewed and presented several more times, but without success, which caused several young members to abandon the society and join the Rochambeau Council of the USJB[21] or other more advantageous societies. After a few years, the number of members diminished gradually because of the young ones leaving and the old ones passing away. In the end, after serious consideration, the members who had fought against affiliation realized that a change was needed, and in the month of July 1908, by unanimous vote, the society decided to affiliate itself with the Union St.-Jean-Baptiste d'Amérique.

---

[21] Translator's note: The Union St. Jean Baptiste d'Amérique (USJB) was established in Woonsocket, R.I. in 1900 with the goal of uniting the many smaller French Catholic societies and clubs established in Franco-American enclaves across the United States under one umbrella organization.

CHAPTER XIII

Public Life—The Cercle Canadien

In 1876, there were 3,500 Canadians in Southbridge, a well-organized parish, a school, a charitable society, etc. At that time, in most French-Canadian communities, associations were formed with the goal of working actively to advance our compatriots in social and political life. Southbridge did not want to be behind, so on March 10, 1876, our village formed a new organization called the "Cercle Canadien" ("Canadian Club") whose motto was: "Join together, Learn together, and Have fun together."

Here are a few articles from the constitution and rules:

Article I

This association will be known as the Cercle Canadien of Southbridge, Mass.

Article II

The goal of this association is to unite French-Canadians in this locality and to employ the most appropriate methods for learning while having fun.

Article III

To become a member of the Cercle Canadien, you must be Roman Catholic, French-Canadian by birth or origin or recognized as such, know how to read and write French or English, be at least fifteen years old, be sober and be generally respected by your compatriots.

Founding members: Dr. Théophile Bélanger, Joseph Blanchard, Clément Bégin, Dr. J.A. Robillard, Camille Métras, J.W. Robinson, Salomon Labonté, J. St. Martin, Emile Robillard, Damase Bourassa, Joseph O. Bourque, Alexandre Lataille, Alexis Deslauriers, J. Edmond Hêtu, Paul Blanchard, Charles and Eusèbe Prunier, H. Hébert, Hubert Labelle, Joseph Quevillon, Edmond F. Lamoureux, Edmond H. Goddu, Henri Lavoie, Michel Surprenant, Edouard Parent, Victor St. Onge.

Shortly after its founding, Antoine Farland, Théophile Tremblay, François Tremblay, Ed. Devillers, Isidore Gervais, and Felix Gatineau were admitted as members of the association.

At an assembly held on March 10, the following officers were elected: Dr. Théophile Bélanger, president; Joseph O. Bourque, vice-president; Dr. Joseph A. Robillard, secretary; Alexandre Lataille, treasurer; Edouard Parent, authorizing commissioner.

At that same assembly, a committee was created to work on

"naturalization," another to choose a play and organize a performance.

The naturalization committee organized a meeting for Canadians and brought in Mr. Ferdinand Gagnon to give a speech on the importance of naturalization and the necessity of becoming a citizen; during that same year and the following year, more than sixty Canadians were naturalized.

The committee that was supposed to take care of the performance chose for its first play a drama entitled "The Curse," along with a comedy, "The Four Plums," both directed by Mr. Edouard Parent.

This performance was an artistic success, but the audience could have been bigger, for at that time, people cared less for dramatic evenings than they do today; young people were more or less apathetic, their literary tastes being underdeveloped.

In the fall of 1877, an evening school was organized by the members and some friends in order to teach English and to perfect our usage of the maternal language. Members did their best to take the classes, even businessmen, and in short time progress was truly notable. After a while, a series of discussions on various topics was organized in order to teach the rules of elocution. This was one of the most important activities of the club, and it continued to yield very satisfactory results for a number of years. Also, there were mock trials with the aim of acquainting people with the legal system; these were also a source of amusement for the members. Several young people came to hold very lucrative positions thanks to the influence of the Cercle.

For several years, the Cercle organized a series of lectures during the winter; these speakers were certainly of value in our little village, teaching some and improving the knowledge of those who were better educated, for the committees took great care to select speakers with excellent reputations. Our Southbridge Canadians, and those from other Franco-American centers in the area, benefited from them.

Even before the lectures, which started a good ten years after the Cercle was founded, several literary evenings had been organized, sometimes by the Cercle and other times by the parish or the St. Jean Baptiste society.

The first lecture was given in 1872 by Rev. Fr. A. Barrette, pastor of North Grafton and previously the first pastor of the first mixed Catholic parish in Southbridge.

In 1873, Rev. Fr. Primeau gave a talk on "Fortune-Tellers," for the benefit of the choir; in that same year, another lecture for the benefit of the choir was given by Judge Joseph Leboeuf of Cohoes, NY, who talked on the subject of education. From 1870 to 1880, Mr. F. Gagnon was invited from time to time to attend meetings, assemblies, etc., and he was asked to speak on a variety of subjects of interest to Canadians.

In 1875, a lecture was given by Mr. L.A.W. Proulx, who lived in Millbury, Mass., on the topic: "Repatriation."

In 1879, Southbridge was visited by Felix Poutré,[22] who organized an interesting discussion, under the auspices of the Cercle, on the subject of the turmoil in 1837-38.

Other Lecture Topics

1880. Lecture, *Naturalization*, by Ferdinand Gagnon of Worcester.

1881. Lecture, *Patriotism*, Odilon Desmarais, lawyer, from St. Hyacinthe.

1882. Lecture, *Naturalization*, Judge H.A. Dubuque, Fall River; *Our Duty*, F. Gagnon; *Politics*, Victor Bélanger, Worcester.

1882. Lectures, September 3, *The French Ethnicity*, Dr. Desjardins, Boston; March 5, *The Northwest*, Rev. Fr. Malo, missionary.

1884. Lecture, *The Rights of Citizens*, H.A. Dubuque.

1885. Discussion, *Troubles in the Northwest*, Gabriel Dumont, Metis and friend of Louis Riel.

1886. Lecture, December 31, *Napoléon Bonaparte*, Henri Boland, speaker from France.

1887. Lecture, January 25, *The Canadians of the United States*, Henri Boland.

1888. Lecture, December 11, *Faith, Civilization and the Canadians*, Charles Thibault, from Canada.

1889. Lectures: March 22, *Repatriation*, L.A.W. Proulx, Montréal; March 31, *Our Best Qualities and Our Flaws*, Emile Tardivel, lawyer, Worcester.

1893. Lecture, July 27, *The Future of Canada*, Honoré Mercier,[23] Canada.

1895. Lectures: January 9, *Patriotism*, Dr. Camille Côté, Marlboro; January 27, *Our Rights and our Duties*, L.O. David, Montréal; February 25, *Ways to Improve Our Standing in the United States*, Dr. L.P. Degranpré; March 12, *Our History*, Rev. Fr. E. Roy, Hartford; March 23,

---

[22] Translator's note: Félix Poutré took part in the 1837-1838 rebellions, was imprisoned and escaped. He was hailed as a folk hero and famed author Louis Fréchette even wrote a play about him. In 1913, it was revealed that he was actually a British spy among the "Patriotes" and he was labeled a traitor. Note that Louis Fréchette visits Southbridge to give a talk on a different work in 1905.

[23] Translator's note: Honoré Mercier was Prime Minister of Québec from 1887 to 1891. He was a strong critic of the Canadian government's treatment of Louis Riel.

Honoré Mercier, his Life, his Works, Léon Rheims; March 27, *Colonization*, L.E. Carufel, Montréal.

1896. Lectures: January 12, *The Future of Canadians in the United States*, Rémi Tremblay, Montréal; January 23, *The Canadian, Who He Is, Who He Should Be*, Father J.E. Cartier, New Haven; February 7, *The Future of Our People*, Father P.E. Roy, Hartford; February 22, *Home Economics*, Charles T. Roy, Lowell; March 10, *Our Best Qualities and Our Flaws*, J.E. Cartier, New Haven; March 30, *Fraternity*, Alphonse Gaulin, Woonsocket.

1897. Lectures: January 10, *American Pioneers*, Clément Bégin; January 24, *Education*, Dr. J.E. Ferland; February 7, *Palestine*, F.X. Tétreault; February 21, *The Effects of Alcohol*, Dr. J.A. Généreux; March 7, *History of the Canadians of Southbridge*, Clément Bégin and Felix Gatineau; March 15, *Hygiene*, Dr. Leriche.

1898. Lectures: March 22, *The Future of the Canadians*, Joseph Blanchard; March 29, *Napoléon at Sainte Hélène*, Alfred Galipeau.

Rochambeau Council, Number 12, USJB in 1903: J.B. St. Germain, Z. Desrosiers, J. Leblanc, L. Langevin, P. Caron, P. Berthiaume, J. Duhamel / Dr. J.A. Généreux, J. Faure, F. Gatineau, H. Dorval, J.L. Coderre, H. Lavoie

Rochambeau Council, Number 12, USJB, 1919: O. Bélanger, A. Langevin, J. Leduc, C. Potvin, A. Paradis, J.L. Berthiaume, H. L'Homme / N. Leblanc, Rev. L.O. Triganne, F. Gatineau, N. Leduc, N. Lavallée

Officers of the Cour Laurier F.F.A, 1919: O. Matte, W. Dupuis, E. Belair, P. Caron, E. Belair, N. Lepain, L. Cloutier, P. Benoit, Dr. J.G.E. Page, L. Dupuis, A. Boulanger

Paul Revere, represented by F. Gatineaux, 1896

An allegorical float (or carriage) on the ocassion of the feast of St. Jean Baptist, 1917

CHAPTER XIV

Lectures (Continued)

1900. Lectures: January 7, *The Future of Canada*, Benjamin Sulte, Ottawa; January 14, The *American Republic*, attorney Israël Bélanger, Cohoes; January 28, *The Wonders of Paris*, Alphonse Gaulin, lawyer, French Consulate; February 11, *Patriotism*, Rev. A.M. Clément, Fiskdale; March 18, *Our Duties*, Rev. G. Brousseau, Manchaug; December 13, *Reminiscences and Observations*, H.A. Dubuque, Fall River.

1901. Lectures: February 10, *The United States at its Apex*, Israël Bélanger, lawyer, Cohoes, NY; February 25, *The Duties of the American Citizen*, Joseph Monette, lawyer, Lawrence;[24] March 10, *The French Ethnicity*, Mr. Léopold Mabilleau, professor at Harvard University.

1902. Lectures: January 20, *Joan of Arc*, Germain Martin, France; February 15, *The French Language*, Professor Joseph Dumais, Montréal; April 20, *Travels in Europe*, Rev. G.P. Desrosiers, Lanoraie, Québec Province.

1903. Lecture, *A Page in Our History*, Rev. Fr. Louis Lalande, Montréal.

1904. Lecture, January 17, *The Beauty of the French Language*, Robert Duprey, professor at Harvard University.

1905. Lectures: February 10, *Crémazie*, Louis H. Fréchette, Québec; March 15, *Health for All*, Dr. L. Lachapelle, specialist from Montréal.

From 1905 to the present day, this custom of organizing lectures was abandoned, to the great regret of the members who were actively engaged in these literary soirées. However, on various occasions, there were still some literary delights. During the winter of 1911, Miss Lilianne Tétreault and her brother, attorney Henri Tétreault, gave talks with illustrations on the chateaux and the aristocracy of France, because the year before they had traveled in Europe.

In 1912, Felix Gatineau gave a talk, with projections, on "The Deportation of the Acadians"; that same year, Dr. Charles Tétreault gave an interesting talk with projections on "The Customs and Habits of the Philippines," where the doctor had spent four years as a surgeon in the American army.

In 1913, during the months of February and March, the Cercle

---

[24] Translator's note: Grandfather of latter day Franco-American writer Paul Monette.

organized a series of lectures that were given in turn by Dr. Zéphyr
Potvin of Webster, who spoke about patriotism; the lawyer Télesphore
Leboeuf, also from Webster, gave a lecture on "Our Duties as Citizens";
and Arthur Surprenant, attorney from Pawtucket R.I., selected as his
topic "An Opinion on Our Shortcomings." These young speakers were
very interesting; and their success equaled their talents as orators. They
were even more appreciated given that Mr. Potvin and Mr. Surprenant
were born in the parish, while members of the family of attorney
Leboeuf were also from Southbridge.

In March 1917, Mr. J. Anatole Caron gave a talk on a trip to
Louisiana that he had recently taken. Mr. and Mrs. Caron had attended
the great "mardi gras" carnival in New Orleans. This talk was well liked
by the attendees.

In that same year, Mr. Alexandre Désaulniers and Mr. J.B. Demers
took a trip to California and British Columbia, and upon their return,
there was a special assembly to hear an account of their experiences. We
have attempted to give our reader this general overview of the works of
the Cercle in order to show everyone the role that this organization has
always played among us and the good that it did for our compatriots by
teaching and entertaining them.

CHAPTER XV

The Cercle Canadien—Theatrical Performances

Even before the founding of the Cercle Canadien, there had already been several plays offered under the direction of Edouard Parent, Clément Desmarais, Abraham Marchessault and Clément Bégin, for the benefit of either the parish, the choir or the Saint-Jean-Baptiste society; but since its founding, the Cercle Canadien endeavored to offer proper performances, not only with the aim to entertain but also to allow its members to improve their study of their native language, to learn to perform in public, and finally to realize sufficient revenue to ensure the persistence of this organization.

There is perhaps no other French-Canadian association in the United States that has such a great number of talented amateurs among its constituents than the Cercle Canadien. The number of plays performed by this society is so great that it would be difficult for us to list them all. We hope it will suffice for us to list the plays for which we have been able to identify the titles.

Titles of the Plays:[25]

La Malédiction, 1876-77
Les quatre prunes, 1876-77-92
L'Expiation, 1877-87
Vildac, 1877-79
Les Fourberies de Scapin, 1877
Le Divorce du Tailleur, 1877-79
Jean le Maudit, 1878
Felix Poutré, 1878-79-1902
Les jeunes Captifs, 1878
Duel à Poudre, 1878-1902
Désespoir de Jocrisse, 1879
Le Proscrit, 1880
Les Châteaux en Espagne, 1880
Les Pirates de la Savane, 1881

---

[25] Translator's note: Original French titles listed. The plays are by a mix of French and French-Canadian authors, including several classic French comedies by Molière and dramas from 19th-century French playwrights Étienne Labiche and Émile Augier, as well as works by authors from Québec, like Philippe-Joseph Aubert de Gaspé and Louis H. Fréchette.

La Berline de l'Emigré, 1881
La Famille du Perruquier, 1881
Malédiction d'une Mère, 1882
Partie de Campagne, 1887-90
Les Deux Rivales, 1887
Papineau, 1883
Le Forgeron de Strasbourg, 1883
La Revanche d'un Charbonnier, 1884
Les Vengeances ou Ton Kourou, 1885-88-91-98-1902-1907
Erreur n'est pas compte, 1885
Le Mascotte, 1885
Le Conscrit, 1885
Le Siège de Colchester, 1888
Une scène politique, 1885
L'Homme aux deux domestiques, 1885-88
Michel Strogoff, 1885-88-91
Le Départ de la Californie, 1885
Les Boucaniers, 1888-1904
Un Bureau de Placement, 1888
Monté Cristo, 1890
Les Anciens Canadiens, 1892
Une Cause Célèbre, 1893-1903
Marie-Jeanne, 1894-95, 1900-1901-1902-1912
La Mort du Duc de Reichstadt, 1894-95
Les Pauvres de Paris, 1894-98
La Taverne du Diable, 1895
L[e] Chapeau d'un Horloger, 1895
Le Maître de Forge, 1895-1917
Une minute trop tard, 1895
Le Gentilhomme Pauvre, 1899
Embrassons-nous Folleville, 1899, 1918-1919
Le Voyage de M. Perrichon, 1901
L'Ami Fritz, 1901-1911
L'Orpheline des Pyrénées, 1901
Le Gendre de M. Poirier, 1904, 1906, 1911, 1917, 1918
Le Château de Kanil-Wortt, 1905
Les Piastres-Rouges, 1906
Le Drapeau Carillon, 1907
Les Fiancés d'Albano, 1910
Les Crochets du Père Martin, 1914
La Marraine de Charlie, 1914-1915
Le Chapeau de Paille d'Italie, 1915

Un ministrel du 20e Siècle, 1915
Un notaire à marier, 1916-1918
La Voleuse d'Enfants, 1917
L'Avare de Molière, 1917-1918
La Lettre Chargée, 1917
Le Malade Imaginaire, 1919

   Directors of dramatic plays since the founding of the Cercle
Edouard Parent, Dr. J.A. Robillard, Joseph L. Brissette, Joseph Duhaime, Alfred Galipeau, Camille Métras, Philippe Dagenais, Philias Casavant, Edmond Pelletier. These members, in particular, have rendered a great service with their skills on stage and as directors. Their devotion equaled their success, and they contributed a lot to building the funds necessary for the continued existence of the Cercle.

  In addition to the lectures, dramatic performances, etc., the Cercle Canadien organized several political assemblies and outdoor festivals.

  In 1893, thanks to the influence of the Cercle, we were able to invite as a speaker Honoré Mercier, ex-Prime Minister of the Province of Québec, who was also visiting Southbridge thanks to the St. Jean Baptiste Society. On that occasion, on July 27, 1893, there was a great general assembly at the City Hall. Mr. Felix Gatineau, who was then selectman, presided over the assembly, and after a few patriotic songs, our distinguished visitor gave a lecture on "Canada's Independence." The hall was full, and a number of compatriots from nearby Franco-American centers had come to hear the speaker, who was always very interesting. People say that even some of our English-speaking fellow citizens attended this event. After the lecture, there was a banquet at the Dresser hotel, a banquet that all of the local manufacturers, professionals and businessmen attended. This little party was an historical event for the Canadians of Southbridge; at the banquet, Mr. Gatineau welcomed the guests and introduced the dignified speakers in order of their importance.

  Joseph Olney, president of the selectmen, in a few words praised the French-speaking community in Southbridge; he said that the Americans of our city were honored to welcome such a distinguished guest as the ex-Prime Minister of the Province of Québec, Mr. Honoré Mercier.

  Senator Eben Stevens gave a toast to the state.

  Mr. Chester A. Dresser, George W. Wells and C. Paige toasted the manufacturers and business owners; Joseph Blanchard, the United States; F.X. Tétreault, the schools; Léon Rheims, France; attorney Odilon Desmarais from Sainte-Hyacinthe, who was accompanying the speaker, gave a little gem of a speech with a toast to Canada. Finally, the day's hero, Honoré Mercier, spoke in English "on the situation in Canada, concerning political views and economic relations." He spoke for over an hour and was often interrupted by outbreaks of applause. The event ended with several patriotic tunes: "The Marseillaise," "O Canada," "The Star Spangled Banner," performed by the Grenier-Péloquin orchestra. All who had the opportunity to go to this banquet left the hall saying that it was the most beautiful party they had ever attended.

The next day, Mr. Mercier and his companion visited Dupaul Young and the American Optical Company, as well as several prominent compatriots. In the afternoon, our visitors left for Worcester where Mr. Mercier spoke in front of 14,000 Franco-Americans who were gathered along the shores of Lake Quinsigamond.

In 1896, the legislature of Massachusetts had by law abolished an official holiday called Fast Day that used to exist in the state on the first Thursday in April; this holiday was replaced by another, Patriot's Day, in memory of the battles of Lexington and Bunker Hill.

Joseph Leclair, then president of the Cercle, was always full of enthusiasm and came up with the idea to celebrate this new legal holiday in Southbridge; a committee was formed and Mr. Alfred Lalime of Worcester, manager of the Syndicat Français [French Worker's Union], was appointed to head the organization.

Invitations were sent by memo to all of the surrounding Franco-American centers announcing the program of events for the celebration which was to be held on Sunday and Monday, April 18th and 19th. This event drew some attention in the State, as Southbridge was the first city to observe this day, better known as "Paul Revere Day."

On Sunday, in the evening, there was a band concert by "Martel's Brigade" of Worcester, and the next day as well. Throughout the town there was a profusion of decorations; early in the day, visitors started to funnel in. Those who were supposed to be in the British army were already set up in great numbers on the main streets, wearing red suits. Early in the evening, a special convoy from Worcester, Webster and other centers arrived with several hundred people. *Paul Revere*, the hero of the day, was to sound the alarm warning of the arrival of the British and calling forth the defenders of the colony, all along the route from Webster to Southbridge.

Charles Wilson was leading the British army and Captain Goodell commanded the colonists. *Paul Revere* was brought to life by Felix Gatineau and while he was en route to Southbridge, a young American charged by on a white horse, a horse that *Paul Revere* was supposed to have ridden but that was refused him at the last minute for certain reasons. These reasons were very apparent: the young man wanted to use the horse himself to trick the crowd that was anxiously awaiting the event. All of a sudden, the young *Paul* charges by at full speed shouting:

"To arms!" The excitement was at its peak, gunshots rang out, all around there were lights and flares, etc. The two armies met and engaged in battle! The cannon thundered, the bells announced the arrival of the British! You would have thought the city were under attack. After the battle, however, calm returned, and just as the young trickster completed his frenetic ride, all of a sudden *Paul Revere* arrived on his "bronco," a horse that was afraid of everything and was terror-stricken by the slightest noise, jumping fences and throwing himself on the ground because he was so scared of the cannon blasts; when the hero of the event arrived in Southbridge itself, it was fairly dark and already a certain number of compatriots were aware of the trick that had just been played on them. They were out of gunpowder by then and the fireworks had finished, such that our pitiful and dismayed *Paul Revere* entered the town in the shadows and without a sound, leading his white filly back to the stable of its owner, John Bowlen, with a recommendation that he train it; as a reward for his devotion, *Paul Revere* was unable to walk for almost a week, a consequence of his bumpy ride from Webster to Southbridge, mumbling swears at the president Joseph Leclair for having roped him into such a hellish chore.

After the outdoor activities, there was a great gathering at the City Hall where Louis XVI, incarnated by Mr. Joseph Blanchard, appeared with his court. There was singing and dancing and a speech by Judge Andrew J. Bartholemew; this was the highlight of the first celebration of Paul Revere Day in Southbridge, an event that was a topic of conversation for several years. They say that over 5,000 people attended this celebration.

CHAPTER XVI

The Cercle Canadien (continued)—Silver Anniversary of

Monsignor Brochu

In 1898, members of the Cercle, along with other societies, participated in organizing a great banquet for the silver anniversary of Monsignor G. Elzéar Brochu. The banquet was held in the Edwards hall on Monday, May 30th; among the many invited guests were a lot of priests from the Springfield diocese and surrounding region.

F. Gatineau was elected president of the banquet and C. Bégin president of the party, which was held in the city hall and consisted of an elaborate musical program prepared for the occasion.

An appropriate speech was given by Father E. Roy, pastor of Hartford and today auxiliary bishop of the diocese of Québec; the address was read by Mr. Clément Bégin, who presented Mgr. Brochu with a superb chalice worth $400 and other precious gifts. The host of the party was touched by this token of gratitude from the parishioners and used the moment to offer an historical overview of the history of the parish during the last twenty-five years of its existence. His eloquence, his warm and vibrant voice, made a strong impression on his listeners, who were very moved, some to the point of tears.

This congenial party left warm and sweet memories in everyone's hearts.

Monument to Honor Dr. J.A. Robillard

In 1884, members of the Cercle Canadien installed a monument to honor Dr. J.A. Robillard who passed away in December 1883 and had devoted so much of himself to this young association.

In 1907, the Cercle also erected a commemorative marble statue to remember Alfred Galipeau, deceased on March 29 or that same year; his father, J.B. Galipeau had his young son join the Cercle at the age of sixteen, and in short time this young man became a consummate actor. Within a few years, he amazed all his listeners with his eloquence and debate skills.

He was the drama director of the Cercle for a number of years, and each time he took on an important role, the Cercle was sure to have a crowd at the performance. He outdid himself especially in the role of *Rusard* in *"Vengeances,"* in the role of *Ivan Ogaref* in *"Michel Strogoff,"* as *George Bergeau* in *"Le Forgeron de Strasbourg,"* as *Bertrand* in *"Marie-Jeanne,"* and as *Jean Renaud* in *"Une Cause Célèbre."*

He died young, at the age of 42, and was mourned not only by the members of the Cercle but by the entire Canadian population of Southbridge.

A monument was also installed in 1912, by members of the Cercle and other friends, in memory of Dr. Joseph A. Généreux who had been an active member of the Cercle from his arrival in Southbridge in 1886 until his death on December 22, 1911. This monument was a tribute to our compatriot and an expression of gratitude for his service to the Franco-American community here over the past quarter century.

Over time, the Cercle Canadien organized anniversary parties and dramatic performances for members and friends; in 1916, there was a great celebration for the fortieth anniversary of the existence of the association. There was a magnificent banquet held in Edwards hall; all of the founding members now abroad were invited and all were present, *all eleven of them*, except one who was indisposed due to illness and old age. Representatives from a number of Franco-American groups in New England honored the Cercle with their presence. There were delegations from the following clubs: Montcalm, from Lawrence; Calumet, from Fall River; Gagnon, from Webster; Brightwood, from Springfield; Bon Ami, from Worcester; Athletic, from Putnam; Dramatique, from Marlboro; Cercle National, from Woonsocket; Rochambeau, from Holyoke. There were also a number of young priests, raised in the parish, as well as Mr. Alexandre Bélisle, representative from the newspaper *L'Opinion Public* and Mr. George Grant from the *Southbridge Press*.

In politics, the Cercle played an important role; its influence could be felt in many elections and, with few exceptions, all of the Canadians elected to important positions in the city and in the state were members of this association. Today there are 250 members, including manufacturers, businessmen, clerks and employees in the factories.

The members are all quite friendly with each other; however, it should be noted that the new generation is, in a way, transforming the society. Today, the Cercle is operated more as a social club than as a literary society.

This is regrettable, of course, but it stems from the fact that young people today are less interested in self-improvement than their elders; having had the opportunity to attend school for a longer time, they do not feel the same need to enlighten or educate themselves. In passing, we might dare to say that several of our young Canadians might have better positions if they thought a little more about educating themselves and a little less about entertaining themselves. It is deplorable for our ethnicity and our country! Further, this should be rectified as soon as possible!

CHAPTER XVII

Social Clubs—The Temperance Society

In 1884, a certain number of young people aged fifteen to twenty, including Napoléon Giroux, Louis Giroux, François Bélanger, Elzéar Bélanger, Henri L. Brousseau, Albert Brousseau, Ludger Martel, Placide Laliberté, and Hormisdas Tremblay, organized an "Entertainment Club" called the "Jolly Club." The aim of the members of this association was to practice sobriety and to entertain themselves with comedies, farces, comic speeches, etc. This little club, which in short time had forty to fifty members in its ranks, developed talent that would later be showcased in performances given by the Cercle Canadien and other societies.

Elzéar Bélanger, Narcisse Gamache and Albert Brousseau became premier "clog" dancers. Placide Laliberté, several years later, played the lead role in dramatic plays. Hormisdas Tremblay soon become a skilled actor, excelling in comedic roles, speeches, and songs. A unique character, he even turned this into a profession, performing for several years in various centers in New England and in Sainte-Hyacinthe county in Canada, where he lived.

There were also others who learned music, for the headquarters of this association was located in the hall of the "Fanfare Canadienne" band, above the Southbridge Journal office on Central Street. Several members later became excellent musicians who played in different bands and orchestras in Southbridge.

CHAPTER XVIII

"Les Chevaliers de St. Pierre"—1887

On January 1st, 1887, a certain number of Franco-Americans called an assembly in the hall of the old *Southbridge Journal* building with the goal of founding a temperance society. After several remarks about the importance of such a society, a committee was formed to submit the group's rules and regulations to the parish pastor, Rev. Georges Elzéar Brochu. After careful examination, he added certain clauses including: "that members would commit to 'Holy Communion' at least every three months." Even though the promoters of this organization were good Catholics, there were some among them who did not want to impose this obligation and the rules were not adopted. Several months later, this society was transformed into a society for charity and temperance under the name *Société des Chevaliers de St. Pierre* of Southbridge.

Here is its act of incorporation:

Act of Incorporation

"Let it be known that we, the undersigned, have joined together with the goal of forming an association by the name of Chevaliers de St. Pierre, in order to create and maintain funds to assist members who are ill, for burials, to support widows and their children, and for any works of charity, morality and temperance. We agree to the statutes set forth and provided for these cases, as attests the certificate of the officers of this corporation.

"This certificate duly and legally approved by the insurance commissioner and registered with his office.

J. Robert Jannery, M.J. Surprenant, J.A. Généreux, M.D., Sal. Ste. Marie, Joseph A. Allard, Michel Bachand, Rosario Paquin, Bazile Proulx the 2nd, Gilbert Thériault, Joseph Thériault, Bazile Proulx the 1st, Augustin Robidoux, Jules Tremblay.

"This is why we, William M. Olin, secretary of the state of Massachusetts, certify that the above-signed association of men and their successors are legally organized and established and are declared by those present to be a corporation existing under the name Chevaliers de St. Pierre, with all powers, rights and privileges.

"In good faith, we affix the seal of the state of Massachusetts this first day of March, in the year eighteen hundred ninety-three.

"Signed, Wm. M. Olin, Secretary of State."

In short time, this society became prosperous, financially as well as in number of members; but all of a sudden, in 1891, there were several disputes among the members due to certain articles of the rules pertaining to temperance. In the end, about twenty members submitted their resignations and that same year laid the groundwork for the *Cour Jacques-Cartier, Forestiers d'Amérique*.

After this failure, the temperance society started to lose its prestige, and since there were several societies and new ones were always popping up, in 1906, by unanimous vote, they decided to disband the organization and to remit a sum of $20 to each member, his share of the account.

CHAPTER XIX

"Temperance Society"—1889

Monsignor Brochu, who was a man of exemplary moral rectitude, had an aversion, if we might call it that, for drunkards and drinkers. So, during the thirty-two years that he spent in Southbridge, he condemned them more than once. He often refused to give them the sacraments, wanting to treat them the way they deserved. Through his sermons on drunkenness, quite often on the eve of an election, he was able to prohibit the granting of certain licenses.

God knows that, in all his polemics, he always had at heart a desire for the spiritual and worldly well-being of his parishioners; this is why he advised so strongly that drinkers turn to temperance and encouraged in any way possible the formation of temperance leagues and associations to combat the devastating scourge of drunkenness. His calls were finally answered when in 1889 several citizens formed an "anti-alcohol society" with the following premise:

"Under the patronage of the Sacred Heart of Jesus, this first of March in the year 1889, we have laid the foundation for a society called: 'Union du Sacré-Coeur de Jésus,' and have established rules for its members.

"As this society is of a religious nature, and since its goal is above all the spiritual health of its members, we have chosen as patron the Sacred Heart of Jesus. Further, we select the pastor of the Notre Dame congregation of Southbridge as its irrevocable leader; the chaplain will be named by the aforementioned leader, as he wishes.

"We choose as a banner for this society that of the Sacred Heart, the flag will be that of the Holy Pontiff, and the insignia of the members will be the *Greek cross*."

Franco-American doctors: Daniel Plouffe, Charles Tétreault / Jos. G.E. Pagé / Charles Simpson, Victor Potvin / Joseph Donais

Franco-American dentists: J. Rock Lepage, E. Céleste Thresher, Arthur Gravel / Oswald Grégoire / Hector Péloquin, Arthur Larochelle, Zéphir Potvin

Franco-American lawyer: Georges Proulx, Arthur Surprenant / Louis O. Rieutard, Alternate Judge / Stephen Benoît, Henri Tétreault

Survivors of the Civil War / C. Provost, H. Leveillé, Pierre Giroux, Israël Ledoux

Group from the Spanish-American War: A. Bélanger, A. Paquin, N. Garceau, W.P. Lacroix, J.B. Caplette / A.N. Gélineau, A. Montminie

Names of the founding members:
Hubert Lavallée
Alex. Montminy, Sr.
Joseph Proulx
Alexis Boyer, Sr.
Alfred Potvin
François Surprenant
Salomon Labonté
Paul St. Laurent
Arsène Robillard
J.-Baptiste Robillard
Louis St. Martin
François Sansoucy, Sr.
George J. Lamoureux
Hector Collette
Paul Phaneuf
Michel L'Homme
Louis Desrosiers
Damase Périgord
Arthur Petit
Edmond Hêtu
Georges Cabana, Sr.
David Duclos
Octave Desrosiers
Théophile Lamoureux
Salomon Larivière
Pierre Allard
Nap. L'Homme
Edouard Demers
Wilfrid Lamoureux
Amédé Lamoureux
Thomas Lavallée
Uldège Gagnon
J.B. L'Homme
Pierre Dumas
Pierre Gaucher
Moïse Garceau
Edouard Bibeau
J.B. Proulx
Pierre Carmel
Charles Garceau, Jr.

Hormisdas Montminy
François Paul
Joseph Lamoureux
Bazile Proulx
Nap. Duquette
Alfred Roy
Gilbert Larivière
Alfred Larivière
Eusèbe Demers
Ulric Donais
Arthur Boucher
Henri Duclos
Joseph Gagnon
Charles Thibodeau

According to the rules, each member paid 25 cents per year and the society paid $10.00 for a service upon the death of a member and $10.00 for an anniversary service.

They elected officers every semester, in January and July each year.

Here are the results of the first election: Chaplain, Monsignor George Elzéar Brochu; President, Edouard Larivière; Vice-President, Louis Desrosiers; Secretary, Alfred Potvin; Corresponding Secretary, Salomon Labonté; 1st Commissioner, J.B. L'Homme; 2nd Commissioner, Octave Desrosiers; 1st Auditor, J.B. Robillard; 2nd Auditor, Fr. Sansoucy; 3rd Auditor, Paul St. Laurent.

This society, which was established with a good number of members, made little progress from 1889 to 1893.

When taking the oath to follow the rules of our temperance society, each member received a cross. We still see temperance crosses today in our good Canadian homes, and many have continued to stay faithful to the solemn promises they made when they entered this association, one that has done immeasurable good in the parish.

The first Sunday of the month of January 1893, Monsignor Brochu, pastor of the parish, wished his parishioners a happy new year; while describing all that happened in the previous year, he spoke of problems in Southbridge; he railed against drunkenness above all and warmly called upon his flock to unite and to form societies with the main goal of combatting this malady that was afflicting our best families.

The following Sunday, January 8th, after vespers, there was a great assembly called by the "Temperance Society"; there were many speeches: they spoke of everything, but especially of the importance of joining the society. At that assembly, they then elected officers who vowed to work with all possible force to recruit new members.

Here are the results of that election: Chaplain, Monsignor Georges Elzéar Brochu; President, Pierre Bachand; Vice-President, Napoléon Duquette; Secretary, Joseph Demers; Treasurer, Joseph Berthiaume; Collector, Paul St. Laurent; Commissioner, J.B. L'Homme; Zealots: Louis Desrosiers, Pierre Allard, Paul Berthiaume, Joseph Berthiaume, Alexis Demers.

The officers fulfilled their promises, for in less than three months the society had over three hundred zealous and punctual members ready to do their duty; they often went to confession and frequented the Holy Table in great number. But this society was no exception to the reality that temperance groups are difficult to sustain, and gradually the number of members declined. Those who were determined continued to take the straight path lost their courage little by little, so that in the end there were only forty or fifty members.

Election of officers on June 19, 1904: President, Paul St. Laurent; Vice-President, Napoléon Giroux; Treasurer, Alexandre Désaulniers; Correspondent, Louis Bourdelais; 1st Commissioner, David Hufault; 2nd Commissioner, Edouard Deslauriers.

At that assembly, since the society had a healthy sum of money in the bank and since the number of members was considerably reduced, it was decided that each member would receive $19.00 and the rest would be put in the society's treasury.

There were a few meetings between June and December of that year, but attendance proved clearly that the members had lost all interest in the society, and on December 18, there was a final assembly to dissolve the society and it was decided that the furniture belonging to the association be sold and the money be used to say a high mass in honor of Monsignor Brochu. The remaining funds in the account were distributed among those who were still members in the end.

CHAPTER XX

Jacques Cartier "Court"

On January 29, 1891, an assembly was called to lay the foundation for a branch of the Foresters of America.

The following signed as founding members: William Giard, Hormisdas Lavoie, Auguste Lucier, J.-Bte. Pinsonneault, Alfred Galipeau, Joseph Demers, Dr. J. Pontbriand, Dr. J.A. Généreux, Henri L. Brousseau, Edmond Pelletier, Joseph Métras, Joseph Leclair, Omer Grégoire, Joseph Larivière, Alfred Langevin, Octave Ethier.

It was resolved that the branch would be called the Jacques Cartier Court, Number 7922, which was later changed to number 56.

Here are the results of the first election of officers: Chief Ranger, William Giard; Vice Chief Ranger, Henri L. Brousseau; Financial Secretary, Alfred Galipeau; Recording Secretary, Hormisdas Lavoie; Treasurer, Joseph Métras; 1st Visitor, Joseph Larivière; 2nd Visitor, Alfred Langevin; Interior Guard, Auguste Lucier; Exterior Guard, Octave Ethier; Physician, Dr. J.J. Pontbriand.

A few months later, this association had seen considerable growth, and in less than a year, there were over two hundred members, most of the young people were full of passion and enthusiasm and spared nothing in promoting their association.

According to the rules of the aforementioned society, a sick member would receive $5.00 per week for fifteen weeks a year, and upon the death of a member, the family would receive $100.00. This was a top notch fraternal society, and with careful administration it had soon accumulated a very substantial financial reserve.

In 1905, there was a general convention in Buffalo, N.Y., and at that meeting it was resolved that going forward there would be only one official language for the administration of the society, that being the English language. Until that time, since the society was composed of different nationalities, each group had the right to manage its own court as it wished, using their maternal language. This change, they say, was made for financial reasons, to save money on the cost of printing the rules, manuals, forms, etc.

Franco-Americans found this decision extremely disagreeable, and several French-language "courts" separated from the high court to later form the Franco-American Foresters.

In 1907, the Jacques Cartier Court became an independent society and continued through April 15, 1908 when it became affiliated with the Union St. Jean Baptiste d'Amérique, under the name of the Jacques Cartier Council, Number 58. Today, this council has 250 members, is well managed and is certainly one of the most prosperous councils in the Union.

CHAPTER XXI

Naturalization Club—Saint-Joseph Union

In 1892, a presidential election year, a naturalization club was organized in order to work towards the advancement of Canadians by introducing them to the country's political system. Mr. Joseph Anatole Caron was elected president; Médéric Duhamel, Secretary and F.X. Tétreault, Treasurer.

Throughout the year, this club made decent progress, but like all political organizations, it did not last long. It was reorganized in 1900 for the next presidential election and was disbanded after the election.

Saint Joseph Union

At a popular assembly called on April 9, 1893 to found a society called the Saint Joseph Union, it was resolved that Mr. Horace G. Gravel would be named president and Joseph N. Arpin secretary of the assembly. Remarks were made by Joseph N. Harpin, Michel J. Bachand, Dr. J.E. Généreux, Dr. J.E. Ferland, L.E. Dionne, Joseph A. Allard and others. Sixty-three fellow citizens requested to become members of the new society, and the main article of the constitution and rules read as follows:

"The aim of this society is to provide assistance in the form of a weekly allocation to members who are unable to work or must leave their regular jobs due to an illness or accident or other event requiring aid, also ensuring support and protection for widows and heirs of all persons belonging to the society or to those who will belong to it in the future."

Results of the election of the first officers: Chaplain, Monsignor Georges Elzéar Brochu; President, Michel J. Bachand; 1st Vice-President, Rémi Chartier; 2nd Vice-President, Aimé Vary; Secretary, Joseph N. Harpin; Assistant Secretary, William Pagé; Correspondent, Edmond Lippé; Treasurer, Michel Surprenant; Assistant Treasurer, Michel Bachand; Collector, F.X. Larivière; 1st Officer, J.B. L'Homme; 2nd Officer, Camille Caron; Collector, Joseph A. Allard.

In less than three months, the society had over 200 members. Each new member had to pay 50 cents per month and received $5.00 per week if ill, for the first six months, then $4.00 per week for the following six months, and $2.50 per week if the illness continued after that. When a member died, the other members would pay a special contribution of one dollar to his spouse or heirs, and upon the death of the spouse of a member, the other members would pay him 50 cents each within one month after his wife's death.

This society offered multiple advantages, so during the enthusiasm of its early days, they unfortunately admitted a number of fellow citizens who were in somewhat poor health or who were over 50 years old. From those first years, it became difficult to cover expenses with the regular revenue coming in, and since there were a number of prosperous groups in Southbridge at that time with younger members, it became almost impossible to enroll young people, and even some who had initially signed up later left this new society.

After a certain amount of time, through mutual agreement, the St. Joseph Union merged with the Union St. Jean Baptiste, on condition that each member would continue to have rights based on the terms of the original society.

CHAPTER XXII

"Cercle Académique"—Lafayette Guard

In 1895, a Cercle Académique [Academic Club] was organized by representatives of each of the Franco-American societies, with the goal of giving lectures and energizing the national movement.

Mr. F.X. Tétreault, Dr. J.A. Généreux, and Mr. Alexandre Désaulniers were selected as its first dignitaries.

Several interesting assemblies were held: lectures, debates, naturalization, etc. The aim of the Cercle was clear and defined: to inspire love for the maternal language and to show our compatriots its beauty. This association was a great asset to Southbridge, but was unfortunately abandoned in 1902.

The Lafayette Guard

In the fall of 1895, a dozen or so friends wanted to create an association for recreation and to support the advancement of their compatriots and thus established the "Lafayette Guard," with the following members: Anthime Desrosiers, Alexis Giard, Amédé Bonin, J.N. Arpin, Alfred Giard, Alfred Langevin, Joseph Desrosiers, Louis Péloquin, Joseph Leclair, Alfred Galipeau, Placide Laliberté, Alfred Allard, Arthur Lamoureux, Godfroi Lamoureux, Louis Duquette, Isidore Lataille, Joseph St. Pierre.

These friends, at various times, organized social gatherings, dramatic and musical performances. They also brought in foreign theatrical troupes to give performances in Southbridge.

On January 3, 1899, the famous troupe of the Cercle National Dramatique from Woonsocket gave a performance entitled: "Le Dompteur" ("The Tamer"), under the direction of M.J.B. Savard, director of the Cercle. This play, presented by artists, was a resounding success; promises were made to have the artists return and entertain us more often. In spring of that same year, they did so, and on June 6 the same troupe performed a play entitled "Le Martyr" ("The Martyr") by Adolphe d'Ennery, under the direction of M.J.B. Savard. Our compatriots from Woonsocket were crowned with glory a second time; this also had the happy result of motivating our people in Southbridge by showing them that there were other good "dramatic groups" outside of Southbridge.

In 1900, this young organization was disbanded and reorganized the following fall of that year during the presidential election. The goal of the society then was to bring together businessmen, without concern for political affiliations, in order to discuss the best ways to exert more influence in local and state politics. It involved promoting our Southbridge compatriots for municipal posts and even having them play an important role in statewide affairs. This was a noble goal and worthy of consideration. This group was organized under the name "Les Intimes" ["Close Friends"] but was better known later as "Pinaro."

This association, over the years, played an important role in local politics and, thanks to its influence, several of our compatriots were elected to important positions. Gradually, the situation changed and the group became more of a social club, which was not condoned by a great number of its members who eventually left the organization. A number persisted as members, however, but like the last time, members engaged in some unsavory activities, including the abuse of alcohol, so the municipal authorities authorized the chief of police to close the doors, which happened on March 30, 1914.

CHAPTER XXIII

St. George Court, F.C.—Rochambeau Council

On June 15, 1896, the Order of Catholic Foresters of Chicago created a court of their organization here called the Court St. George, number 593.

Dr. L.E. Dionne of North Brookfield was selected by the superior court to come establish the court and the following officers were appointed:

Chaplain, Rev. L.A. Langlois; Chief, F.X. Larivière; Vice-Chief, Hormisdas Bédard; Secretary, Anthime Desrosiers; Treasurer, Salomon Labonté; Treasurer-Secretary, Médéric Duhamel; Supervisors, Siméon Pagé, Joseph Brodeur; Guards, Alex. Blais, Auguste Lucier; Physician, Dr. J.S.E. Farland; Managers, J.B. Bonin, Louis Durocher, Stanislas Plante.

At that same assembly, twenty members signed the charter and vowed to work towards the advancement of the new society. A committee was formed to work with the members of the Jacques Cartier Court in order to use their hall; after the meeting, there was a reception for visitors which included speeches by Rev. L.A. Langlois, Mr. F.X. Larivière, Dr. Farland, Mr. Médéric Duhamel and Dr. L.E. Dionne from the superior court.

The St. George Court, in short time, developed a decent membership and played an important role among the local societies. It was represented in the state court for six years by Mr. Joseph Leclair. He was succeeded by Mr. W.J. Lamoureux, city council member, who held this position for four years.

The Order of Catholic Foresters has 150,000 members in both Canada and the United States and is one of the most influential societies on the American continent.

Rochambeau Council, Union St. Jean Baptiste of America

The Rochambeau Council, number 12, of the Union St.-Jean-Baptiste of America, was the first council organized within this society. It was established on March 12, 1900. Before this date, eleven societies and clubs had joined the new federation. Dr. J.A. Généreux and Felix Gatineau were delegates to the convention, and Felix Gatineau was chosen as one of the officers of the board of directors. This board applied to the state of Rhode Island to obtain a charter. This charter was obtained on May 1st, 1900, the official date of the formation of the Union St.-Jean-

Baptiste.

The officers also requested a permit from the state of Massachusetts, which was obtained in the month of May 1901, a time when members of the Rochambeau Council were beginning to pay their contributions.

Before the founding of the Council, given that the goal of the Union St. Jean Baptiste of America was to unite all the old societies under one umbrella, steps had been taken to encourage the old St.-Jean-Baptiste Society of Southbridge to join the federation. Several members were in favor of this change, others considered their society to be prosperous and expressed some doubts about the value of the new society. Even though the majority of members favored the change, according to the rules a two-thirds majority was needed, and the proposal failed. This caused some members to resign and to join the Rochambeau Council, which in just a few years had over 500 members.

Mr. F.X. Tétreault was the first president and was a devoted member until his death on September 9, 1913. Mr. J.A. Généreux, F. Gatineau, Médéric Duhamel, Napoleon Giroux, Philias Caron, Honoré Dorval, J.A. Caron, Jos. G.E. Pagé, M.D., Alfred Galipeau, Paul Berthiaume and others were among those who promoted the Council, which had sixty members at the time it was founded.

The Council has 550 members, with a reserve of $11,500, and is recognized as one of the most prosperous councils in the Union St.-Jean-Baptiste of America for its financial situation as well as for its membership.

CHAPTER XXIV

Artisans—Southbridge Branch

In 1902, there were some Canadian members of the Society of Artisans in Southbridge. Mr. Zéphirin Lepage, then a foreman at the "American Optical Company," was a former member, for he had joined while in Canada, in the early years of the organization of this society, and it was thanks to his initiative that a branch of the Artisans was established here.

At the first meeting on December 15, it was resolved to request a charter, to invite representatives of the society to come establish a branch in Southbridge, and to install officers.

Here is the list of officers: Honorary Chaplain, Monsignor Elzéar Brochu; Chaplain, Rev. L.A. Langlois; President, J.Z. Lepage; Vice-President, Paul St. Laurent; 2nd Vice-President, Joseph Pariseau; Treasurer-Secretary, Archille Langlois; Commissioners, Euclide Dupuis, Louis Bourdelais; Censors, Emery Ménard, Auguste Gaudette, George Normandin; Physician, Dr. J.B. Goyer.

A good number of attendees, of both sexes, were present for the installation assembly; there were also several visitors from surrounding Franco-American communities. Mr. L.Z. Lepage warmly thanked the members for the honor bestowed on him by naming him president and promised to do everything in his power to promote the new society which, in short time, became quite prosperous.

The following people also spoke at this event: Father L.A. Langlois, P. Perreault from Worcester, Mr. Alain Chaput from the Worcester newspaper *L'Opinion Publique*, André Lajoie, President of the Worcester branch, O.A. Bourque, organizer of the Artisans in the United States, Alfred Roy of Worcester. The main speaker was Mr. Henri Roy of Montréal, who spoke about the origins and history of this society. After the meeting, there was a reception for visitors; at this very friendly reception, there was music and singing.

The Southbridge branch was honored on several different occasions at the general convention, which according to the rules was always held at the headquarters in Montréal. It also has the honor of having in its membership Mr. Ronaldo Guilmette, manufacturer, who is one of the organizers and general directors and has held this prestigious post for six years. This branch currently has 225 members who belong to the French-Canadian elite in Southbridge, and it is without doubt one of the most well managed of all of the societies.

The Society of Artisans is pretty much the most powerful French-language society on the continent, for it has over 45,000 members in Canada and the United States.

The current officers are: Executive Council Representative, Louis Meunier; President, Wilfrid Richard; Vice-President, Basile Proulx; 2nd Vice-President, Alfred Deneault; Secretary, H. Ravenelle; Collection Treasurer, Médéric Duhamel; 1st Commissioner, Edouard Péloquin; 2nd Commissioner, L.F. Cloutier; Censors, Alfred Lapierre, Télesphore Duquette, Donat Petit.

CHAPTER XXV

Brochu Council, USJB of America—St. Cécile Branch, Artisans

On December 11, 1902, the second women's "council" of the Union St.-Jean-Baptiste of America was established in Southbridge. The first "council" of this kind was established in Newburyport, V.T. on November 11 of this same year.

At the meeting of this society in Southbridge on July 22 and 23 of 1902, it was decided that councils composed of women would be organized, following the same conditions as the men, and shortly after this meeting, the women of Southbridge took the initiative to organize a council; however, there was a certain delay caused by the printing of the rules and regulations that were to guide these councils. Finally, the Brochu Council was established on December 11, 1902 in honor of Monsignor Georges Elzéar Brochu, pastor of the parish for thirty-two years.

Mr. Henri Langelier of Woonsocket, R.I., acting "executive president" of the society came to install the officers in Southbridge, assisted by Mr. F.X. Tétreault who was then president of the Rochambeau Council.

Here are the names of the distinguished people who were installed on this occasion: Chaplain, Monsignor G. Elzéar Brochu; President, Mrs. Clara Gamache; Vice-President, Miss. Blanche Richard; Secretary, Albina Larivière; Treasurer, Elsie Jolicoeur; Collector, Arzélie Girard; Inspector, Laura Gatineau.

After the installation, there was singing, music, speeches, refreshments; as soon as this council was organized, enthusiasm was at its peak for the members. In short time, the number of members increased beyond even the most optimistic expectations, and soon the Council was one of the largest of all of the women's councils in the Union St. Jean Baptiste, a title it continues to hold today as it now has over 425 members.

There have been significant payments made to heirs of deceased members and to the sick, and there is a reserve account of several thousand dollars held in local savings banks.

The dignitaries who currently run the society are: Spiritual Director, Rev. L.O. Triganne; President, Mrs. Henri Robida; Vice-President, Mrs. Philias Gauthier; Dean, Mrs. J.A. Généreux; Honorary President, Mrs. Clara Plouffe; Secretary, Mrs. Florina St. Martin; Assistant Secretary,

Mrs. François Giard; Collector, Olympe Dupuis; Treasurer, Mélina Leblanc; Mistress of Ceremonies, Rosilda St. Martin; 1st Commissioner, Evélina Berthiaume; 2nd Commissioner, M. Aimée Ferland.

The council also has a permanent committee that takes care of members and others who are living in poverty. During the last war, a number of them devoted their time to making clothes for the orphans in France. On several occasions, they also organized recreational evenings for their members. These ladies subscribed a sum of $50 for Assumption College in Worcester; they bought a certain number of "bonds" from the government, and they are always ready to support parish work and other initiatives.

St. Cécile Branch of the Artisans—1907

The Sainte Cécile Branch was organized on March 11, 1907 by Mr. O.A. Bourque, executive organizer for the society in this country. Rev. L.T. Rodier was chosen as chaplain and Dr. J.R. Goyer, medical examiner.

The other dignitaries were: Marie-Louise Métras, Alphonsime St. Onge, Azana Plouffe, Célina Larivière, Henriette Lantagne, Delta Delâge, Exilda Gauthier, Octavie St. Martin, Octavie Langevin, Yvonne Bessette, Georgianna Lamoureux.

On several occasions throughout the twelve years that have passed since its founding, members have organized literary and social gatherings. The branch has 45 members and is administered by highly qualified officers.

Chaplain, Rev. L.O. Triganne; Executive Council Representative, Délia Lavallée; President, Maria Laperle; Vice-Presidents, Aldéa Carpentier, Florina Tavernier; Secretary, Henriette Lantagne; Treasurer, Parmélia Daigle; Managing Com., Délia Tremblay, Florence Carpentier; Censors, Florence Gervais, Florine Surprenant, Alexina Tavernier; Medical Examiners, Dr. J.G.E. Pagé, Dr. J.E. Donais.

Soldiers who died in service to their country: W. Girouard, A. Dufault, P. Donais / Dr. E. Tétreault, P. Talbot / P. Fontaine, Sargent A. Riendeau, A. Bibeau / S. Desmarais, S. Boisvert, T. Proulx, J. Girouard / G. Giard, L. Bibeau, Art. Laflèche, Capt. T.J. Proulx

Soldiers and marines: Art. Allard, F. Girouard, J. Paulhaus, R. Proulx / W. Dumas, Capt. C. Tétreault, A. Bail / L. Allard, H. Généreux, A. Caron, V. Lemoine, L. Lemoine

Soldiers and others from the World War: J. Desmarais, E. Parent, W. Bail, C.E. Garceau / Lieutenant A. Généreux, Emma Riendeau, Lieutenant E. Coderre / M. Capistrand, W.C. Lacroix, J. Paradis, Geo. Gatineau

Group of soldiers from the World War

Group of soldiers from the World War

Group of soldiers from the World War

CHAPTER XXVI

Triganne Council, USJB of America—Laurier Court, FFA

Thanks to Mr. Joseph Leclair's initiative, the Triganne Council, Number 240 of the Union St. Jean Baptiste was created on September 6, 1908 in the presence of Mr. Elie Vézina of Chicago, Ill., Vice-President of the Society, assisted by Mr. Emile Leroy Audy of Chicago as Master of Ceremonies. A sizeable delegation of representatives from the West attended the ceremony. These delegates were on their way to the Holyoke conference, which was to take place the following day, and took advantage of the occasion to visit Southbridge. They were welcomed by the Brochu, Jacques-Cartier and Rochambeau councils. On Sunday, September 6th, in the evening, there was a big public assembly at the city hall, and after the ceremony for the Triganne Council, there was singing, music and speeches. The "Rochambeau gang" was in attendance in full force, making this a quite spirited event.

Rev. Fr. Triganne, pastor of Notre Dame, extended a cordial welcome to the visitors; he congratulated all of the different councils for their activity and their enthusiasm. Dr. Oswald Grégoire, who presided over the evening's events, gave a rousing patriotic speech and introduced the speakers: Father Poissant from St. George, Ill., Father Gélinas from Chicago, and Father Simard from Aurora, Ill. each took the podium. Mr. Elie Vézina, who was the main speaker, gave an overview of the activities of the Union St. Jean Baptiste; he highlighted the good that this organization had already done for our compatriots and the role that it was called to play in society. He congratulated the Franco-Americans of Southbridge for having joined the society in such great numbers, having "five councils" and 1,500 members to their credit. He remarked that wherever he would be asked to speak, he would always cite the Canadians of Southbridge as an example of patriotism, as he has done many times before. This speaker, whose reputation precedes him, captivated the audience, and this evening was one that would go down in the annals of history for Canadians in our city. The Triganne Council, composed mostly of young women, lasted for seven years, but since it was hard for these girls to attend assemblies, because of their other activities, it was suggested and decided that the Council would join together with the Brochu Council. The fusion of the councils occurred in 1915, much to the satisfaction of all. It became clear yet again that *"in unity, there is strength."*

Laurier Court, Franco-American Foresters—1911

On April 12, 1911, the Laurier Court was organized thanks to the initiative of Dr. J.G.E. Pagé, Louis G. Dupuis, Joseph Tremblay, J.B. Nadeau, Michel McDermott and others. This court, which is the youngest of the Franco-American societies in Southbridge, has made a lot of progress since its inception and currently has 135 members. We can say that it is growing with each day. The Order of Franco-American Foresters, although it has only existed for a few years, has nearly 10,000 members spread across different Franco-American centers in New England.

CHAPTER XXVII

French-Canadian Conventions in the United States

After living in the United States for several years, French Canadians felt the need to join together, to unite, at first to know each other better and to organize themselves better, but then to study ways to improve their situation, to more strongly defend themselves in the fight to preserve their language, their ancestral customs and their national character. It became a sacred duty to send delegates and representatives from all cities where sufficient numbers of our compatriots lived to participate in the great assemblies called for these ends.

The first big and important conventions for French Canadians in the United States were held in New York in 1865 and 1866; in 1867, there was an assembly in Troy, N.Y., and in 1868, in Springfield, Massachusetts, and during that meeting it was decided that the "Federation of French-Canadian Societies" would be founded. This was realized at the convention in Detroit, Michigan in 1869.

In 1870 the St.-Jean-Baptiste society of Southbridge was founded, and in that same year, Mr. Alexandre Lataille was the first of our compatriots to attend one of the big conventions, the one held in St. Albans, Vermont.

In 1871, our delegates to the convention in Worcester, Mass. were Mr. Alexandre Lataille and François X. Casavant.

In 1872, Mr. Alexandre Lataille attended the convention in Chicago, Ill., and submitted the name of the St.-Jean-Baptiste Society of Southbridge to the federation of societies; this same delegate was sent to the convention in Biddeford, Maine.

In 1874, the convention was held in New York and the delegates from Southbridge were Mr. Alexandre Lataille and Mr. Georges J. Lamoureux. These two were authorized by our local society to terminate all affiliations with the federation since we received no benefits from it and, on the contrary, it was a considerable expense to belong to it. For one reason or another, however, we remained affiliated with the federation.

Here are the delegates who were sent to each convention:

Holyoke Convention, 1876, Alexandre Lataille, Victor Lamoureux.

Northampton Convention, 1879, Alexandre Lataille, Georges et Victor Lamoureux.

Springfield Convention, 1880, Felix Gatineau, Théophile Tremblay.

Fall River Convention, 1881, Joseph Blanchard, Clément Bégin, Georges Goddu, G. Lamoureux, Camille Métras, Michel Surprenant.

Boston Convention, 1884, Georges Goddu, Isaac St. Martin, François Tremblay.

Albany Convention, New York, 1884, Clément Bégin, F. Gatineau.

Holyoke Convention, 1885, Joseph Blanchard, Felix Gatineau, Camille Métras, Joseph Lareau, Léon Rheims, Joseph Proulx.

At this last convention, it was decided that the next convention would be held in Southbridge in 1887, and an organizing committee was formed as follows: President, Joseph D. Blanchard; Vice-President, Dr. J.B. Niquette, Northampton; Secretary, Léon Rheims; Treasurer, Felix Gatineau.

In 1886, Mr. Joseph Blanchard, delegate from the Cercle Canadien, attended the convention in Rutland, Vermont, where he was named to one of the most important committees: a committee to explore the creation of a national alliance of St.-Jean-Baptiste societies in America. He took an active role in various parts of the project. The Southbridge convention was held in Dresser hall on August 9, 10, and 11 of 1887.

Names of the Delegates

Chicopee Falls, A. Désautels, J.N. Lamoureux, Dr. Louis Dionne, Amable Monjeau, Fr. Durocher, Fr. E.M. Messier.

North Brookfield, Adolphe Laventure, E.B. Tétrault.

Holyoke, J.A. Potvin, Israël Potvin, E. St. Jacques, Ulric Perrault, Aimé Bénard, L.S. Paquette.

Indian Orchard, Dr. L.J. Roy, Alfred Brouillet, E.J. Gendreau, E. Tétreault.

North Adams, Dr. J.G. Lussier, Pierre Sorel, J.A. Gendron.

Southbridge, M.J. Surprenant, A.T. Lamoureux, Georges Goddu, Joseph Goddu, Joseph Ouimette, Sr., Alex. Lataille, Ernest Decelles, A. Caron, I. St. Martin, Joseph Leclair, J.L. Brissette, C. Bégin.

Ware, A.C. Larose, Ernest Dumontel.

Three Rivers, Thomas Chènevert, A.P. Trudeau.

Manville, Dr. L. de Grandpré, J.L. Duhaime, E.H. Désilets, Dr. J. Larivière, J.B. Morin, E. Mandeville, Louis Goulet, F.J. Landry.

Fall River, B. Janson, E.F. Lamoureux, P.F. Péloquin, Dr. P.C. Collette, G.J. Desjardins, Alf. Plante, Arthur E. Fournier, U.J. Dufault, H.A. Dubuque, S. Quintin, Nazaire Piuze, Elzéar Lamoureux, A.O. Marien, T. Dupont.

Boston, Dr. L. Da Silva, Wm. Filiatrault, S. Vannier.

Centreville, Dr. M.J.E. Legris, Joseph Fontaine, Moïse Leclerc, Joseph Salois.

Pawtucket, André Blanchard, Pierre Bourassa.

West Gardner, Dr. J.H. Palardy, Bruno Grandmont, L.E. Robillard.
West Warren, H. Hébert, Dr. V. St. Germain.
Fitchburg, W.F. Demers, J.A. Deslauriers, G.C. Des Rivières.
Woonsocket, O.T. Paradis, Dr. Maranda, Côme Tétrault, Elz.
Gingras, Dr. J.A. Gagnon, L.P. Demers, L.L. Malhiot, J.U. Giguère, J.
Bourdon, C.A. Lussier.
New Bedford, J.C. Patenaude, A.P. Lagassé.
Taunton, Geo. Badeau, A. Milot, Dr. L.C. Bussière.
Millbury, E. Desmarais, Charles Thibault.
Salem, J.A. Chabot.
Spencer, Louis Dupuis, P. Lavallée, André Ledoux, E. Mineau, J.B.
Gendreau, F. Collette, D. Parent, F.X. Dansereau, Nap. Mandeville, H.A.
Larue, Dr. M. Fontaine, Joseph Richard, P. Richard, P.J. Martin, C.S.
Trahan.
Central Falls, F.F. Lamarine, André Faucher, Rev. N. Leclerc.
North Grafton, Dr. J.A. René.
Worcester, P.L. Paquette, J.R. Jannery, J. Vaudreuil, Jr., A. Bélisle,
Jr., Nap. Vincent, L. Guérin, Dr. F.D. Fontaine, A.G. Lalime, Joseph
Granger, J.B. Simard, Rev. Joseph Brouillet.
Fisherville, E. Tétrault.
Westboro, David Richard, A. Gauthier.
Lowell, E.H. Choquette, J.H. Guillette, J.W. Paradis, A.
Bourbonnière.
Northampton, Olivier Dragon, Dr. L.B. Niquette, Narcisse Paquin,
A. Ménard, Alf. Parenteau.
Fiskdale, Pierre Mondor, Isidore Houde, Charles W. Giard, Ant.
Marcille, Alphonse Leclair, J.B. Forand.
Grafton, Victor Chapdelaine, Elie Tétrault.
Chicopee, A. Nantais.
Members of the Clergy
Worcester, Rev. Joseph Brouillet, Rev. Joseph Marchand.
Fiskdale, Rev. Jules Graton.
Central Falls, Rev. N. Leclerc.
West Gardner, Rev. C.E. Brunault.
North Adams, Rev. Louis Leduc.
St. Hyacinthe, Rev. N. Leduc.
Nicolet, Rev. H. Brunault.
Representatives of the Press
Woonsocket Reporter, F.A. Bélisle.
Southbridge Herald, X.E. Lescault.
Le Courier de Worcester, E. Brodeur.
L'Indépendant, H.A. Dubuque, Dr. M. Fontaine.

Le Travailleur, A. Bouvier, A. Choquet.
Télégram, Wm. Walsh.
La Petite République de Manchester, L.O. Morasse.

"Our Conventions"

"We must congratulate the French-Canadians of Southbridge for the enthusiasm they have demonstrated and the spirit of collaboration that has marked their organization of this convention. The members of the executive committee should be proud that their efforts have made this convention one of the best organized and most practical meetings that has ever been held in the United States. All of our conventions have had their practical results in different areas, but we can state that there is one commonality in all of the conventions which is to let others know what a convention is. Each important Canadian center should make it their duty to hold a convention if possible. This would be an appropriate way to dispel certain prejudices among those who are opposed to these assemblies of delegates in different Canadian centers in New England. What Canadian in good faith could oppose the idea of a meeting of key influential citizens who are the most capable of understanding the various questions relating to the interests of the French-Canadian nationality dispersed throughout a foreign country? It is a well-known fact that the conventions have accomplished good things in the past and their mission is to play an important role in the destinies of Canadian people in the United States. It is in the course of these meetings that we reignite our patriotism and our strength to fight the daily battles we face; it is here that we find the best way to dispel prejudices that others have of us; it is in these meetings that we find the way to rebuff the insults that a few ignorant or fanatical people hurl at us. In these conventions, we examine and we try to resolve various problems that we might have to confront. We are certain that we will be proud of the results of this convention that will benefit our nationality as a whole, and we hope that Southbridge, in particular, will enjoy a share of the rewards to be had from this Canadian convention. Hats off to all of you, our compatriots who understand their duty so well that you sacrifice your time and your money in order to promote the well-being of your fellow men. Hats off to the executive committee to whom we owe a thousand thank-yous for your organization of this convention which will certainly be a success worthy of the hard work you have put into it." –Xiste F. Lescault

"Our Language"

"Canadians have inherited the French language from their forefathers, this beautiful language, the richest of all modern languages, the one that is glorified by all who seek to distinguish themselves in terms of social status or education. The French language is to civil society what Latin is to ecclesiastical society. The same way Latin is the official language of the Church, French is the official language of civilized nations; it is the language of diplomacy; it is used by the heads of nations to communicate with each other. And we, we who have received this language from our forefathers, a language that is highly valued throughout the civilized world, are we going to abandon it; are we to be embarrassed to speak it, preferring to speak a foreign language, a language that is necessary to know because of the place in which we live, true, but one that has no place in the Canadian home? Let's preserve our language, the language of Hugo and of Veuillot and all of the kings of literature who have brought glory to France over the centuries; it is the language of Berryer and of Montalembert and of all of the kings of the podium whose sublime eloquence has earned the world's admiration for over a century. Is not the French language the most sublime vehicle for human thought? Has it not given us the most beautiful masterpieces of poetry and literature in the modern era? Let us not be embarrassed to speak it, rather let us be proud of it. But our language's intrinsic merit is not the only reason we should preserve it. For Canadians, to preserve our language is to protect our nationality. Experience has proven this to be true, for a Canadian who ceases speaking French, ceases to be Canadian; he grows apart from his compatriots, he renounces his nationality. If we want to remain French-Canadian and if we want to fulfill the mission that Providence has given our ethnicity on this continent, let us keep our language and not allow any other to rule in our homes." –L.O. Morasse, M.D.

At the start of planning for this convention, the committee had to overcome a number of obstacles imposed by the pastor, Monsignor Georges Elzéar Brochu. He did not like conventions, claiming that second-rate orators attended these conventions because they liked to hear themselves talk. He further said that any clergy attending the assembly should avoid coming to see him because he would not receive them. It seems he kept his word, for the priests who dutifully went to greet him at the rectory were given a very cold reception. In spite of all of these obstacles, our fellow citizens were very generous and gave generously to pay the organization's expenses.

This convention was extremely interesting for among the delegates were several men of great merit who were great orators. Speeches were given on the different topics of each day, and even though the discussions were often quite animated, they always remained amicable. The public followed the various debates with great interest; at the closing ceremony, it was decided that the next convention would be held in Spencer in 1889.

In 1888, the following delegates attended the convention in Nashua, N.H.: Dr. J.A. Généreux, Joseph D. Blanchard, C. Métras, Alfred Galipeau, Joseph Leclair, Georges J. Lamoureux, J.P. Davignon, Théophile Lamoureux.

This convention of Canadians was probably the most important one and was a great success. The attorney Emile Tardivel, under the direction of the executive committee composed of compatriots from New Hampshire, visited a great number of centers, especially in the west, with the goal of recruiting all of the French-Canadian groups to send representatives to the big assembly. As a result, there were many delegations and the debates were quite spirited. Resolutions concerning the rights and duties of Canadians in the United States were adopted.

The convention in Spencer, August 1889. Delegates: Georges J. Lamoureux, Felix Gatineau, Georges Goddu, Wm. Girard, Pierre Caplette, Clément Bégin, Camille Métras.

CHAPTER XXVIII

Conventions, Assemblies, etc. (continued)

In 1893, there was a World Exposition in Chicago, and French-Canadians from that city took advantage of it to organize a great "national assembly" on August 22 and 23. All the societies and all the French-speaking groups were invited to send representatives.

Canada was represented by a large delegation. Honoré Mercier was invited as the guest of honor and was accompanied to Chicago by many friends and admirers from Canada who went to attend the big meeting and visit the exposition. Our city also wanted to be represented. Camille Métras represented the Cercle Canadien, Georges Goddu the St.-Jean-Baptiste Society, and Clément Bégin the parish.

In the month of February, 1899, Dr. J.A. Généreux and Felix Gatineau were chosen as delegates to attend a meeting called by the St.-Jean-Baptiste Society of Holyoke. The aim of this meeting was to examine ways to create a "federated society," to improve the standing of several charitable societies whose insurance systems were unable to meet the needs of their members. It was important to fix this as soon as possible, for our compatriots were losing confidence in the Canadian societies and many were enrolling in English language societies that offered more security. A committee was formed to change certain constitutions to this end, and these changes were adopted at another meeting held in Woonsocket on March 27, 1900, at which the foundation was laid for the Union St.-Jean-Baptiste d'Amérique. The citizens of Southbridge who were delegates to that meeting were Dr. J.A. Généreux and Felix Gatineau. Felix Gatineau was elected to the board of directors.

In the month of October 1901, there was a great Franco-American assembly. We wanted to explore all possible ways to exert pressure on ecclesiastical authorities to assign French-speaking priests to Franco-American parishes. Nearly 1,000 delegates were present and a number of very important questions were discussed; a permanent committee was named and authorized to contact Rome to request that Franco-Americans, when there were sufficient numbers of them, be served by priests of their own nationality.

The following delegates from Southbridge attended the conference:

St.-Jean-Baptiste Society: Felix Gatineau, Clément Bégin, Georges Lamoureux, L.A. Lataille.

Cercle Canadien: Joseph Métras, F.X. Tétreault.

Chevaliers St. Pierre: Alexis Boyer, Jr., Joseph Ouimette.

St. Jacques: Ed. Lareau, Arthur Larichelière.

Naturalization Club: Joseph Leclair, Joseph A. Allard, Amédé Bonin.

Temperance Society: Joseph Berthiaume.

Cercle Académique: Hormisdas Lavoie, Alexandre Désaulniers.

Catholic Foresters: Dr. J.E. Ferland, W.J. Lamoureux.

Les Intimes: Dr. J.A. Généreux, Alfred Galipeau.

Rochambeau Council: J.A. Caron, Médéric Duhamel.

The Parish: Dr. J.G.E. Pagé, Dr. J.R. Goyer, Alfred Allard, J.Z. Lepage.

Second Conference of the Union St.-Jean-Baptiste

The second conference of the Union St.-Jean-Baptiste d'Amérique was held in Southbridge, Mass., on July 22 and 23, 1902. Since the founding of the society, the progress that was made surpassed even our most optimistic expectations. Reports from that time show that the number of members was 3,712 and the bank reserve was $11,475.90. Fifty-eight councils and societies were represented, with 92 delegates.

The delegates from Southbridge were: F.X. Tétreault and Médéric Duhamel, Rochambeau Council; Dr. J.G.E. Pagé, Council #22, Marvistic, Michigan; J.A. Caron, Council #31, Bourbonnais, Illinois; Alfred Galipeau, Council #37, St. Albans, Vermont; Paul Berthiaume, Council #58, Clinton, Massachusetts; Dr. J.A. Généreux, Council #25, Ludington, Michigan.

These councils did not have delegates, and according to the rules, the delegates listed above were appointed for the conference.

There was a high mass dedicated to the delegates, celebrated by Rev. M. Clermont of Newport, Vermont, assisted by Rev. L.M. Prud'homme of Cadillac, Michigan as deacon, and Rev. M. Bourassa as assisting deacon. The masters of ceremony were Fr. Alfred Potvin of Lewiston and Fr. L.A. Langlois. In the sanctuary were seated Monsignor Elzéar Brochu, Rev. A.M. Clément of Fiskdale; C. Crevier of Holyoke; F.X. Chagnon of Champlain, New York; M. Frigon of Montréal; Vaillancourt of Windsor, Québec and J.E. Marcoux of Fitchburg. A very strong choir sang at the third solemn mass of Leprovost, under the skillful direction of Rev. M. Chicoine who was then vicar of Southbridge.

During the offering, Miss Eugénie Tessier, the famous singer from Albany, New York, beautifully sang "Saint Cécile's Vision."

The main homily was given by Rev. Charles Crevier of Holyoke. After cordially welcoming the delegates, he spoke about the religious and patriotic feelings that should always inspire Franco-Americans in the

United States. He praised the Union St.-Jean-Baptiste and did so with remarkable talent. The preacher concluded by calling God to bless the conference and the society. The collection was taken up at the church by young boys and girls from the parish. After the mass, the societies, led by a marching band, escorted the delegates to the city hall where the conference was held.

At the opening of the convention, Mr. Antoine Farland, a member of the city council, welcomed the delegates and offered them the use of the spacious hall in the building, saying that they should "make themselves at home" in Southbridge. The Franco-American population, as well as members of the city council, did everything they could to make the delegates feel comfortable during their stay.

At this convention, Mr. Felix Gatineau of Southbridge was elected president of the Union St.-Jean-Baptiste, a position that he held until December 1911.

At the end of the conference, it was proposed that thank-yous should be sent to the city councilmen, the Rochambeau Council and the parishioners for their warm welcome and the kindness they extended to the delegates. This resolution was adopted amidst enthusiastic applause.

CHAPTER XXIX

Union St. Jean Baptiste Conference

The third conference of the Union was held in Willimantic on September 27 and 28 of 1904. The delegates to the conference from the Rochambeau Council were: Mr. Hormisdas Lavoie, Mr. Honoré Dorval, Mr. C. Brochu, Mr. Napoléon Giroux.

Fourth Conference—1906

The fourth conference of this society was held in Woonsocket on September 25-27, 1906. The delegates from the Rochambeau Council were: Dr. J.R. Goyer, Frédéric Delâge, Clément J. Potvin, Honoré Dorval, Joseph L. Berthiaume.

Council Brochu: J. Anatole Caron, Joseph L. Coderre, Dr. J.A. Généreux.

For this fourth conference of the Union St.-Jean-Baptiste, there was to be a large public demonstration and the Rochambeau Council, with its honor guard and brass band, attended this demonstration, which promised to be an immensely successful event. Man proposes but God disposes, says the proverb, and so the great dreams of the organizers were dashed by a torrential rain that threw a wet blanket on all of the excitement. There was supposed to have been an outdoor mass, but this important part of the program, of course, was omitted; it also rained on the parade.

Fifth Conference

This conference was held in Holyoke, Mass., on September 8 and 9 of 1908. The delegates from Southbridge were:

Rochambeau Council: F.X. Tétreault, Napoléon Giroux, N. Leblanc, Philias Caron, Joseph L. Coderre.

Council Brochu: Rev. L.O. Triganne, Dr. J.A. Généreux, Clément J. Potvin, Dr. C.M. Pomerat.

Council Jacques-Cartier: Dr. J.G.E. Pagé, Joseph Leclair, Hormisdas Lavoie.

Council St.-Jean-Baptiste: Alexis Boyer, Jr., Bazile Proulx, Louis St. Martin.

Sixth Conference

This conference was held in Manchester, New Hampshire, on September 6-7, 1910. Delegates from the Rochambeau Council: Joseph Faure, Alexis Boyer, Joseph Berthiaume, Clément Potvin, Napoléon Giroux; Council Jacques-Cartier: Isidore Leblanc, Joseph Laflèche; Council Brochu: Joseph Coderre, Dr. J.A. Généreux, Oscar Gatineau; Council St.-Jean-Baptiste: Bazile Proulx; Council Triganne: F.X.

Tétreault.

Special Conference in Providence, December 12, 1911
Delegates: Wilfrid Lamoureux, F.X. Tétreault, J.A. Caron, Joseph Laflèche, Joseph Coderre, Isidore Leblanc, Alexis Boyer, Oscar F. Gatineau, Joseph Métras.

Fall River Conference, September 1912
Delegates: Rochambeau Council: F. Gatineau, F.X. Tétreault, Joseph L. Berthiaume; Council Jacques-Cartier: Isidore Leblanc, Felix Lavallée; Council Brochu: Joseph Tremblay, Philias Caron; Council St.-Jean-Baptiste: Clément Bégin; Council Triganne: Joseph Laflèche.

Eighth Conference, Worcester, September 14-15, 1915
Delegates: Rochambeau Council: Felix Gatineau, Médéric Duhamel, Hervé L'Homme; Council Jacques-Cartier: Dr. J.G.E. Pagé, Philias Gauthier, Edmond Pelletier; Council Brochu: David Blain, Valmore Tétreault; Council St.-Jean-Baptiste: J.B. Nadeau.

Ninth Conference, Springfield, November 18, 19, 20, 1918
Delegates: Rochambeau Council: W.C. Poirier, C.J. Potvin, A. Paradis, Hervé L'Homme; Council Jacques-Cartier: Henri Robida, Joseph Tremblay; Council Brochu: Isidore Leblanc, Joseph Coderre, Ph. Gauthier; Council St.-Jean-Baptiste: Joseph D. Proulx.

Blanchard family orchestra

Southbridge Brass Band, 1897

Michel Girard Family: Eleven Brothers

O.J. Paquette, Manufacturer

Hector Leclair, Manufacturer

CHAPTER XXX

Music—Instructors

The first person to teach piano in Southbridge was Mr. Georges W. Papillon, and that was in 1883; Mr. Papillon, though still young, dedicated himself to studying piano, and after persevering for several years in his studies, he began to give piano lessons, which he still does today, quite successfully if you judge by the number of his students.

Miss Emélie Surprenant taught piano and organ starting in 1888; still young and gifted with a remarkable musical talent, she shared her talents with her compatriots on several occasions. Miss Surprenant was the first organist of the Notre Dame parish in 1889, much to the delight of the parishioners who had long wished for an organist of their own nationality.

From 1890 to 1900, Miss Albina Surprenant and Mrs. Dr. Dionne and Mrs. J.A. Pontbriand were instructors.

From 1900 to the present day, Alice Guilbert, Joséphine Bonneau, Elosia Lamothe, and Angéline St. Onge were instructors.

Today, our music teachers are: Prof. Eugène Tapin, organist, Georges W. Papillon, Alcide Bell, Edgar Proulx, Laurina Lizotte, Stéphanie Lippé, Bernadette Parent, Mrs. Joseph Lavallée, etc.

Brass Bands and Orchestras

Instrumental music is important in Southbridge and several of our Canadians have made a career of it, including: Joseph Bourque, Henry Bronze, John B. Desgreniers, L. Langlois, Adolphe Péloquin, Joseph Lataille and Arthur Blanchard. Some were part of theatrical companies, others were in various musical groups in the area.

The first brass band of Southbridge was organized by the Hamilton Woolen Company in 1861, called the "Hamilton Woolen Cornet Band." It was at the start of the Civil War, and since there were numerous patriotic demonstrations during that era, this band, which was largely comprised of employees of the company, was often called to participate in the demonstrations. The first director was Wm. Hargrave, supervisor of the factory. In 1866, the war ended but the band was reorganized as the "Globe Village Cornet Band," with Wm. Marcy as director; in 1871, it went by the name of "Mechanics Band," Henry Pellett, director. A few Canadians were involved in it; the first was Albert Giard, who was a member of the first band in 1862. Mr. Victor Lamoureux was also in it in 1866. A little later, we see the names of Joseph Bourque, Xavier Bourque, Salomon Blanchard, Alexandre Sénécal, Pierre Surprenant and

Pierre Giard, Jr. listed in the "Globe Village Cornet Band."

In 1874, the "Mechanics" band, which had a dozen Canadian members, accompanied the St.-Jean-Baptiste Society to the great assembly in Montréal on June 24. Back in Southbridge, a few Canadians who were members of this band, along with other young folks who wanted to learn music, came up with the idea to create a predominantly Canadian brass band. Edmond Lamoureux, Salomon Labonté and Isidore Gervais were the organizers, and in the month of October 1874, a musical association called the "Southbridge National Band" was formed with Joseph Bourque as director and the following members: Edmond Lamoureux, Henri Lavoie, Narcisse Sénécal, Salomon Labonté, Misael Goddu, Moïse Monette, Isidore Gervais, Georges Goddu, J.B. Robillard, Joseph Bourque, Edmond Goddu, Anthime Robillard, Xavier Bourque, Joseph Goddu, Flavien Cabana, Edmond Hêtu, Pascal Sénécal, Napoléon Vincelette, Joseph Gamache, Napoléon Couture, Evariste Péloquin, Osias Patenaude, Cléophas Parent, Joseph Bibeau, Elzéar Hêtu, André Blanchard, Camille Métras, Pierre Benoit, Pierre Peck, John B. Giroux.

In short time, this musical association made rapid progress; in 1875, it was the musical group for the St.-Jean-Baptiste Society's celebration of the patron saint. In 1876, they participated in several parades, including one for the soldiers on May 30, one for St.-Jean-Baptiste day on June 24 and one for the national holiday on July 4th, and they also marched in parades organized by different political parties during the presidential election.

In 1877, 1878 and 1879, the brass band enjoyed a period of great prosperity; in 1879, the association members wanted to raise money to buy uniforms and instruments, so they organized a series of parties. Unfortunately, people turned to dancing for entertainment, and since the pastor of the parish, with good reason, utterly detested this type of entertainment, he gave them a dressing down and as a consequence, the brass band was immediately disbanded.

In 1880, the group was reorganized under the name "Cadet Band," with Prof. Olivier Bisson as director; among the members of this new brass band were: Ernest Decelles, Jules Trudel, Elzéar Bélanger, Josué Blanchard, Léon Young, Georges Ferron, J.B. Desgreniers, Fr. Delâges, Louis Delâges, Louis Duquette, Joseph Lamothe, Joseph Blais and others.

In 1882, Prof. Bisson moved to Lowell and was replaced by Mr. Léon Young as director.

In 1888, there was the "Cadet" band, comprised of Canadians, and the "Mechanic" band, which was mostly Canadians. Since it was hard to maintain two musical organizations, the two groups united and called themselves the "Southbridge Brass Band." Several other Canadians joined the new band, including: Thomas Plante, Adolphe Péloquin, Albert Brousseau, Alfred Boucher, Joseph Desrosiers, Pierre Lavallée, Henry Bronze, Zoël Delâge, L. Langevin. Mr. Albert Brousseau was named drum major, and Augustus Cook, former director of the "Mechanic" band, became the director of this new organization for a time. He was replaced by Mr. Léon Young, who was director for two years. J.B. Desgreniers was the next director for six years, then Gélas Guillet for two years, followed by Louis Delâge who has been the director for twenty-two years.

The "Southbridge Brass Band" has been in existence for thirty years; it is comprised mostly of Canadians and is recognized as one of the most important musical groups in Worcester County, especially known for French music.

In 1910, during the Manchester conference, this band gave a great concert in the public park on the eve of the "Labor Day" demonstrations. More than 25,000 people attended that concert, and the band won much acclaim that day.

St. Joseph Brass Band—the "National Band"

In 1893, thanks to the initiative of Dr. J.E. Ferland, who was a passionate music lover, and several others who wanted to learn music, a brass band called the "St. Joseph Brass Band" was formed with the following members: Dr. J.E. Ferland, Gédéon Pinsonneault, Joseph Casaubon, Edouard Demers, Alexis Demers, Napoléon Arpin, Wilfrid Casaubon, John B. Lippé, Omer Bélanger, Edouard Barolet, Felix Lavallée, J.B. Demers, Zénon Desrosiers, Joseph Desrosiers and others.

Dr. Ferland was the director and J.B. Lippé the drum major. In 1898, Dr. Ferland, who was the heart and soul of the organization, returned to Canada, much to the regret of the members, and there was no more band.

In 1896, a new brass band was organized by the Blanchard brothers, called the "National Band." Most of the members were Canadians; in short time, the organization became very prosperous and was able to accept several engagements in Southbridge and elsewhere. It existed for ten years, but since the Blanchard's had to dedicate more and more time to their orchestra and their theater, the brass band was disbanded in 1906. Brothers Salomon, Alfred and Arthur Blanchard took turns as directors.

CHAPTER XXXI

Music (continued)—Orchestras

In the fall of 1871, the first orchestra was formed in Southbridge, called the "Southbridge Orchestra." The director was Mr. Joseph Bourque, and the members were as follows: Salomon Blanchard, Alexandre Sénécal, Xavier Bourque, Newton D. Putney, Chauncey Rose, and Major Woodbridge. This orchestra lasted until 1895, when it was reorganized and named "Blanchard's Orchestra," and still exists today, providing music at the Blanchard theater. This musical organization soon became a first-class orchestra. It enjoys an excellent reputation in our city and in surrounding Franco-American centers. The orchestra is directed by Mr. Alfred Blanchard, assisted by Salomon Blanchard, Louis, William and Arthur Blanchard, this last brother is also the manager of the "Blanchard" theater.

In 1880, there was the "Bisson" orchestra, which lasted for two years. In 1888, an orchestra comprised of young Canadians was founded and named "Grenier & Péloquin Orchestra." These two fellow citizens were skilled musicians, and for a number of years, this musical association enjoyed a very good reputation. Since 1914, it has been called the "Imperial Orchestra," and it is directed by Prof. A. Péloquin, a top-notch violinist.

From 1890 to 1900, there was the "Palin Orchestra," and the "Ferland Orchestra"; in 1905, the "Bélanger" orchestra was created, Omer Bélanger, director. Léonce, Edmond, Eugène and Alphonse Pelletier organized an orchestra in 1913; director, Léonce Pelletier, accompanist, Arthur Proulx.

Mr. Joseph Bourque was the first Canadian to teach violin and instrumental music in Southbridge. He started in 1871 and continued through 1882, when he accepted a position as conductor of the "Duprey & Benedict" troupe, and he traveled until 1893; he returned here and continued to teach until his death on October 29, 1898.

Mr. Olivier C. Bisson also taught violin here, from 1879 to 1883, and directed the brass band. He left Southbridge in 1883 to go live in Lowell.

Miss Aurore Lacroix participated in numerous famous concerts in Boston, Montréal, Toronto and New York from 1915 to 1919. She has the reputation of being one of the most famous pianists in New England and in the entire country. She has always been highly praised for the concerts in which she has participated. She has many admirers everywhere she goes.

CHAPTER XXXII

Musical Groups (continued)

During the past fifty years, several musical groups were formed in Southbridge; concerts were organized to benefit the parish, national societies, etc.

Early in the year 1885, a musical group was formed by the "Cercle Canadien" called "The Orphéon of the Cercle Canadien." The director was Mr. Ernest Decelles, and the members were as follows: Jules Trudel, J.A. Caron, Raymond Dostaler, Edmond Pelletier, Joseph N. Lareau, Edmond Lareau, A. Montminy, Joseph Pinsonneault, Alfred Galipeau, Joseph Desrosiers, Joseph Leclair, Camille Métras; Sophroie Gravel, Clara Lord, Sophie Lord, Maria Leroux, Olivine Leroux, Marie Pinsonneault, L.O. Morasse, Ella Sénécal and Delphine Rémillard.

On May 18, 1885, a musical performance was offered by the Cercle Canadien in order to raise funds needed for the purchase of sheet music, etc. This event included an operetta entitled "A, B, C, D," "Les Soirées de Québec," "La Mascotte," "La Retraite," and other national songs. This was a great evening for Canadians, and our members, who were encouraged by this successful first event, went right back to work.

On November 18, the Orphéon gave another performance: Mr. Jules Trudel and Miss Séraphine Gravel sang "Chrétienne et Musulmane" with great enthusiasm; Mr. Joseph Loiseau was also applauded for this bass solo.

In the month of December 1886, the Orphéon again organized a concert; on the program, among others, were: Mr. Alfred Deserre, famous violinist, and Mr. E.H. L'Africain, both from the Boston Conservatory.

Early in the year 1887, the Orphéon was reorganized and renamed "The Montagnards," with Ernest Decelles as director. On December 11, this group gave a concert with the help of Mrs. Joséphine Lespérance of Worcester; Dr. Valmore St. Germain, baritone, of St. Hyacinthe; Mr. Médéric Lefebvre of Lynn, Mass., and Napoléon Amelotte of Spencer. This performance was a godsend for our community and from that moment on, the "Montagnards" were well-known and were invited to give concerts on Worcester, Woonsocket, and other nearby centers.

In 1890, the "Montagnards" were reorganized again and renamed the "Union Musicale," comprised of men and women. Mr. Ernest Decelles was named director and Mrs. Dr. J.A. Pontbriand accompanist.

On December 16 of that same year, a big concert was given by a strong choir featuring Eugénie Tessier, the famous blind singer who used to sing at the cathedral in Albany, N.Y., and Mrs. Dr. Bardy Dionne, renowned pianist. Among the soloists featured at this concert were: Mr. Arthur Riendeau, Mr. Joseph Lavallée, Mr. Edmond Pelletier, Mr. A. Bouchard, Mr. Ernest Decelles, Mr. Joseph Loiseau, Mr. Albert Sénécal, Miss Albina Dupaul, Miss M. Anna Pinkham, Miss E. Bouchard and Mrs. Dr. J.A. Pontbriand. The Péloquin orchestra offered the music.

From 1890 to 1895, the "Union Musicale" organized several performances and volunteered to sing at various conferences and patriotic festivals. By the month of December, the "Union Musicale" no longer existed.

From 1895 to 1898, there were several musical performances organized under the direction of Mrs. J.R. Jannery with Miss Albina and Miss Emélie Surprenant. In that time, there was a number of young women with remarkable musical talent, including: Marie Surprenant, Elodia, Corina and Yvonne Leclair, Amanda Lavoie, Albina Dupaul, Jessie Sénécal, Emélia and Elise Duclos, M. Anne Pinkham, Albina and Ida Surprenant, Marie-Anne Parent, Eva Thériault, Emma Martel, Alice Guillet. Among the men known for talent in the musical world in Southbridge, we note Dr. Oswald Grégoire, M.J.H. Martel, Zéphir Potvin, Arthur Riendeau and Joseph Martel.

A concert was given by members of the Notre Dame choir, under the direction of Rev. L.A. Langlois, on February 22, 1898 in Edwards hall. A choir of forty voices, accompanied by the "Péloquin and Degreniers" orchestra, sang "La Chasse aux Hussards" and "La Patrie des Hirondelles." Then, there were various selections sung by Elise and Amélie Duclos, Mrs. Clara Péloquin, Albina Dupaul, Emélie and Herminie Bonneau, Amélia and Elise Péloquin, Olivier Lamothe, Zéphyr Potvin, F. Lavallée.

On December 28, 1900, under the direction of Rev. J.A. Frédette, there was a magnificent concert in the city hall to benefit the Brochu Academy. Eugénie Tessier, M.H.J. Faucher, violinist, M.E.N. L'Africain, cornetist from Boston, were the most famous people to perform.

From 1900 to 1907, there was nothing remarkable in the world of music in Southbridge, but in the spring of 1907, Miss Joséphine Bonneau, who was then the organist of the Notre Dame parish, organized a concert with the choir. It was well-known that this concert, thanks to Miss Bonneau's initiative, was an immense success.

On December 13 of 1908, the Union St.-Jean-Baptiste of America organized a concert to benefit Eugénie Tessier, who, in particular, was the focus of the event.

On December 15 of 1908, Miss Lillias Chapdelaine, a student at the Boston Conservatory, gave a concert in the Rochambeau hall with the help of several other renowned artists. Having just turned 13, this young virtuoso already had an admirable voice, which would later become her livelihood.

In April 1908, another concert by Miss Joséphine Bonneau and the choir. Notable people in this concert: Eugénie Tessier, Dora Boucher, Cécile Viau of Woonsocket, R.I., and Rachel Garceau.

On January 20, 1910, Paul Dufault and Joseph Martel of New York gave a concert. On January 19, 1911, another performance by Alma Désautel of Springfield with several other artists.

Chaminade Club

In 1914, around thirty young women who liked music organized a musical association called the "Chaminade Club." After a few months of preparations, this club, directed by Miss Cora Gatineau with Irène Allard, accompanist, gave their first concert at the "Plaza" theater on June 2, 1914. On that occasion, the young ladies were offered many congratulations.

On April 25, 1916, another concert offered by the club, under the direction of Dr. A.J. Harpin of Worcester, assisted by A.J. Hackett, eminent tenor, and Miss Sara Girardin of Worcester.

On January 25, 1917, another concert offered by this association with the following slate of out-of-town artists: Joseph Martel of New York; Mrs. Agnès Gaulin-Pouliot, Miss Léonora Boulay of Woonsocket; Irène Chagnon, Springfield.

On June 7, wishing to organize a fundraiser, the club offered a concert to benefit the "Red Cross" under the direction of Dr. A.J. Harpin. During the war, members of this young association offered free music and singing at various patriotic assemblies and public demonstrations. They also made clothes for the soldiers and orphans in France and Belgium.

On May 15, 1916, the Chaminade Club organized a big religious concert in the new Notre Dame church for the dedication of the new organ. The director was Eugène Tapin, parish organist.

The Chaminade Club was organized as follows: Cora Gatineau, Director; Gertrude Allard, Blanche Pagé, C. Gatineau, Accompanists; Maximilienne Tétreault, President; Ida Gatineau, Secretary; Gertrude Allard, Treasurer; Florence Coderre, Collector; Léontine Généreux, Librarian.

Names of other members: Emma Allard, Irène and Gertrude Allard, Anna Bachand, Anita Bélanger, Blanche Bertrand, Yvonne and Anna

Bédard, Agnès Berthiaume, Ella Brousseau, Jessé Boiteau, Anna
Coderre, Florence Coderre, Cécile Daigle, Eva Daigle, Blanche Daigle,
Béatrice Daigle, Mina Leblanc, Antoinette Delâge, Rosaline Delâge,
Alice Desrosiers, Antoinette Desrosiers, Lena Désaulniers, Corinne
Duchesneau, Thérèse Farly, Rita Gamache, Emma Gatineau, Ida
Gatineau, Cora Gatineau, Léontine Généreux, Mérilda Guillet, Eveline
Guillet, Valida Giroux, Irène Lamoureux, Valida Lamoureux, Alice
Langevin, Fabiola Lareau, Nathalie Lareau, E. Larivière, Imelda Lataille,
Ed. Langlais.

Other names not mentioned here are listed in the summary of the
dedication of the Notre Dame church.

Guilmant Chorus

We are delighted to also make mention of Notre Dame church's
"Guilmant Chorus," the most recently formed musical group in
Southbridge and perhaps the most impressive. It is the work of a maestro,
a former student and worthy disciple of Guilmant himself: Prof. Eugène
Tapin, organist of the Notre Dame parish. There is no need to sing the
praises of our compatriot, but he has certainly earned congratulations
from the Southbridge community who has been charmed and entertained
by his expert melodies, etc. many a time. Still fresh in our memory is the
success of the first annual concert of the Guilmant Chorus held on June
8, 1919. Before the echoes of this charming evening fade away, may we
attend another concert just like it!

CHAPTER XXXIII

Savings and Cooperative Banks

Wanting to encourage our compatriots to save money and, above all, to teach young people about saving, several parishioners organized a savings society in order to open a savings bank. This society was organized on July 1, 1892 by members of the Cercle Canadien, requiring that each shareholder give $1.00 per week to the treasurer, to be deposited at the bank on Mondays, so that after one full year, each shareholder will receive the amount he deposited: that is, $52.00 plus accumulated interest.

Mr. J.D. Blanchard was elected president, J. Anatole Caron was vice-president, and Felix Gatineau collector and treasurer. All went as planned and within a year a total sum of $2,600.00 had been deposited in the bank, a sum that was returned to each shareholder because this society only lasted for one year. After time, some wanted to continue to save because, they said, "we were able to save a certain amount of money without even noticing it." However, the collectors found that it was too much imposition to be there each week to collect the money, and they no longer wanted to do this work, so the society was disbanded.

In the month of February 1898, another savings society was organized with the same terms and conditions, and this society was called the "French-Canadian Association." After a year had passed, the funds were again returned to the shareholders and the association terminated.

Cooperative Bank

At the start of 1910, a few Franco-Americans met to try to organize a cooperative bank. The project seemed to be of interest; a committee was formed to take the necessary steps to obtain a charter from the state, and in short time the charter was obtained and the bank, named the "Southbridge Cooperative Bank," was incorporated on March 8, 1910.

At an assembly of shareholders, held on April 7 of 1910, the following officers were chosen: President, W.J. Lamoureux; Vice-President, F.X. Tétreault; Secretary and Treasurer, J.A. Caron; Consulting Attorney, Louis O. Rieutard; Directors, Joseph A. Benoit, H.U. Bail, Clément Bégin, J.B. Demers, A.L. Désaulniers, Honoré Dorval, Felix Gatineau, W.P. Gendreau, Aimé Langevin, Om. Micheli, Elzéar Ouellette, A.J. Paquin, Napoléon Blanchard, Joseph A. Richard, F.A. Wald; Auditors, Alexis Boyer, Sr., Origène J. Paquette, O.F.

Gatineau; Finance Committee, E. Desrosiers, W.P. Gendreau, Stanislas Matte; Safety Committee, H.U. Bail, A.L. Désaulniers, J.B. Demers.

The first series began in the month of April 1910, and the bank has prospered ever since. For the 19th series in the month of April 1919, 700 new shares were sold, and the monthly revenue was $3,500, with a total reserve of $143,803.99 at that time.

The officers for 1919 are: President, J.A. Caron; Vice-President, Ronaldo Guilmette; Secretary-Treasurer, Ed. Desrosiers; Safety Committee, A.L. Désaulniers, H.U. Bail, J.B. Demers; Auditors, Geo. F. Douner, Joseph Métras, J.A. Martin; Directors, three years, Antoine Duplessis, A.H. Dubey, F.A. Bouvier, U.J. Lamoureux, Edgar Larichelière; Directors, two years, J.B. Demers, A.L. Désaulniers, R. Guilmette, F. Gatineau, Joseph L. Berthiaume; Directors, one year, H.U. Bail, L.O. Rieutard, Victor Laperle, Elz. Ouellette, S. Matte.

This bank's funds are invested in first-class mortgages, and today, after eight years of existence, this financial institution is one of the most prosperous cooperative banks in the state.

Southbridge Savings Bank

In 1912, after the defalcations at the Southbridge Savings Bank, Mr. Alexis Boyer, Dr. J.G.E. Pagé, and Mr. Alex. Désaulniers were chosen to become members of the corporation; Mr. Joseph Larivière and Mr. Philias Renaud, trustees.

In 1917, Louis O. Rieutard was elected director of the "Southbridge National Bank" for one year. Mr. Joseph Laflèche began work as an accountant in that same bank on May 12, 1919.

"Southbridge People's National Bank"

This bank was founded in the month of June 1919. Léon Young was elected President; Wilfrid Lamoureux, R. Guilmette, H.L. Bédard, Directors; Elzébert Ouellette, Jr., Assistant Cashier; Anna Bédard, Annette Lamoureux, employees.

CHAPTER XXXIV

Legislature—Canadians of Southbridge, Representatives in the State Legislature

Mr. François X. Tétreault, elected Representative to the "Legislature" in 1902 and 1903, was a candidate for State Auditor in 1904. He had a lot of influence among members of the Democratic party, and was in the electoral campaign for his party on several occasions.

Mr. F. Gatineau was named member of the legislature in 1906; he was also named to a special commission to codify insurance laws in the state by J.M. Cole, President of the House; in 1907, he was named to a two-year term as trustee of the home for mentally retarded children in Waverly by Governor Guild. In 1909, he was again named to this position by Governor Draper, for a term of three years, and he has been a member of that corporation ever since.

Legislature and Senate

Mr. Alexis Boyer, Jr., was elected Representative to the "Legislature" in 1907-08. In 1910, he was the Democratic party's candidate for State Auditor; in 1914, he was elected Senator for the Hampden and Worcester districts. He was also a member of the State Democratic Committee. His political influence among members of his party was almost unparalleled. We can state without a doubt that Mr. Alexis Boyer, Jr. is one of the most notable figures that Southbridge has ever known. He was duty and honesty incarnate; the good that he did for his fellow citizens during his too-short political career is immeasurable. Several of our compatriots owe him eternal thanks. He had many friends of all walks of life, and people of all races and religions loved and admired him. It is thanks to him that Mr. Joseph Métras of Southbridge and Mr. Eugène Marchessault of Spencer were named postmasters.

Senator Alexis Boyer, Jr.

F.X. Tétreault, First Canadian in the Legislature, 1902

Etienne Richard, First Canadian Manufacturer in Southbridge

F.X. Sansoucy, Councilor

Wilfrid J. Lamoureux,
President of the Councilors

Rev. J.B. Plante, S.J.

Clément Bégin, first Canadian elected to a municipal post in 1879

His dedication to charity was exemplary, and he never encountered a problem without doing everything in his power to solve it; many of the poor have benefitted from his donations, which he distributed right and left, always forbidding people to speak publicly of them. His death, which arrived prematurely, sent the entire population of Southbridge into mourning and profound consternation.

Here is what the local newspaper published about him on June 13, 1917, at the time of his death:

Mr. Alexis Boyer Just Died in Southbridge

"The deceased was taken in the prime of his life after a full career—Mr. Boyer brought honor to the Franco-Americans of Southbridge and to his entire ethnicity—he had been Selectman for 13 years and held the position of Deputy in the Legislature and State Senator—Sympathy to the Boyer family.

"Southbridge, June 13, 1917. With much regret, that we are sure our readers will share, we inform you of the death of Mr. Alexis Boyer, Jr., Selectman and former State Senator, who died this morning at 1:45am in his residence at 108 Hamilton Street.

"Mr. Boyer was 42 years and 4 months old. He had been sick for eighteen months. The deceased had attended parish schools and had graduated from the high school in 1894. He was a Selectman in Southbridge for 13 years; Representative to the Legislature in 1907 and 1908, and State Senator in 1914. He was a member of the Rochambeau Council and the St. Jean Baptiste Council of the USJB of America, of the Cercle Canadien, of the Red Men, of the Eagles and of the Knights of Columbus. He was a member of the Democratic Committee of the state, as well as President of the Democratic Committee of his city.

"The deceased was a profoundly religious man, and at the time of his death, he was given all of the consolations and support that the Church provides for its children. Mr. Boyer was of exemplary piety. Last week, he expressed a desire to go to Montréal to ask Brother André to intercede with the All-Mighty in order to cure him.

"Apart from his father, the deceased leaves behind a brother, Mr. Oliva Boyer, and a sister, Miss Laurencia Boyer.

"We all bow with respect, sadness and regret before the body of one who held the flag of our ethnicity high and proud for so many years, and we offer our most sincere condolences to his grieving family."

Mr. Wilfrid Lamoureux was named Justice of the Peace in 1898 by Governor Greenhalge, Notary Public in 1906 by Governor Douglass, and was elected to the legislature in 1910, 1911-1919. When the troubles occurred at the "Southbridge Savings Bank," he was called to take part in a special commission charged with undertaking an investigation and with safeguarding the interests of depositors. Mr. Lamoureux played an important role in the political arena in Southbridge and was always interested in the advancement of our people. He was born here on December 13, 1869, and is the son of George J. Lamoureux and of Domithilde Bourdeau. From a young age, he received an excellent education, having studied in Watertown, N.Y. and in Montréal, Canada. He first worked at "American Optical," where he was very popular; on June 16, 1900, he went into business, along with Joseph E. Lareau and his brother Arthur Lamoureux. He is now the sole owner of the store, which is a very prosperous establishment today.

Mr. Louis O. Rieutard, attorney, arrived in Southbridge in 1902 to practice law. In 1903, he was named Justice of the Peace by Governor Wolcott, and shortly thereafter was nominated as Notary Public. In 1908, he was named "Master in Chancery" by Governor Guild; in 1912 and 1913, he was elected to the legislature, reelected in 1917 and, in a special session in 1918 to revise the state constitution. Named to the important post of Deputy Judge of the district court in 1919 by Governor Coolidge, he was recognized as one of the best lawyers in Worcester county and was held in high esteem by the citizens of Southbridge.

Thanks to the influence of Franco-Americans in Southbridge, Mr. Joseph Laflamme of Sturbridge was elected to be a member of the legislature in 1914 and 1915.

CHAPTER XXXV

Business—Advertisements—Franco-Americans in Business and

Professional Life in Southbridge

Insurance Agents: Edouard Desrosiers, Oscar F. Gatineau, Valmore Tétreault

Architect: Oswald Laliberté

Artistic Photographer: Ad. Benoit

Real Estate Agents: Jean B. Proulx, Eugène Gabrie; V. Tétreault

Lawyers: Louis O. Rieutard, Henri Tétreault

Doctors: Dr. J.G.E. Pagé, Joseph Donais, Charles Tétreault, Charles Simpson

Contractors and Builders: H.U. Bail, A. Boyer and Son, Charles Proulx, Pierre Allard, Joseph Proulx and Son

Barbers-Hairstylists: Alfred Adam, Walter Girard, Tougas and Dugas, U. Larouche, Ph. Tétreault, Ernest Martel, Fabien Brodeur, Pierre Bachand, Arthur Geoffrion, Théo. Lefebvre, Guertin and Tremblay, Arthur Chapdelaine

Jeweler: George E. Proulx

Laundries: J.B. Hébert, Alb. C. Favreau

Bakers: J.E. Demers, Arcade Richard, Georges Richard, H. Massé

Shoe Stores: H.L. Bédard, F. Bouvier, Joseph Blais, Omer Bédard, H. Courtemanche, Stephen Dufault, O.L. Désaulniers, Gédéon Grégoire, Wm. Hamel, Hilaire Lavigne, Elz. G. Lavallée, Alexandre Paquin, Joseph Robichaud

Dentists: Roch Lepage, H.L. Desmarais, Arthur Gravel, H. Péloquin, Arthur Grégoire

Milk Delivery: Théo. Bonnette, Louis Dionne, L.F. Favreau, H. Cournoyer, J.B. Beaudreau, etc.

Electrician: Aimé J. Larochelle

Grocers and Butchers: Joseph E. Benoit, Joseph Berthiaume, Fr. Brissette, Pierre Cournoyer, Mrs. Wm. Chicoine, Ephrem Chicoine, J.B. Demers, J.B. Proulx, Sénécal Brothers, Joseph L. Demers, A.L. Désaulniers, Joseph Desrosiers, Noé Ethier, J. Gaumond, Wilfrid Gendreau, Joseph Jacques, Joseph St. George, Joseph Therrien, Ad. Laporte, Pierre Larochelle, Joseph Lippé, Auguste Loomis, Odilon Lavoie, Georges W. Lavallée, G. Pinsonneault, Isidore Rémillard

Tinsmiths-Plumbers: Joseph A. Allard, Proulx and Co.

Blacksmiths and Drivers: H. Lemmelin, Ernest Collette, E.J. Gibeault, Giroux Brothers

Saddlers: Aimé Parent, Oscar L. Désaulniers, Henri Désaulniers

Clothing: H.L. Bédard, Dufault & Co., Joseph F. Larivière, A.J. Paquin, J.B. Bonin, Victor Pelletier

Garages: Girard Brothers, F.W. Paquin, Hamel & Co.

Hotels: Hotel Newman, Alfred Allard; Central Hotel, Labelle and Sons; Nipmuck House, Joseph A. Larivière

Civil Engineer: Arthur Généreux

Fruit and Candy Shops: George Favreau, David Gamache, John B. Julien, Clarinda Chagnon, Elz. G. Lavallée, Hubert Lavigueur, Victor Pelletier, etc.

Fashion Boutiques: Mrs. Clara Lord Péloquin, Mrs. M. Gaumond, Mrs. Julie Dufresne, Mrs. Arthur Grégoire, Mrs. Marie Delâge, Mrs. Alfred Lapierre, Mrs. Ida Campagna, Miss Eva Montigny

Milliners: Maximilienne Labossière, Adelpha Casavant

Novelty Shops: Mrs. Pierre Allard, Mrs. J.O. Berthiaume, Mrs. John Boyle, Mrs. Wm. Therrien

Furniture: Julien Gabrie, Iréné Beauregard, W.J. Lamoureux

Brick and Cement Work: Pierre Allard Jr., Pierre Benoit, Noé S. Carpentier, Albert Lamarine, Aimé Langevin

Ophthalmologists (born here, moved away): Olivier Lavallée, Boston, Mass.; Wm. Girard, Worcester; Henri Lavoie, Brockton; Théo. Gagnon, Providence R.I.; Edgar Martel, Laconia, N.H.; Georges Ferron, Hartford, Ct.; E. Decelles, Montréal; Emery Brodeur, Holyoke, Mass.; M. Rhéaume, in Virginia. Those who live in Southbridge: W. Blanchard, Moïse Gagnon, Pierre Lafortune, Noé Tétreault.

Painters: Antoine Farland, Louis E. Farland, Arsène Girard, Ad. Girard

Pharmacists: Théodore St. Onge, J.A. Larivière

Restaurant Owners: Houde and Proulx, J. Labelle, Oscar Antaya, Louis Péloquin

Pool Halls and Billiards: Alfred Adam, Wilfrid Brousseau, Alpha Fontaine, N. Péloquin, Louis Péloquin, J.B. Proulx

Bowling Alley: Alex. Parent

Funeral Undertakers

The Canadian first funeral home owner was Mr. François X. Casavant; even before 1870, he was employed with Samuel Williams, furniture salesman, who was also an undertaker. Often, when there was a funeral in the Canadian population, he would replace Mr. Williams.

Mr. Raymond Dostaler, born in Canada, opened an undertaker's office in spring of 1886.

Mr. F.X. Larivière, of Fall River, arrived in Southbridge in July 1892 and opened an undertaker's office in Southbridge, and he was an undertaker for 21 years.

In 1899 and 1900, there was Blais and Lafortune, undertakers from Holyoke.

Lafortune and Savaria, 1901-1902.

Brassard and Savaria, 1903 to 1907.

Brassard and Sansoucy, 1907 to 1909.

F.A. Sansoucy, 1909 to 1919.

Philippe Dagenais, graduated in 1915, currently an undertaker.

Alfred Martel, undertaker for five years, lives in Lawrence, Mass.

CHAPTER XXXVI

Professionals—Born in Southbridge—Biographies

Mr. Victor Potvin, born in Southbridge to Georges Potvin and Marie Dumas on February 5, 1885. After attending the parish schools, he left for college in Sainte-Thérèse and later studied at Laval University, where he entered the medical profession on June 20, 1909. He now lives in Claremont, N.H. where he has a robust clientele.

Dr. Daniel Plouffe, born in Southbridge to Daniel Plouffe and Marie Lavallée on November 9, 1882. He completed classical studies at the College of Sainte-Thérèse, then studied at Laval University in Montréal, where he received his medical diploma on May 13, 1910. He currently lives in Montréal and is a doctor at the Hôtel-Dieu general hospital.

Mr. Zéphir Potvin, born in St. Ours, Canada on September 25, 1875 to Georges Potvin and Marie Dumas. He studied at the College of Sainte-Thérèse, at Laval University in Montréal, and at the University of Baltimore. He entered the profession on June 21, 1901 and currently lives in Springfield, Mass. where he owns a successful establishment.

Mr. Arthur Larochelle, born in Southbridge on January 15, 1893 to Napoléon Larochelle and Marie Sénécal; after attending the parish schools, he left for the Seminary of Sainte-Hyacinthe, then later studied at Tufts College in Boston. He became a dentist in the month of June 1918. He opened an office in Webster, Mass., making the Franco-Americans of Southbridge proud.

Dr. E. Robillard arrived in Southbridge in 1870 at the age of two. He studied in the parish and municipal schools; he then left for Canada to complete classical studies; later he entered Laval University in Montréal and became a medical doctor in 1894. He moved to Leeds, South Dakota, where he practiced for twelve or thirteen years, then went to Louisiana, where he currently lives.

Mr. Arthur M. Surprenant was born in Southbridge, Mass. on November 20, 1887 to Michel Surprenant and Marie Potvin. He studied at the Sainte-Marie-de-Monnoir Seminary in Canada, then at Harvard Law School. He graduated on May 25, 1912, and currently lives in Pawtucket, R.I.

Mr. Antonio Delâge, born on August 2, 1890, to François Delâge and Elzire Chapdelaine. An employee at the Hartwell pharmacy, after a few years he completed coursework at the Boston Pharmacy College, received his degree as a pharmacist in 1916; and in 1917, he enrolled in the medical corps of the American army.

Georges Elzéar Proulx, Attorney

Mr. Georges Elzéar Proulx, attorney, was born in Southbridge, Mass. on June 13, 1890 to J.B. Proulx and Marie Simpson. He obtained diplomas and degrees at the following three institutions: the Notre Dame parish school in Southbridge in 1906; the Bancroft School in Worcester in 1914; Boston University School of Law in Boston in 1917. He passed his exams to become a lawyer on September 11, 1917 and was admitted to the state bar. Mr. Proulx is admired by his fellow citizens for his initiative. He is currently President of the Federation of Franco-American Societies in Leominster, one of the directors of the Model Comb Co., Leominster, and a probation officer.

Stephen Benoit, Attorney

Mr. S. Benoit was born in Southbridge in 1887 to Pierre Benoit and R. Anna Richard. He went to Boston Law School and became a lawyer in the month of September 1912. He currently practices law in Worcester, Mass. The Benoit family has been living in Worcester since 1895 and their ancestor is Pierre Benoit, who arrived in Southbridge in 1839.

André Blanchard, Deputy Sheriff

Mr. André Blanchard arrived in Southbridge at a young age; he worked in the optical factories for a while, then was employed in the store owned by his brother, J.D. Blanchard, and took on an active role in the national movement. A few years later, he went to live in Pawtucket, R.I. and there was named to the important position of Deputy Sheriff, a post he held for twenty-six years. He was also a bailiff in the Superior Court of Rhode Island for several years. He died in Pawtucket on March 21, 1917. Mr. Blanchard was a man of immense respectability, a real Canadian. He was only 58 when he died. At his funeral, the St.-Jean-Baptiste church was full of the faithful come from all parts to pay a final tribute to the memory of a man who was one of the most devoted patriots, one of our oldest pioneers whose personal qualities earned him an enviable place in the hearts of his fellow citizens and his compatriots.

Mr. Victor Lamoureux, merchant, was named Deputy Judge by Governor Russell in 1894; he held this position until his death on June 2, 1919.

Mr. Louis O. Rieutard, attorney, was named by Governor Coolidge to become Deputy Judge of the First District Court of Southern Worcester on July 1, 1919.

Post Office

Mr. Joseph Métras, Head Postmaster, was born in St.-Michel-de-Napierville, Québec Province, on March 15, 1872 to Jacques Métras and

Mathilde Poissant. He arrived here in 1874. He went to the parish school, and later was employed at Bugbee & Wheeler, then at American Optical Co. and J.D. Blanchard & Co. He was named postmaster on January 3, 1914 for a term of four years and named again in 1918 for another term. Mr. Métras is very interested in fraternal work and is involved in several mutual aid societies, especially the Cercle Canadian where from a young age he has actively participated in dramatic plays; he has held several titles as an officer and was the president in 1916 for the fortieth anniversary celebration.

Before Mr. Métras, one of our Canadian women, Miss Corinne Tétreault, remarkable for her initiative, held the position of First Assistant in that same office for several years. Miss Tétreault was the first French-Canadian woman to obtain a diploma from the high school in 1894. She was employed at the post office in 1893 and left her position in 1909, much to the regret of her compatriots, for she had been of great service to her compatriots in numerous circumstances.

From 1875 to 1890, we note that several Canadians, including Joseph Quevillon, Hormisdas Hébert, Felix Gatineau, Théodore St. Onge, Alexandre Richard and Alexandre Lataille, were employed by P.H. Carpenter, who owned a grocery store and was also postmaster at the same time.

Among the current employees who have taken the government exam, we find a number of our compatriots: Léon Gagnon, Urgèle J. Gaumond, Oscar F. Gatineau, Napoléon Bachand, Georges Dumas and Hector Hébert, who was employed at the post office in Boston for thirteen years and who is the son of Hormisdas Hébert, who was employed by the Southbridge post office in 1875.

Pharmacists—Professionals—Biographies

Franco-Americans of Southbridge who have obtained their certificates, diplomas and degrees as pharmacists in the state.

Certificates: Emile Robillard, 1878; Dr. J.A. Letourneau, 1883; Felix Gatineau, 1883; Zotique Leclair, 1887.

Diplomas and Degrees: Herménégilde Demers, 1892; Théodore St. Onge, 1893; Edmond Chapdelaine, 1902; Armand Brissette, 1904; Léo Dumas, 1908; Elzéar Cabana, 1910; Paul Mongeau, 1913; Ladislas Lavallée, 1914; Antonio Delâges, Armand Dupaul, 1915; Anatole Demers, J.A. Larivière, Alfred Péloquin, 1917.

References: The first Canadian from Southbridge to receive a pharmacist's certificate was Mr. Emile Robillard, and that was in 1878. After spending a few years working at the Robinson Pharmacy in Southbridge and in East Brookfield, from 1874 to 1882, he later moved to Gardner, where he still owns a very successful establishment.

Mr. Théodore St. Onge received his diploma in 1893; after establishing pharmacies in Gardner, Chicopee and Millbury, he has owned his establishment in Southbridge since 1905.

Mr. F. Gatineau, an employee at the Robinson pharmacy from 1879 to 1882, received his certificate as a pharmacist in 1883.

Mr. Zotique Leclair received his certificate in 1887 and moved to East Brookfield.

CHAPTER XXXVII

Manufacturers—Their Employees

The first Canadians to settle in Southbridge were employees in the Hamilton factories. This is why today we find names like Mailhot, Leblanc, Marois and Giard listed in the registers of this important company. These families were employed there from 1830 to 1835. A little later, we find other Canadians employed at the Dresser factory, better known at the time as the Paige factory, and at the Columbian factory.

In the early days, people worked twelve hours a day, from five in the morning until half past seven in the evening, with thirty minutes for meals, and there was no time off on Saturday afternoons. The salaries for children were from $8 to $10 per month, and from $10 to $18 per month for those who were older. Each mill had a general store where the employees would buy their provisions and were they settled up their accounts every three or six months. At that time, they would get the remainder from their salary earned, and very often they found themselves owing money. They had to promise the factory authorities that they would be more frugal. As you can imagine, work in the factories was not easy, and sometimes families would spend entire years in debt to the company because of some misfortunate incident or due to their lack of judgement. Further, in some cases, it was the manufacturers who had advanced the families money to pay for their transportation from Canada to Southbridge. In the early days, the trip from the homeland to the United States was made by carriage or train, with a certain distance covered by boat on Lake Champlain.

However, despite the relatively insignificant salaries of those times, through frugality several Canadians accumulated savings and, after several years, returned to the land of their fathers to live peacefully on their farms.

Furthermore, in those times, children were not required to attend school, so they started work at a very young age. The consequences of this were that, because of overwork or lack of care, many contracted deadly illnesses, often consumption or tuberculosis, which sent them to their graves.

For a while, there was a continual coming-and-going between Canada and the United States; it really was this vagabond emigration that caused so many troubles and so much misery among our compatriots.

People would wildly spend the little money they had saved, earned by hard work and misery, during these pointless trips. Other less fortunate families were never able to return to Canada, feeling like exiles because they did not have enough money; however, other families soon arrived and since the manufacturers held these so-called exiles in high regard, a sense of calm slowly spread and soon there was a much more stable and permanent immigration.

The Americans, meaning the English-speaking colonists who were already living here, also encouraged Canadians in many ways; in 1852, it was an American, Wr. Edward, who donated the land to build the first Catholic church in Southbridge. In 1869, the Hamilton company donated the land to build the Notre Dame church, the old church, and later, the one that was in the location where the old convent now stands.

In 1893, during the great economic depression that was in all countries, the Maison Edward & Co. alone donated over $2,000 in clothing that was distributed among the very poor. Proof that our compatriots, from all eras, were well treated by our manufacturers is that a good number remained in their employ for many years. At the Hamilton factory, there are currently some Canadians who have been working there for over forty years. Mr. Joseph Goddu, after fifty years of service in that factory, resigned in 1916 and receives a lifetime pension.

At the American Optical Co. today, of the total 3,050 workers, 1,503 are Canadians. Some have been working there for twenty-five or thirty years. Among those who have been there over forty years, we note: Louis Delâge, Moïse Gagnon, Alfred Langevin, Napoléon Peck, Daniel Plouffe, Pierre Lavallée, John B. Bonin, Joseph Bertrand, and others. In the month of August 1918, Mr. Alexandre St. Martin, Mr. Louis Bibeau and Mr. Joseph Pinsonneault each received a gift of $100 in gold for having worked at the company for fifty years.

In the month of September 1917, the company offered a great banquet to honor Mr. Pascal Sénécal for his fifty years of service; 125 guests attended this banquet. Mr. C.M. Wells, President of the American Optical Company presided over the festivities and took the opportunity to present the hero of the evening with a sack of $100 in gold, congratulating Mr. Sénécal and all of the Canadians employed at the factory for their dedication to their work.

Franco-American Manufacturers

Mr. Etienne Richard was the first Canadian to open a factory in Southbridge; in 1862, he established a cutlery factory in Sandersdale, later moved to Brickville. In 1897, he formed a corporation with his sons Stephen and Joseph; a factory was built on Elm Street and called "Richard Manufacturing Co." In 1911, he transferred his interests in the company to his two sons who, in 1918, turned it into an association bearing the same name, of which Mr. Eugène G. Bartel of Gardner is President and Mr. Origène Paquette is Treasurer and Manager. Knowing the enterprising nature of the officers of this new corporation, we rightly believe and hope that this old institution will continue to exist and to prosper.

Control of the Hyde Manufacturing Company, organized in 1881, passed to Joseph Lacroix, one of the principle stockholders of this corporation, upon the death of J.P. Hyde in 1895. Over the past several years, this company, which manufactures knives, has entered into a very prosperous era; the headquarters are now located in a modern building that was just constructed. This company employs 125 people, of which 80% are Canadians. The officers are: Joseph Lacroix, President; M. Clémence, Treasurer; Arthur Lacroix, Superintendant.

Dupaul Optical Company. In 1888, Mr. Joseph Anatole Caron, Mr. Joseph N. Dupaul and Mr. Léon Young, three of our young compatriots who possessed both an enterprising spirit and experience in the glasses industry, laid the foundation for this type of factory, calling it "Dupaul & Young Optical Company." Their modest beginnings soon led to progress, and today this factory is one of the most successful in Southbridge and a source of pride for our fellow citizens. The current officers are: Léon Young, President; J. Anatole Caron, Treasurer; Joseph N. Dupaul, Superintendant; Salomon Labonté, Director. This factory employs 150 people; 85% are Canadians.

In 1881, Joseph Proulx, one of our well-known fellow citizens, opened a business selling slate and everything needed for the construction of roofs. After several years, this company was organized under the name of "Southbridge Roofing Company," and thanks to the skill of our compatriot and his two sons, Arthur and Roméo, who have an interest in this corporation, it is making great progress.

In 1890, Joseph D. Blanchard and Clément Bégin oversaw the manufacturing of knives and shoemaking instruments, under the management of Mr. Hector Lepage. Two years later, the manager left this position to go live elsewhere, and since our two owners were already in business for themselves, they decided to suspend operations and to liquidate the holdings.

In 1895, Mr. Ernest Decelles specialized in working with glasses; he moved into the old N.E. Putney store on Central Street. This company flourished for in short time, Mr. Decelles went to live in Providence.

Southbridge Optical Supply Company

Mr. Zéphirin Lepage, formerly of Montréal, went to live in New York with his family in 1890 and there he opened a factory to make cases for lenses. In 1897, he arrived in Southbridge to work on this type of manufacturing for the American Optical Co. In short time, this department developed very rapidly for when he left his position in 1911 to go work in Newark, N.J., he had 250 employees. For the past several years, Mr. Lepage has been superintendent of the Southbridge Optical Supply Company, makers of glasses for motorists, aviators, etc.

Ouimet Optical Company

In 1895, Joseph Ouimet began selling prescription glasses; in 1900, he organized a wholesale department, which he continued running until 1919 when he incorporated the company for $50,000 to manufacture lenses under the name "Southbridge Toric Lens Company." This is a business that is on track for growth.

Central Optical Company

For the past several years, a few Franco-Americans from Southbridge have been contemplating a project to raise capital for spectacle manufacturing.

The organizers met on November 12, 1900 and at that first assembly, Mr. Alfred G. Galipeau was named President of the organization and it was decided that the next meeting would be on the 16th and all interested parties should attend.

The archives show that at that meeting, Alfred G. Galipeau, Felix Gatineau, P. Narcisse Leclair and François X. Tétreault addressed the assembly to promote the new enterprise. In order to bring this good work to fruition, the seven following directors were named: François X. Tétreault, Edward D. Desrosiers, P. Narcisse Leclair, Pierre Peck, Alfred Galipeau, Joseph Renaud and Joseph F. Larivière. At this meeting, it was also decided to call this new factory "Central Optical Company." Next, officers were chosen and among the directors named above, they elected François X. Tétreault as President, Alfred G. Galipeau as Vice-President, P. Narcisse Leclair as Treasurer (a position he occupied at various times over eight years), and Edward D. Desrosiers as Secretary, and Pierre Peck as Manager.

The first glasses were manufactured in the building formerly occupied by the Blanchard Optical Company, on Elm Street. The limited experience of the founders in this new industry and the strong competition they encountered made the early days of this company very difficult. However, thanks to their perseverance, they succeeded in creating such demand for their products that in 1901, they had to look for a bigger space and the workshops of the Southbridge Manufacturing Co., on that same street, were purchased; the company still occupies this site.

It was in that same year, on October 16, that the company was incorporated for fifty thousand dollars in the state of Maine, but the pressing business needs required that, in August 1904, the capitalization was changed from fifty thousand to one hundred thousand dollars.

Of our fellow citizens, those who were part of the administration for two terms or more as members of the board of directors are: P. Narcisse Leclair, François X. Tétreault, Pierre Peck, Joseph F. Larivière, Clément Bégin, Alexandre L. Désaulniers, Noé Ethier, Dennis A. Arsenault, Mathias Langevin, Aimé Langevin, Renaldo Guilmette, Hormisdas Pontbriand, Alonzo J. Leclair, Hector M. Leclair, John B. Demers.

The current officers are: Ronaldo Guilmette, President and Director; Hector M. Leclair, Treasurer and Director; Edward L. Leclair, Secretary; and John B. Demers, Director. They have been in the administration since 1911 and are happy to have successfully continued the work of their predecessors. The Central Optical Company today has an enviable reputation in the business world and thanks to the enterprising spirit of its officers, its products are sold throughout the universe. In addition to a complete line of glasses, it also manufactures safety lenses of all kinds; shop glasses for mechanics, aviators, cyclists, motorists, wind glasses, etc.

We are right to be proud of an organization that is the work of our people and that contributes to the good reputation of our nationality, to the prosperity of our city, and to the prestige of our country in international commerce.

Doctor T. Bélanger, First President of the Cercle Canadien

J.A. Caron, President of the Cooperative Bank"

Joseph Métras, Postmaster

Joseph Ouimette, Jr.,
Manufacturer

Ronaldo Guilmette, Superintendant
and Director, Central Optical Company

Owners and Directors of the Dupaul-Young Company: L. Young, J.A. Caron, J. Dupaul, F.H. Horr, deceased

Antoine Ferland, City Assessor

Napoléon Giroux, Chief of Police

Southbridge Cigar Company

In 1908, a few Canadians laid the foundation for an association to manufacture cigars. This enterprise, after several years, was abandoned due to lack of experience. In 1912, it was closed.

Southbridge Commercial Press Company

In 1911, a few energetic young compatriots formed a corporation named Southbridge Commercial Press Company. It was a printing shop; under the skilled direction of the manager, this shop progressed from day to day. The officers are: Mr. Origène Paquette, President; H. Tétreault, Secretary-Treasurer; A.J. Paquette, Manager; Arthur Cabana, Dominique Paquette, Directors.

Mr. Albert Bonnette began to make glasses on his own, on Worcester Street in 1913. Alfred Lapierre founded an establishment on Crane Street in 1914 named Eastern Optical Co; in 1916, Wilfrid Lavoie moved to Hartwell Street, where he can currently be found.

Is it possible to prove any more categorically what an enterprising spirit our Southbridger fellow citizens possess. In just a few years, some will hold prominent places in the industrial world. Congratulations to them! Congratulations for their accomplishments!

Population of Southbridge

According to the censuses of the federal government.

Date	Population
1816, year of incorporation	830
1820	1,056
1830	1,444
1840	2,031
1850	2,824
1860	4,131
1870	5,208
1880	6,464
1890	7,055
1900	10,025
1910	12,592
1915, State census	14,217

French-Canadian population according to various censuses taken by the parish.

Date	Population
1852, date of St. Peter's parish	322
1860	510
1867	1,010

1869, the founding of Notre Dame parish	1,550

Censuses taken by Rev. Georges Elzéar Brochu

1887, 622 families	3,380
1889, 700 families	3,714
105 owners, 210 voters	
1891, 769 families	4,077
125 owners, 270 voters	
1893, census taken by Rev. P. Genest	5,143
936 families, 175 owners	
1900, census by the Cercle Canadien	6,027
1,154 families	
1905, 1,330 families	6,650
1907, 1,458 families	7,177
1908, division of the parish	

1919, according to the city census, out of a population of 15,000 people, there are 9,000 Franco-Americans.

CHAPTER XXXVIII
Memorable Dates and Historical Facts

Captain Papillon

The property of the Notre Dame Church was sold by Captain Papillon to Moses Marcy in 1732, one year before his death.

Captain Papillon, famous for his battles with the privateers who riddled the Caribbean, bought 6,000 acres of land in 1720, land that is today the center of Southbridge.

The Captain, who came from Salem as noted in the State archives, was the first land owner in Southbridge. He bought the property in question from James Blackwell, who had been granted it by the British Crown. Captain Papillon, who is credited with having rid the Atlantic of pirates, died in 1733 and received full military honors. His body rests in the old cemetery in Salem. People say that he paid for the land he purchased with Spanish silver which came from the spoils he seized from the privateers during his encounters with them.

Southbridge was incorporated on February 15, 1816.

The first municipal assembly was held on March 16, 1816.

The saw mill was built at the "Globe Village" lock on the Quinebaug river in 1732, and the Dugas family lived on the top floor of this building when they first arrived from Grandpré in 1755.

The honorable William F. Marcy, who was a juris consult, Governor of the State of New York, United States Senator, and Secretary of State under President Polk, was born in 1786 on the property where we find the Notre Dame church today.

Salomon Labonté, Director
of the Dupaul-Young Company

Dr. J.A. Robillard, Founder of the
Cercle Canadien

E.D. Desrosiers, Treasurer of

A.L. Désaulniers, Director of the

the Cooperative Bank   Cooperative Bank

P.N. Leclair, A Founders of the
Optical Company

H. Bédard, Director of the Central
People's National Bank

Southbridge takes its name from the bridge that crosses the Quinebaug river on Central Street; before the incorporation of the city, this bridge was known as the bridge in the south (south-bridge).

Before the incorporation of Southbridge in 1816, the colony was known as "Honest Town."

The first hotel in Southbridge was built in 1825 in the location of the fire station, Elm Street, and was known as "Freeman's Tavern."

The first newspaper in Southbridge was published in 1828.

Globe Village gets its name from the Globe Village Manufacturing Co., predecessors to the Hamilton Woolen Co., which was incorporated in 1831 with a capital of $200,000.

The glasses industry was started in Southbridge in 1831 by William Beecher, who had a jewelry store on Main Street, in the location of the Hartwell pharmacy.

In 1835, David Perus, a young emigrant to Southbridge, enrolled in the American Marines for a term of four years.

The first city hall in Southbridge was built in 1839. The current city hall was built in 1888 in the same location.

The National Bank opened in 1836 with 95 shareholders and a capital of $100,000. Reorganized in 1865 according to federal laws.

The Southbridge Savings Bank was incorporated in 1848.

In 1848, Charles Daigle, an employee of the Hamilton company, died while moving a barrel of cider down into a cellar.

In 1852, the Catholics of Southbridge established a parish.

In 1856, the inhabitants of Globe Village attempted to separate from Southbridge to create their own city.

In the month of April 1859, there was a fire in the stables of the Edward hotel; forty-three horses were burned to death.

In 1860, on December 31, there was a fire in the pension house and other buildings of the Hamilton company. Twenty-eight horses burned to death.

During the Civil War, from 1861 to 1865, Southbridge supplied 237 soldiers, including nine in the Marines, and contributed $34,000 towards the war effort.

Rev. Fr. Migneault, who was one of the first missionaries in Southbridge, was also the chaplain in one of the Army regiments of the Civil War and was wounded by a gunpowder explosion that burnt his face.

In 1863, in the month of April, the Healy Tavern and several other buildings on Main Street, from Central Street to Foster Street, including the Baptist church, caught fire.

On November 9, 1863, there was a fire in the Edward hotel and other nearby buildings.

Abraham Lincoln, the President of the United States, was assassinated in Washington D.C. on April 14, 1865.

In 1866, on November 9, the first convoy of railroad passengers arrived in Southbridge.

In 1866, Clarice Dupaul, a young girl only nine or ten years old, was working at the Hamilton factory and lost her life when her clothing and hair were caught in a belt. Her death was instantaneous.

In 1868, there was an explosion of a gas tank at the Hamilton company; five people died including a young Canadian, Michel Larochelle, who was from Canada.

Sandersdale, before 1868, was known by the name African, and the train station was called Ashland.

In 1869, Antoine Laroche was killed by a rail car while working on the railroad between Sandersdale and West Dudley.

In 1869, in the month of November, the French-Canadians established a parish; it was the fifth French-Canadian parish in the United States.

The first Notre Dame church was opened to worshipers on Christmas day, in 1870.

In 1870, on May 23, there was a fire in the Dresser factory.

In 1871, in the month of October, Louis Robert, brakeman for a convoy used to repair the railroad between Webster and Southbridge, fell between two wagons and died. It was his last day of work for that corporation.

In 1874, on December 27, the Dresser opera caught fire.

In 1876, on May 9, Paul Blanchard died while building a stone wall across from the old Notre Dame church; a crane broke and he was crushed by a heavy stone.

In 1879, Rev. Georges Elzéar Brochu organized a mission in Fiskdale.

On August 21, 1880, Antoine Duplessis lost his life because of a glare while working on the construction of the first aqueduct reservoir in Southbridge.

Two brothers, Egile and Joseph Papillon, served in the American Marines from 1880 to 1887.

James A. Garfield, President of the United States, was assassinated in Washington D.C. on July 2, 1881.

On August 23, 1881, a mission of the community of Sisters of Sainte Anne was founded in Southbridge, the second in the United

States.

In 1883, on August 14, there was a fire in the freight depot of the New York & New England railroad, in the barn of the Hamilton company, in the barn of Dr. Curtis and in fifteen or twenty houses in various parts of the village.

In 1884, on August 9, the Columbian factory caught fire.

In 1886, on July 7, the skating rink on the corner of Marcy Street and Hamilton caught fire. The St. Mary's and Notre Dame churches were almost damaged by this fire.

In 1888, on April 2, Company K, 6th Regiment, M.V.M., was organized, and it took part in the Spanish-American War in 1898.

In 1891, on April 6, the electorate of Southbridge voted against the distribution of licenses, the only time in the town's history so far.

In 1891, in the month of August, a mission of the community of Sisters of the Assumption was established in Southbridge, replacing the Sisters of Sainte Anne.

In 1892, on June 1, death of Monsignor O'Reilly, first bishop of Springfield.

In 1894, on August 25, Monsignor Brochu bought the Marcy property in order to build a church.

In 1894, on November 25, a train filled with young people who were going to attend a football game was hit by a convoy of passengers crossing the train tracks on Central Street; several were killed or injured. A young Canadian, Charles Gauthier, instantly died.

In 1897, in the month of August, the electric rail between Sandersdale and Fiskdale began operation.

In 1898, on April 5, the post office vaults were exploded by robbers who stole $110.00.

In 1899, Monsignor Brochu bought the St. Georges cemetery.

William McKinley, President of the United States, was assassinated in Buffalo, N.Y. on September 6, 1901.

In 1902, on October 19, the electric rail from Worcester to Southbridge began operation.

Monsignor Georges Elzéar Brochu died on September 26, 1904.

In 1907, on July 5, the electric rail from Springfield to Southbridge began operation.

In 1908, on December 1, division of the Notre Dame parish and formation of the Sacred Heart parish.

The Cooperative Bank of Southbridge was incorporated on May 9, 1910.

In the month of June 1910, the Cercle Juneau of the Lacordaire Society was organized in Southbridge. This club disbanded in the year

1912.

Unveiling of the monument for soldiers of the Civil War on July 4, 1914.

In 1914, on August 1, Germany declared war against Russia, on August 3 against France, and the same day Belgium was invaded.

In 1916, from July 1 to 4, the centenary celebration of Southbridge.

In 1916, on July 2, the new Notre Dame church was dedicated.

In 1917, on April 3, the United States declared war against Germany.

In 1918, from June 17 to 24, fundraising week to support Assumption College. Franco-Americans of Southbridge contributed $3,368.65.

In 1918, on November 11, the armistice was signed between Germany and the allied countries and the peace treaty was signed on June 28, 1919.

From 1917 to 1918, during the World War, Southbridge supplied 912 soldiers, of which twenty-six died on the battlefield.

Contributed in liberty bonds	$3,186,950.00
Contributed to the Red Cross	$86,276.45
War stamps	$75,341.97
K. of C. and other war funds	$67,878.63
Y.M.C. Association	$18,000.00
Total	$3,434,447.05

The People's National Bank was incorporated on May 1, 1919.

In 1919, on September 1, celebration in honor of the soldiers of Southbridge who enrolled in the American Army to defend the Allies against Germany.

Sunday, October 5, 1919, Adélard N. Ferron and Lionel Gaumond, two young soldiers recently released from the American Army lost their lives in an automobile accident. Mr. Lionel Gaumond had served in France.

In 1919, on November 27, celebration of the fiftieth anniversary of the founding of the Notre Dame parish and the St.-Jean-Baptiste Society.

--End--

APPENDIX I

Presidents of the Cercle Canadian from 1876-1916
(enlargements of individual images)

1
Dr Théophile Belanger
1876.

2
Clément Bégin
1877 81 84 87 88 82
1900 01 08.

3
Alexandre Lataille
1877

4
Joseph D. Blanchard.
1878 80 97.

Dr. J. K. Robillard
1879.

Francois Tremblay
1880.

Félix Gatineau
1881 88 96 97 98
1912-13.

Xiste Lescault
1881 82-86.

9
Édouard De Villers
1882.

10
Charles St Pierre
1883.

11
Hormisdas De Celles
1883.

12
Camille Metras
1884-91.

13
Dr. E. O. Morané
1882.

14
Joseph L. Brissette
1887.

15
William Pagé
1888.

16
Joseph Le Clair
1830 1831 02 03 04
1905.

17
Francais X. Tetrault
1890-91-92-93-98
1900-06-07.

18
Joseph L. Codere
1893-1894.

19
Wifred J. Lamoureux
1894-1904-09-10-11-12.

20
Alfred Gatineau
1895.

21
Joseph N. Lareau
1898.

22
F. Anatol Caron
1898.

23
Pierre Métras
1902.

24
Stanislas Math
1907 1908.

25
Egisbert Ouellette
1808-1868.

26
Philippe Duchenais
1814-1915.

27
Joseph Metras
1810-1816.

28
L.Émile Robillard
Fondateur

APPENDIX II

Additional images from C/W MARS library system and Via Appia Press.

Felix Gatineau delivering goods for P.H. Carpenter

Felix Gatineau photographed at his store front, 1901

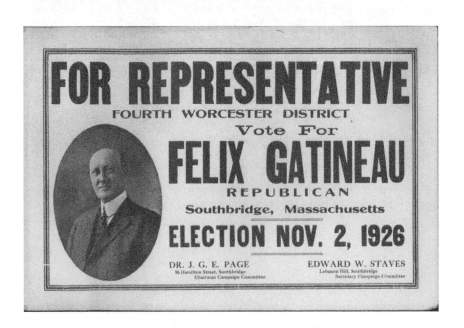

Blanchard barber shop

Blanchardfamily

Blanchard Building, 1920

Interior of the Blanchard Theater

A full house at the Blanchard Theater

Blanchard Block – Strand Theater fire.

Made in the USA
Columbia, SC
08 October 2018